Russian politics today

Manchester University Press

Politics Today

Series editor: Bill Jones

Russian politics today

The return of a tradition

Michael Waller

Manchester University Press
Manchester and New York

distributed exclusively in the USA by Palgrave

Published by Manchester University Press
Oxford Road, Manchester M13 9NR, UK
and Room 400, 175 Fifth Avenue, New York, NY 10010, USA
www.manchesteruniversitypress.co.uk

Distributed exclusively in the USA by
Palgrave, 175 Fifth Avenue, New York,
NY 10010, USA

Distributed exclusively in Canada by
UBC Press, University of British Columbia, 2029 West Mall,
Vancouver, BC, Canada V6T 1Z2

British Library Cataloguing-in-Publication Data
A catalogue record for this book is available from the British Library

Library of Congress Cataloging-in-Publication Data applied for

ISBN   0 7190 6414 7   *hardback*
EAN   978 0 7190 6414 2

ISBN   0 7190 6415 5   *paperback*
EAN   978 0 7190 6415 9

First published 2005

14 13 12 11 10 09 08 07 06   10 9 8 7 6 5 4 3 2

Typeset by R. J. Footring Ltd, Derby
Printed in Great Britain by CPI, Bath

Contents

Contents

Figures

Tables

Boxes

Acknowledgements

My thanks are due to Christopher Binns for reading a draft of this book; to Stephen White and Jekaterina Young for help on many occasions; to the *Courrier International* for arranging permission to print the drawings from the Russian press; and to Florence and Manon Waller for their technical help and advice.

Abbreviations

AD	autonomous district
CEC	Central Electoral Commission
CICA	Conference on Interactions and Confidence-building Measures in Asia
CIS	Community of Independent States
CPSU	Communist Party of the Soviet Union
EES	United Energy Systems
EU	European Union
FAPSI	Federal Agency of Government Communication and Information
FNPR	Federation of Independent Trade Unions of Russia
FOM	Public Opinion Foundation
FSB	Federal Security Service (successor to the KGB)
GAS Vybory	state automated system elections
GATT	General Agreement on Tariffs and Trade
GDR	German Democratic Republic
GKO	government treasury bond
GUUAM	Georgia, Ukraine, Uzbekistan, Azerbaijan and Moldova
IMF	International Monetary Fund
KGB	Committee of State Security
KP	*Komsomolskaya Pravda*
KPRF	Communist Party of the Russian Federation
LDPR	Liberal Democratic Party of Russia
MNVK	Moscow Independent Broadcasting Company
MVD	Ministry of Internal Affairs
NATO	North Atlantic Treaty Organisation
NAUFOR	National Association of Stock Market Participants
NGO	non-governmental organisation
NKVD	People's Commissariat of Internal Affairs
NPSR	People's Patriotic Union of Russia

NTV	Independent Television
ODKP	Organisation of the Agreement on Collective Security
OIC	Organisation of the Islamic Conference
OMON	military detachments for special assignments
ORT	Russian Public Television
OVR	Fatherland–All Russia
PR	public relations
RF	Russian Federation
RKS	Russian Communal Systems
ROMIR	Russian Public Opinion and Market Research
RSPP	Russian Union of Industrialists and Entrepreneurs
RTR	Russian Television and Radio
SCO	Shanghai Cooperation Organisation
SOTSPROF	Union of Socialist Trade Unions
SPS	Union of Right Forces
TNK	Tyumen Oil Company
TPP	Chamber of Commerce and Industry
TVS	Television Sotsium
UN	United Nations
UR	United Russia
USA	United States of America
USSR	Union of Soviet Socialist Republics
VTsIOM	All-Russian Public Opinion Research Centre

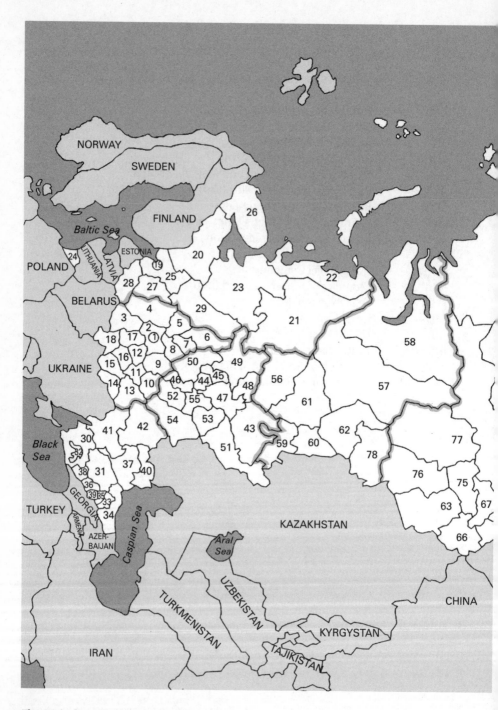

The 88 'subjects' of the Russian Federation
Key overleaf. Note position of Kaliningrad (numbered 24), between Poland
and Lithuania. A more detailed map of the Caucasus appears on p. 78.

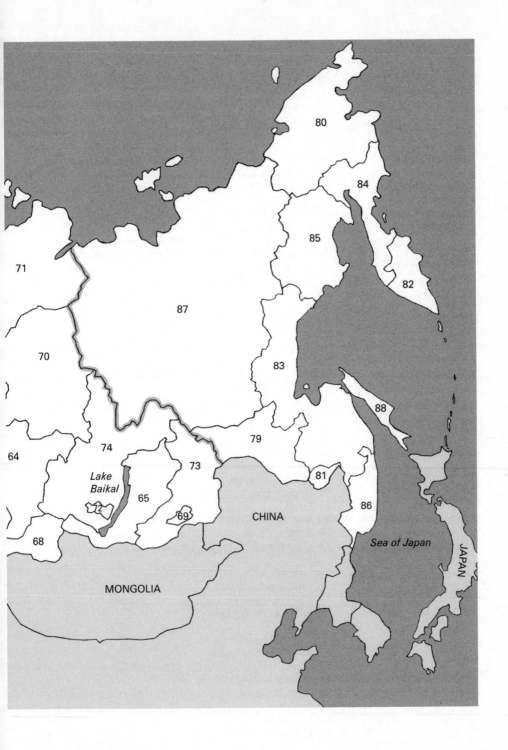

Lake Baikal

MONGOLIA

CHINA

Sea of Japan

JAPAN

71

70

64

74

73

65

72

69

68

87

85

80

84

82

83

88

79

81

86

Key to map on pages xiv–xv

Subjects of the Russian Federation, numerical and alphabetical order.
AD, autonomous district; Rep., Republic.
All the rest are oblasts except for the few krais, as listed.
The Jewish autonomous oblast is a one-off anomaly.

Numerical order

Central Federal District
1 Moscow city
2 Moscow oblast
3 Smolensk
4 Tver
5 Yaroslavl
6 Kostroma
7 Ivanovo
8 Vladimir
9 Ryazan
10 Tambov
11 Lipetsk
12 Tula
13 Voronezh
14 Belgorod
15 Kursk
16 Orel
17 Kaluga
18 Bryansk

North-western Federal District
19 St Petersburg city
20 Karelian Rep.
21 Komi Rep.
22 Nenets AD
23 Arkhangelsk
24 Kaliningrad
25 Leningrad
26 Murmansk
27 Novgorod
28 Pskov
29 Vologda

Southern Federal District
30 Krasnodar krai
31 Stavropol krai
32 Adygeya Rep.
33 Chechen Rep.
34 Dagestan Rep.
35 Ingush Rep.
36 Kabardino-Balkar Rep.
37 Kalmyk Rep.
38 Karachaevo-Cherkess Rep.
39 North Ossetia Rep.
40 Astrakhan
41 Rostov
42 Volgograd

Volga Federal District
43 Bashkortostan Rep.
44 Chavash Rep.
45 Mari-El Rep.
46 Mordova Rep.
47 Tatarstan Rep.
48 Udmurt Rep.
49 Kirov
50 Nizhni Novgorod
51 Orenburg
52 Penza
53 Samara
54 Saratov
55 Ulyanovsk

Ural Federal Disrict
56 Perm krai (note that it has absorbed an earlier Komi-Permyak AD)
57 Khanty-Mansii AD–Yugra (note new name)
58 Yamalo-Nenets AD
59 Chelyabinsk
60 Kurgan
61 Sverdlovsk
62 Tyumen

Siberian Federal District
63 Altai krai
64 Krasnoyarsk krai
65 Buryat Rep.
66 High-Altai Rep.
67 Khakasiya Rep.
68 Tuva Rep.
69 Aginsky-Buryat AD
70 Evenk AD
71 Taimyr AD
72 Ust-Ordynsk AD
73 Chita
74 Irkutsk
75 Kemerovo
76 Novosibirsk
77 Tomsk
78 Omsk

Far Eastern Federal District
79 Amur
80 Chukot AD
81 Jewish autonomous oblast
82 Kamchatka,
83 Khabarovsk krai
84 Koryak AD
85 Magadan
86 Primorye krai
87 Sakha Rep.
88 Sakhalin

Alphabetical order

Adygeya Rep., 32
Aginsky-Buryat AD, 69
Altai krai, 63
Amur, 79
Arkhangelsk, 23
Astrakhan, 40
Bashkortostan Rep., 43
Belgorod, 14
Bryansk, 18
Buryat Rep., 65
Chavash Rep., 44
Chechen Rep., 33
Chelyabinsk, 59
Chita, 73
Chukot AD, 80
Dagestan Rep., 34
Evenk AD, 70
High-Altai Rep., 66
Ingush Rep., 35
Irkutsk, 74
Ivanovo, 7
Jewish autonomous
 oblast, 81
Kabardino-Balkar Rep., 38
Kaliningrad, 24
Kalmyk Rep., 37
Kaluga, 17
Kamchatka, 82
Karachaevo-Cherkess
 Rep., 38

Karelian Rep., 20
Kemerovo, 74
Khabarovsk krai, 83
Khakasiya Rep., 67
Khanty-Mansii
 AD–Yugra, 57
Kirov, 49
Komi Rep., 21
Koryak AD, 84
Kostroma, 6
Krasnodar krai, 30
Krasnoyarsk krai, 64
Kurgan, 60
Kursk, 15
Leningrad, 25
Lipetsk, 11
Magadan, 85
Mari-El Rep., 45
Mordova Rep., 46
Moscow city, 1
Moscow oblast, 2
Murmansk, 26
Nenets AD, 22
Nizhni Novgorod, 50
North Ossetia Rep., 39
Novgorod, 27
Novosibirsk, 75
Omsk, 77
Orel, 16
Orenburg, 51
Penza, 52
Perm krai, 56

Primorye krai, 86
Pskov, 28
Rostov, 41
Ryazan, 9
Sakha Rep., 87
Sakhalin, 88
Samara, 53
Saratov, 54
Smolensk, 3
St Petersburg city, 19
Stavropol krai, 31
Sverdlovsk, 61
Taimyr AD, 71
Tambov, 10
Tatarstan Rep., 47
Tomsk, 76
Tula, 12
Tuva Rep., 68
Tver, 4
Tyumen, 62
Udmurt Rep., 48
Ulyanovsk, 55
Ust-Ordynsk AD, 72
Vladimir, 8
Volgograd, 42
Vologda, 29
Voronezh, 13
Yamalo-Nenets AD, 58
Yaroslavl, 5

Introduction

This book is an account of the politics of the Russian Federation at a particular moment in the evolution of Russian state and society, when the monopoly of power of the Communist Party of the Soviet Union, acquired in the revolutionary period from 1917, collapsed, and Russia's three-quarters of a century of isolation from the world economy came to an end. The communist period can now be seen as a phase in Russian history, with a beginning and an end, but a phase that none the less carried important threads of continuity from the pre-communist past, just as there are continuities from the communist period into today's Russian Federation.

The start of the process that was to lead to the fall of communism and the birth of the new Russian Federation was the launch of a movement for reform within the existing Soviet system by Mikhail Gorbachev in 1986, the second year of his power as General Secretary of the ruling Communist Party. The crowded events of the two decades since then fall into three phases. The first was one of a political awakening, which brought a surge of optimism as the authoritarian restrictions of the communist system were replaced by the basic mechanisms on which a democratic order could be constructed, among them freedom of association and of the press. By the end of 1991 both the Soviet Union and its Communist Party had passed into history, but the nettle of a complete shift in the economic system from comprehensive planning to the market had still not been grasped. That task was undertaken in a second period, under the presidency of Boris Yeltsin, in the newly formed Russian Federation. The turbulence that the economic reform inevitably caused was aggravated by the way in which it was managed, bringing severe disruption, social deprivation and a steep rise in economic crime. The third period is that marked by the stringent steps that Vladimir Putin has taken to stabilise Russia since his election as President in 2000 (and re-election in 2004).

The book is constructed around three major themes that reflect the process of change. The first is the extent, at present very limited, to which Russian society has been able to benefit from the end of communism and to institute forms of pluralist politics. The second is the counterpoint between change and continuity in the evolution of the Russian Federation. The third concerns the uneven competition between elites that developed in this period of social transformation.

State and society

In approaching the first of these themes, the book examines the extent to which, in Russia's new circumstances, impulses from within society, now able to take organisational form, have been able to gain a political foothold sufficient to withstand the continuing downward pressure of the state, and to establish bridgeheads from which a democratic politics might develop. The task of description is made easy in one sense by the fact that autonomous organisation for political ends was suppressed in the Soviet Union by the ruling party's monopoly of power. This provides a simple baseline, since any gain at all in real citizen involvement (as against the sponsored involvement of the masses of Soviet days) is a clear benefit. It is complicated, however, by the pendulum swing from the enthusiasm and advances of the Gorbachev years to the retrenchment under Putin. Any infringement of electoral rights by the law-enforcement agencies today, for example, is necessarily experienced as a step back towards the past. The book will show that Russian society has not yet been very successful in using the democratic mechanisms that the Gorbachev period made available to develop successful channels of representation, much less to ensure accountability of government. Such sustained autonomous initiatives from within society as there have been, strong during the Gorbachev and Yeltsin periods, have encountered severe checks during Putin's presidency. Putin has set out to provide a framework of law for what could, in his expressed design, become a democratic polity, but in many ways his policies and decisions have militated against the realisation of that design. It is difficult to attribute responsibility for outcomes to particular individuals in a period of political upheaval. None the less, in any historical assessment of Putin as a statesman he must be charged with failing to provide leadership in this regard.

Change and continuity

The subtitle of the book announces the return of a tradition. The chief reason for evoking that term is to emphasise the cultural aspects of political change. The speed at which a society can adjust to change is determined by the extent to which people, both the leaders and the led, can absorb it. The Russian revolution itself was a showcase of the way in which revolutionary ideas can be inflected (distorted, in the view of some) by the existing culture. Leaders can rework political and economic institutions and relationships, but they are hard put to erase the folkways and informal conventions with which people are familiar, and which are needed if change is not to bring chaos in its train. This was all the more so in the case of the transition from Soviet communism, where informal folkways had a greater purchase on political and economic life than the formal constitutional structures had. Moreover, many features of Russia's politics today are rooted in a more distant past, and at times it is possible to make full sense of present events only by assessing them in the light of debates and experiences that took place long ago. Despite the revolution of 1917 and the upheaval caused by the demise of the Soviet Union, Russian society through the centuries has been self-contained and sure of its identity. Traditions and political myths are correspondingly strong.

A new elite?

On 21 August 1991 an attempted coup in Moscow, launched with the aim of halting the process of reform of the Soviet system, was foiled. In the circumstances of change that had already gathered momentum, the failure of the coup broke the back of the ruling Communist Party and led directly to the collapse of the Soviet Union itself, disempowering the existing elite. The radical programme of economic reform in the new-born Russian Federation, with its revolutionary recasting of social relations, seemed to present a seedbed for the emergence and development of a new elite with a base in business, industry and finance. It will be seen in the book how two factors in particular have frustrated that development. The first is that the most prominent beneficiaries of the reform were a group of financial adventurers who appropriated a significant part of the country's wealth, creating an animosity within the population that opponents of the emergence of a new economic elite could exploit. The second factor is the steps taken by Putin as President to do precisely that. He opposed the so-called 'oligarchs' who had enriched themselves in the privatisation of the economy by exiling some and imprisoning others. He also appointed military and security personnel to positions of power throughout the state and, through them and his use of the law-enforcement agencies, he created an atmosphere of fear in business circles, which was an impediment to any collective self-assertion of a new elite drawn from that community.

The structure of the book

Part I of this book describes the formation of today's Russian Federation and provides an account of the mainsprings of the transcended Soviet system. Part II sets out the institutions that today comprise the state, including the constitution and the courts. These last are often despatched to a place at the end of commentaries, but Russian realities make it important to situate them squarely among the instruments that the powerful Russian state uses to secure itself and its policies. Part III deals with the formal mechanisms through which the accountability of government to the people is catered for – though in fact not yet guaranteed. It relates how the Federal Assembly has failed to serve as a buckle that constitutionally links the state to the demands and interests of its citizens; a separate chapter is devoted to the electoral process itself. Part IV focuses on society, on the social effects of the shift from plan to market, and on the role that groups, both formal and informal, play in Russian politics today. It examines also the way in which freedom of the media, the essential mechanism for ensuring the accountability of government, has been increasingly circumscribed in Putin's Russia. The final chapter, which constitutes Part V, is a coda devoted to the place of Russia in the international arena today.

Background and assessments

Each chapter after the first begins with a passage dealing with the background to the chapter's topic, to provide at least some recent historical depth. These passages are intended to sharpen the focus of the more general Chapter 1. Each of these chapters concludes with an 'assessment', which draws out key themes that have arisen in the chapter, so that the wood can be seen as well as its individual trees. This involves making judgements, framed in terms of change and continuity, but which are intended also to situate the topic in the context of discussions among social scientists.

Conventions used

- Russian terms have been reduced to a minimum, but some have been retained where the search for an English equivalent can be misleading. Most frequently encountered will be two terms used in describing the units of the Federation – 'oblast' and 'krai'. These are explained in Chapter 4.
- The transliteration of Russian names has been kept simple (Grigori Yavlinsky for the more formal Grigorii Yavlinskii) or adapted to reduce clumsiness (Alexander for Aleksandr, Alexi for Aleksii). In some names Russian components have been translated (North Ossetia for Severo-Osetinskaya respublika).
- The acronyms of organisations and political parties are given as in the original language but full names are translated (e.g. KPRF for the Communist Party of the Russian Federation).
- At times the journalistic term 'the Kremlin' is used for convenience, to connote collectively the President and the Administration of the President's Affairs. Since emphasis is placed in the text on the relationship between the President and his Administration, 'the Kremlin' is used sparingly, and only where no confusion can arise.

Time of writing

This book describes the process of change through which the Russian political system has been passing, which makes it important to indicate the precise date at which the text was written. It was submitted for publication in the autumn of 2004, but it was possible to include some updating during the proof stages up to December of that year. For the most part recent changes have confirmed the trends outlined in the book.

Sources

Textbooks on Russian politics present two major problems. One is that they go out of date very quickly. The publication of this book has been timed for the moment when Putin has made his first impact and now has a chance to press on with pursuing policies whose general outline can be discerned, however tentatively.

The second problem, which the author shares with the reader, is that of sources. Books appearing when this book was being composed were written some time earlier, which sharply restricts the number of published sources worth referring to. There are, of course, established texts whose value is lasting. Reference is made to these, where appropriate. Some sources for further reading are suggested at the end of each chapter, listed in an approximate order of relevance. For the bulk of the information, however, newspapers, journals and websites have been used. One source is particularly valuable for readers who are not familiar with the Russian language. This is Radio Free Europe's daily bulletins, available on the Internet at www.rferl.org/newsline/. That source scrutinises the Russian press, television, radio and websites, and gives general references. Since most readers of this book will not read Russian, many references are to that source, which enables readers to have access indirectly to a host of sources in Russian. Many references to sources in Russian have also, of course, been included.

Other useful general websites are:

www.rferl.org/reports/rpw (*Russian Political Weekly*)
www.rosbaltnews.com

The most useful journals are *Post-Soviet Affairs*, *Europe–Asia Studies*, *The Journal of Communist Studies and Transition Politics*, *Problems of Post-Communism* and *Communist and Post-Communist Politics*.

General reading

For the historical background:

G. Hosking, *Russia and the Russians: A History* (Cambridge, MA: Harvard University Press, 2001).

R. Service, *Russia: Experiment with a People* (Basingstoke: Macmillan, 2002).

For accounts that offer a perspective on the process of transition from communism:

T. J. Colton and M. McFaul, 'Are Russians undemocratic?', *Post-Soviet Affairs*, 18:4 (2002), 91–121.

P. B. Evans, *Bringing the State Back In* (Cambridge: Cambridge University Press, 1985).

D. R. Herspring (ed.), *Putin's Russia: Past Imperfect, Future Uncertain* (Lanham, MD: Rowman and Littlefield, 2002).

M. McAuley, *Russia's Politics of Uncertainty* (Cambridge: Cambridge University Press, 1997).

M. McFaul, *Russia's Unfinished Revolution* (Ithaca, NY: Cornell University Press, 2001) (this source offers a basis for comparison with other cases of transition from authoritarian rule).

M. A. Weigle, *Russia's Liberal Project: State–Soviet Relations in the Transition from Communism* (University Park, PA: Pennsylvania University Press, 2000).

Supplementary commentaries on Russian politics:

R. Sakwa, *Russian Politics and Society* (London: Routledge, 3rd edn, 2002).

S. White, *Russia's New Politics* (Cambridge: Cambridge University Press, 2000).

Part I

From Soviet Union to Russian Federation

1

The transition from communism in Russia

When Vladimir Putin became President of the Russian Federation in 2000 he faced a formidable task. A process of reform in the Soviet Union under its last President, Mikhail Gorbachev, to tackle the Soviet system's increasingly severe problems, had brought political and economic dislocation as it had gathered its own momentum. The main political and economic mechanisms on which the Soviet system rested having been undermined one by one, at the end of 1991 the Union itself succumbed and was quite simply dissolved. With it the monopoly of power enjoyed to that point by its Communist Party, of which Gorbachev was himself the General Secretary, also passed into history.

It was as President of the Russian Federation – by far the largest of the 15 republics that had constituted the Soviet Union until its dissolution – that Boris Yeltsin presided over a fundamental recasting of the economic system and of property relations. A market economy was introduced, but at a high social price. With wages going unpaid and widespread shortages of food, with consequent strikes among miners and other groups, with financial adventurers sequestering a large portion of the country's wealth, the state appeared to be losing its cohesion, despite the powers given to the President by a new constitution promulgated in 1993. Coming to power, first as Prime Minister in 1999 and then as President in 2000, Vladimir Putin was to set about reversing some of the processes of dislocation that characterised the Yeltsin years.

These three personalities give a structure to the period since Gorbachev's accession to power in 1985, each of them playing a distinct role in the collapse of the Soviet Union and the creation of today's Russian Federation (Box 1.1). This chapter examines the two periods that preceded Putin's call to order: the Gorbachev period, from 1985 to 1991, and the years of Yeltsin's presidency, 1991–99.

Box 1.1 From Gorbachev to Putin

1985	Gorbachev becomes General Secretary of the Central Committee of the Communist Party of the Soviet Union.
1986–91	The period of **the Soviet system's decline and fall.** The Party abdicates from its monopoly of power in the economy (perestroika) and in politics (glasnost).
1991–93	The period of **dual power** as two rival centres of power in the Russian Federation contend. Yeltsin's defeat of the Supreme Soviet leads to the adoption of a new constitution, while the freeing of prices in January 1992 is the landmark for the full shift from plan to market.
1993–99	The period of **economic transition** as the turn to the market is consolidated and Russia enters the world economy. The political reforms are maintained but lead under Yeltsin to a weakening of the state.
From 2000	A period of retrenchment in Putin's first and second presidencies. A **return to Soviet political norms** accelerates sharply in the aftermath of the hostage-taking crisis in Beslan in September 2004 (see Box 2.1, p. 25).

The Stalinist background

Political systems bear the marks of their origins. In the case of the Soviet Union, while it was the Russian revolution of 1917 that brought the Bolshevik founders of the Soviet state to power, the system that was to meet its end in 1991 was established effectively from 1928, the point by which Joseph Stalin had acquired dictatorial power and when two fateful decisions were taken. The first was the adoption of a strategy of industrialisation at a forced pace by submitting the economy to a system of comprehensive planning. The second was the collectivisation of agriculture, which, in the way it was carried through, gave the ruling party control over production in the countryside and over its distribution. The countryside was to pay for industrialisation in the towns.

Through its rigorous mechanisms of political control, the Communist Party mobilised the Soviet people (predominantly illiterate at the time of the revolution) for a monumental drive for economic construction. All production was put in the hands of the state, which meant in the hands of the Party, since it held a monopoly of power. The Party controlled strategic sectors of society – labour and youth, for example – by organising them from above. The soviets – the popularly elected councils that had embodied the power of the workers in the symbolism of the revolution – were subordinated to the Party through its control of elections. These elements of control have been quite over-shadowed in history by the horrors of the 'great purges' of the 1930s and the creation of the labour camps (the gulag), and it is hard to peel that paroxysm of terror away from the story of economic and social development that was taking place and continued when the dictator had died and been replaced by a still repressive collective leadership. Thirty-two years separate Stalin's death in 1953 from Gorbachev's accession to power, and the Soviet Union was in many ways transformed in that period. None the less, it is important to note that the system that confronted Gorbachev in the 1980s was, apart from minor adjustments, the same Stalinist system that had underpinned the construction drive, with all its rigours.

Not surprisingly, the system had by then got completely out of phase with a changing reality. The story of forced labour offers a simple but graphic example. The early tasks had been simple, requiring no great skills – digging canals, lumbering and mining, for example. They could be done by the slave labour of the gulag. But by the late 1950s the economy had developed to a stage where labour could not be wasted in this way. More complex tasks now called for rewards for the skills that the Party could claim to have been developing. It was at that point that the gulag began to empty. Whatever other reasons were involved, the Stalinist system was under pressure to change, and the pressure was to continue in line with the demands and requirements of an urbanised, culturally sophisticated and technology-based society.

The Communist power monopoly

Had the Soviet system really broken down when Gorbachev introduced his reforms? It is paradoxical that the great bulk of expert opinion, inside the Soviet Union and outside it, holds that the system was fatally flawed, yet opinion polls within today's Russia have shown that a majority of respondents still claim that life was better in Soviet times. How can these facts be squared?

It helps to distinguish the social from the political and economic factors. Socially it can be shown that in many respects life for the bulk of the population did steadily improve during the history of the Soviet Union, as a result of processes of urbanisation, the stratification of the workforce, and the accumulation of skills, educational achievement and access to cultural provision. It was in the early days that universal literacy was achieved and, more gradually, the movement of people from countryside to town meant the development of a sophisticated urban culture, though in the countryside, too, the provision of libraries, for example, serves as an indicator of cultural progress. It should not be forgotten that despite the system's undoubted defects, the Communist Party was conducting a pioneering experiment in the provision of social welfare on unprecedented equitable principles, maintaining low income differentials and providing a health service and education at all levels free of charge to the entire population. Prices of essential commodities were pegged at a low level and rents for accommodation, with heating, electricity and so on, were nominal. A system of benefits – pensions, sickness and maternity pay, health and holiday sanatoria, summer camps for the young – covered the entire population and was administered by the trade unions.

It is this equitable social provision that today's older generation in Russia remembers, and the fact that it was at a very low level – nominal rents, for example, very often went hand in hand with sharing a communal flat with a number of other families – does not appear to have extinguished a sense of nostalgia.

Culturally, too, the record of the Soviet Union offered much to be proud of. Funds were pumped into cultural life, and while strong political controls were imposed on the works of the creative intelligentsia, much of their output did not fall under this control, or they found ways of skating round it, which became themselves part of Soviet urban culture, artists and the general public sharing a complicity in the enjoyment of the illicit songs of Bulat Okudzhava or the novels of Yuri Trifonov, both of them dealing with the everyday cares of urban folk, from the trauma of divorce to the heartless stratagems that unscrupulous people could resort to in order to move into a better apartment – or just one of their own. In circumstances of strong controls, art does not have to be very provocative to have an air of the *avant-garde*.

Unfortunately, in the political and economic spheres the record was very different. In both, by the 1980s the usefulness of a system designed for earlier tasks had clearly come to an end, and many of the country's leading economists were foreseeing catastrophe. To explain their alarm at least a little must be said about that failing economic system, which went under the name of central command planning.

Central command planning

With the adoption of a series of five-year plans from 1928, the market was effectively abolished, and instead of making their own decisions on what to produce and in what quantity, firms were given instructions on these matters from a central planning authority via the ministries to which the task of organising the whole of the nationalised economy was now entrusted. The materials that they needed for their planned tasks were allocated to managers by another central authority – the State Procurement Commission – which issued them with chits, against which they would obtain the needed inputs. They were told also where their finished or semi-finished goods were to be sent. Managers could not, in this way of doing things, lift a telephone to order components against payment (unless, as was often the case, they were tapping into some strictly illegal source of supply in the extensive black economy). Nor could they determine their labour costs or fix their prices, since these also were centrally determined.

The social advantage of this highly controlled system was that the price of essential goods, such as meat and bread, could be kept low, and wide wage inequalities could be avoided. Through control of prices the Party could ensure that basic goods were accessible to all. But this advantage was offset by the system's numerous failings:

- Firms that could not cover their costs were kept afloat by handouts from the budget. These handouts concealed the true costs of production, and also undermined efficiency, since managers faced only 'soft' constraints.
- There was inadequate control over the use of energy, which was therefore inefficiently used.
- A lack of incentives resulted in a lack of care.
- Consumer preferences played no part in a firm's decisions, which were instead determined by meeting the indicators set in each year's plan. (According to a common caricature, the manager of a firm making nails, with a plan indicator stated by quantity, would manufacture a mass of tiny nails, while one with a plan indicator stated by weight could rationally produce just one enormous nail.)

Planning depends for its effectiveness on (among other things) the elimination of uncertainties – in the costs of raw materials and labour, and market prices, for example. This the Party achieved by closing the frontier against the movement of goods and people, thus protecting the economy against fluctuations in world prices, against an outflow of the skilled labour that was being trained up – and against the entry of information that would undermine the Party's justification for its monopolistic role and for the sacrifices it was exacting from the Soviet people. Isolation from the world economy and from more general influences, even if it could never be completely achieved, was an essential component of the Soviet system.

A second link between the political and economic systems lay in the fact that the Party's political monopoly enabled it to pinpoint economic targets, and to ensure that the appropriate resources were devoted to those targets even if that meant deprivation in other areas. A dual economy emerged, with the defence industries, and heavy industry in general, draining resources from the consumer sector, without the consumer being able to question the imposed imbalances. Again, political control gave the Party the muscle to ensure that there was movement towards its chosen targets, though its capacity to mobilise the population waned with time.

'The leading role of the Party'

Such an economic structure could not function unless it was supported by a particular kind of politics, and in fact the political and economic systems were closely connected. The political concomitant of central command planning was what was termed 'the leading role of the Party' – that is, of the Communist

Party, which ever since the revolution had banned all rival parties, indeed all autonomous political organisation.

The leading role of the Party rested on two basic mechanisms: control of information and control of strategic jobs. The Party maintained a hierarchy of committees that paralleled the organs of government at all administrative levels and that controlled their work. The committees had key departments dealing, on the one hand, with appointments to important posts (the term *nomenklatura* was used to connote both this list of posts that a Party secretariat was competent to fill and the office-holders themselves, collectively) and, on the other, with the media and cultural matters. Their power extended to the nomination of candidates for election to the soviets and to the appointment of trade-union officials. In the former case, the Party committee would propose a name and organise an election campaign stressing national successes and the Party's role in them. No other nomination was deemed necessary.

In a country where open and free competitive elections were virtually unknown, where literate and administratively competent people were in extremely short supply, and yet where the country's modernising leadership was intent on involving all the people in government, it was not surprising that the Party took on a paternalistic role. The 'masses' were involved, but the Party made sure that its own choice of candidate was elected. In the same way, the trade unions, together with the radio and the other media, were seen as channels of political education, with the Party as teacher and the masses as the pupils. But with time, this educative aspect of the Party's power monopoly became redundant, and indeed began to work against its image. In the 1960s, for example, the Party had to give up sending 'agitators' to harangue cinema audiences on the importance of the latest production figures. Developments of this kind, each one small in itself, were bringing the Party's role increasingly into question and by the time Gorbachev was proposing his reforms a shortage of administrative competence and political awareness could no longer be used as an excuse to deny the electorate the freedom to present candidates for election. Such thinking was hardly appropriate when the Soviet Union was sending rockets into space and winning Nobel prizes.

The Gorbachev years, 1985–91: glasnost and perestroika

Mikhail Gorbachev was appointed General Secretary of the Communist Party and thus the Soviet Union's supreme leader on 11 March 1985. His two predecessors had each died after a little more than a year in that post, and it was during the long incumbency of the General Secretary before them, Leonid Brezhnev, that the problems that were to lead to the Soviet Union's collapse began to emerge. Opinions differ on the main reason for the Soviet Union's collapse, but the foregoing already suggests two prominent ones. The first was the severe checks on the circulation of information. Signals that can ensure an efficient use of resources in an economy, such as a freely operating relationship between supply and demand, were almost entirely ruled out in the system of central command planning. At the same time, the Party's stifling controls on the channels of communication meant that the signals on which rational political decisions could be made were missing. The political system was preventing itself from adjusting to changes in society and from responding to new challenges.

But there was a second reason – the pressures of international competition. The strong performance of Western economies from the 1970s, coupled with a decline in Soviet growth rates to virtually nil by the 1980s, was accompanied by a growing mass awareness of the true standard of life in the West. This led to what Gorbachev himself called a 'pre-crisis' situation. The further technological development of the Soviet economy, including the exploitation of the country's vast reserves of natural resources, required international cooperation, above all in technology. The difficulties in setting up a project for a gas pipeline with European partners, which came up against US refusals to issue licences on essential components, is but one example among many.

Glasnost

These problem areas Gorbachev set out to tackle, under the catchwords glasnost and perestroika. Glasnost derives from the Russian word for 'voice', and it was voice in politics, giving publicity to problems, that Gorbachev was anxious to promote – together with choice in the economy.

When Gorbachev first called for glasnost, in March 1986, it was with a view to making the governmental process more transparent – by putting a window in the administration, as it were. This was the beginning of a process that was to accelerate to seismic proportions. The loosening of the Party's control over the circulation of information had two immediate effects beyond the simple reporting of events and debates.

First, it was impossible to prevent the 'dark pages' of the Soviet Union's history from being opened. Past opposition figures, such as Nikolai Bukharin, were rehabilitated, numerous statues were removed and criticisms of Lenin began to appear. Also, the historical names of some major cities and streets that had been renamed during the Soviet period were restored, Moscow's Gorky Street once again becoming Tverskaya, though it was not until 1991 that Leningrad was given its original name of St Petersburg.

Second, freedom of information was accompanied by legislation establishing freedom of association. Groups known to history as the 'informals' began to form, not necessarily with overt political aims. They were able to print news-sheets and programmes – as far as they could, given the difficulties of acquiring the materials in the still planned economy.

The excitement that these developments caused rose higher when Gorbachev proposed that Party secretaries and the soviets themselves should be subject to open election. In March 1989, the Soviet façade of a parliament was replaced by a new Congress of People's Deputies, in which debate was unfettered. The intense interest and excitement occasioned by the Congress ('I had my heart pills by my side', remarked one commentator) were fully rewarded, as the speakers unburdened themselves of their views and criticisms. But the structure of the Congress illustrated Gorbachev's intention to retain some kind of privileged place for the Communist Party in a democratised system: a third of the seats were reserved for the nominated representatives of 'social organisations' such as the Party. A further third were territorial seats with large constituencies. The city of Moscow was a single constituency, and the winner of that seat would necessarily be endowed with an exceptional authority in the country's politics. It was won by Boris Yeltsin.

Free elections and a reworking of history did not necessarily presage problems for the Soviet Union itself, even if they were going wider and faster than reformers loyal to the old system might have wished. On the other hand, one development from the policy of glasnost categorically contained the seeds of the Soviet Union's destruction in its existing form. This was the revolt of many of its component republics (discussed under 'Ethnic federalism' below).

Perestroika

The whole series of reforms set in motion by Gorbachev has come to be subsumed under the term of perestroika, but it is helpful to attach it particularly to proposals for economic change, to distinguish it from the more political proposals associated with glasnost. In that sense, it can be seen as a move to institute choice in the economy, just as glasnost legitimated 'voice' in politics – that is, both perestroika and glasnost sought to remedy a lack of information flows, which was the main systemic reason for the collapse of the communist system (the other main reason being the Soviet Union's isolation from the world economy).

In the most general terms, Gorbachev called for a more efficient use of resources and for economic mechanisms to be put in place to achieve it. He approached the task at both the macro and the micro levels. At the macro level, the aim was to make enterprises accountable for their own operations. In the system of central planning, the constraints they faced were 'soft' – if they failed to cover their costs the state would cover the deficit (though the manager might be sacked). The Law on the State Enterprise, which came into effect in January 1988, freed enterprises from the ministries of which they had been effectively branches; this enabled them to deal independently, on the basis of their own plans, with other enterprises as well as with the state. From that point, both the industrial ministries and the state planning bodies were put on notice, though reform had to proceed further before they finally left the scene or, in the case of some ministries or their departments, became quasi-governmental corporations. These developments took place still within the framework of state ownership.

At the micro level, one reform simply legitimated an existing practice. The fact that entrepreneurial activity was outlawed in the Soviet Union had had the effect of making it almost impossible to get done the innumerable small servicing jobs that daily life requires, such as plumbing, car maintenance or tailoring. The result was illegal moonlighting on a substantial scale. Legislation in 1986 made it possible to engage in individual privately remunerated work of this kind without falling foul of the law.

A second step involved a more significant move towards private enterprise, by permitting people to set up in business independently of the state but as a cooperative. This could be accommodated within the existing ideology without too much strain (in fact, the collective farms in the countryside had been regulated by a special cooperative code of law since Stalinist days). Under a Law on Cooperatives of 1988 it became possible to open, for example, a restaurant, workshop or more extensive firm, which could hire labour and raise money. This meant the generation of income independently of the state, which in turn meant that taxation, for example, assumed an entirely new character. It was no longer a matter of moving funds around within a state budget, as it had been and still was to a predominant extent. Now the state's officials had to locate the sources of part of the country's wealth and ensure that entrepreneurs contributed to the common purse.

Ethnic federalism

The Soviet Union was constitutionally a federal state made up of 15 republics, by far the largest of which was itself a federation – the Russian Soviet Federal Socialist Republic (Box 1.2). This contained a number of 'autonomous republics', 'autonomous regions' and 'national districts', in descending order in the administrative hierarchy. Each of these units had been created around one of the numerous ethnic minorities that the Soviet Union comprised, with a view to their retaining their group identities until such time as economic and political development, in Bolshevik theory, had overridden ethnic particularisms and had welded them all into a single community. Stalin's constitution of 1936 accorded them substantial formal powers, the Union republics even having a constitutional right to secession. In the circumstances of the time, however, that constitution meant little. The planning system took no account of republican borders and the Communist Party used its apparatus in the republics to stifle any separatist tendencies.

On the other hand, not only were the national minorities given demarcated territories bearing their names but they were allowed quite a high degree of cultural autonomy, with schools and a local press using the minority's language. The official formula that encapsulated this arrangement was 'socialist in form, national in content'. By the 1980s most of the minorities with less than Union

---

Box 1.2 The constituent republics of the Soviet Union

The Union of Soviet Socialist Republics (USSR) was composed of 15 republics: the Russian Soviet Federal Socialist Republic and the Soviet Socialist Republics of:

Armenia	Latvia
Azerbaidzhan (now Azerbaijan)	Lithuania
Belorussia (now Belarus)	Moldavia
Estonia	Tadzhikistan (now Tajikistan)
Georgia	Turkmenistan
Kazakhstan	Ukraine
Kirgizia (now Kyrgyzstan)	Uzbekistan

(Note that the variants Azerbaidzhan, Belorussia, Kirgizia and Tadzhikistan apply to the Soviet period.)

---

republican status had undergone a substantial degree of assimilation, but the Union republics themselves had come to be able to use their institutional base to protect themselves to some extent from Moscow's centralising power.

When glasnost got under way, ethnic loyalties surged in the Union republics. Suddenly, instead of being a text useful only for propaganda purposes, the constitution became the credible basis for claims for independence launched by various 'national fronts'. These movements were strongest in the Ukraine, in Georgia, and in the Baltic republics of Estonia, Latvia and Lithuania, the *Sajudis* movement in Lithuania playing a particularly prominent role.

The end of the Soviet Union

Despite the indecision and uncertainty of the early stages of the reforms, both political and economic change in the Gorbachev period were dramatic. The sudden opening up of choice in the economy and voice in politics had the effect of a dam bursting. As the verse by Ogden Nash runs:

> Shake and shake the ketchup bottle;
> None'll come and then a lot'll.

The final collapse of the system was precipitated by the events of August 1991, when a group of highly placed Soviet political figures took action designed to halt the galloping process of reform. The group included the Vice-President, the Prime Minister, the Minister of Defence, and the head of the security apparatus. Announcing the formation of a State Committee for a State of

Emergency, they declared that Gorbachev was ill and no longer capable of exercising his public functions (he was on holiday in the Crimea at the time) and sent troops into the capital. While the plotters were Soviet officials, it was the leadership of the Russian Federal Republic under Yeltsin that issued a counter-appeal and led an indignant citizenry in a three-day defence of the seat of the Russian parliament and presidency, known as the White House. The coup collapsed, bringing down with it whatever authority the Communist Party now retained. Yeltsin was able during the autumn to capitalise on this turn of events.

Finally, on 7–8 December 1991, a meeting of the leaders of the three Slav republics of the Union – the Russian, the Ukrainian and the Belorussian republics – took place at Belovezha, near Minsk. There they passed an accord stating that 'The USSR as a subject of international law and as a geopolitical entity has ceased to exist', claiming as their authority for taking this step the fact that it was those republics that had established the Union in the first place, in 1922. There was now nothing for Gorbachev to be President of, and Russia left its communist phase to enter a new one.

The Yeltsin years, 1991–99: reaping the whirlwind

Expelled in 1987 from the Communist Party's leadership and from his post at the head of the Moscow Party organisation as a result of his aggressive calls for the pace of reform to be accelerated, Boris Yeltsin made a spectacular come-back when he was elected, as noted, to the Congress of People's Deputies as representative for Moscow city itself. He went on to be popularly elected President of the Russian Republic in June 1991.

With its capital in Moscow, and being the historical homeland of the Russian people, the Russian Republic assumed the attributes of the defunct Soviet Union, such as its seat on the United Nations Security Council, though it shed the 'socialist' and 'soviet' elements of its title (Russian Soviet Federal Socialist Republic) to become simply the Russian Federation. It was as President of this new polity that Yeltsin took the movement for reform into an entirely new phase from the end of 1991.

Four facets of Yeltsin's period in power are particularly worth noting, in view of the later evolution of Russia: his dynamic pursuit of economic reform; his struggle with the hold-over parliament from the Soviet days, which mounted an opposition to his radical moves; the adoption of a new federal constitution in 1993; and his personal style.

Pressing on with reform in the economy

The Soviet system of central command planning had been largely dismantled in the Gorbachev period, but some central elements of it still lingered when the Soviet Union itself was dissolved at the end of 1991. The abolition of the State Commission for the Plan (*Gosplan*) and that for Procurements (*Gossnab*) in January 1992 was merely a matter of setting the seal on their already effective demise. The freeing of prices in the same month, however, was a resolute step towards an open-market economy, which took reform into a new phase. It was a central plank in the policy of 'shock therapy' that was energetically being promoted by Yegor Gaidar, as first deputy Prime Minister, with advice from Western economists.

The detail of that policy, together with its effects in Russia, is the subject of Chapter 11. However, since the aim here is to give an overall perspective on the Yeltsin years in the recent evolution of the Russian Federation, some of those effects must be mentioned. First and foremost, the sharp rise in prices cleared the streets of queues, while putting many goods beyond the financial reach of most people. Access to goods was now graded according to the income of the shopper – as is normal for those living in a market economy. For former Soviet citizens it was novel.

Second, even before the fall of the Soviet Union, the early economic reforms had enabled people in positions of power in the economy to accumulate considerable personal wealth through the workings of a still largely unregulated market system. Then, in Yeltsin's presidency, as a result of the way in which the process of privatisation was conducted, there emerged a number of phenomenally wealthy financial operators, who were able to exercise a powerful influence on government, on the media and on Yeltsin personally. These 'oligarchs' were making their greatest impact on public life – and on public opinion – when, in the mid-1990s, the basics of life were becoming unobtainable for most of the urban population, who at that stage were too stunned and too busy seeking the means of physical survival to react to this pillaging of the nation's wealth by a few individuals.

Confrontation with parliament and the crisis of 1993

The period from Yeltsin's election as President of the Russian Soviet Federal Socialist Republic in June 1991 to the end of that year was one of a period of conflict of power, with Gorbachev exercising his authority at the head of the Soviet Union and Yeltsin installed as leader of its core – Russia. Apart from personal mutual animosity, the leading issues on which the two leaders were opposed included, first, the pace and direction of reform and, second, the future of the Union, Yeltsin's role as President of Russia ranging him with a now generalised movement for 'sovereignty' (the term was used with various interpretations) among the Union's republics. The departure of Gorbachev and the Soviet Union from the scene removed that locus of tension, with its element of dual power, but a new one was soon to develop within the Russian Federation itself, this time between the parliament and the President.

The Congress of People's Deputies elected in the Russian Soviet Federal Socialist Republic in March 1990 had an inner body – the Supreme Soviet – which came to be dominated by the Congress's speaker, Ruslan Khasbulatov. A highly personalised confrontation developed between Khasbulatov and Yeltsin, behind which there lay substantive issues.

One was, again, the nature and pace of economic change. Views on this among the delegates to the Congress, despite their widely varying stances on other matters, came to crystallise into two positions. Support for Yeltsin's radical economic measures came from a loose grouping that had come to be known as the 'democrats'. Against Yeltsin's policies, however, stood an opposition to radical change, whose views ranged from outright support for restoration of the Soviet system to an acceptance of the need for continued change but at a slower pace and lower social price. A polarisation developed on the issue, opposing the President's radical position to a consolidated range of alternatives being championed by the Congress. The fact that the latter had been elected in the Soviet period contributed a good deal to the polarisation (no fresh elections had been held when the Soviet Union broke up in 1991).

A second major issue was the relative powers of the Congress and the President, on which there was confusion in the much-amended constitution of the Republic, which appeared to allocate supreme power to both institutions. The resulting position of dual power was not sustainable in the long or even medium term. One of many sources of weakness in the Congress was that it lacked the coherence that a party system can impart, in terms both of developing leadership roles among the deputies that went beyond personal self-assertion, and of establishing links with society, whether of an organisational or a programmatic kind. In general, it had not had time to generate for itself a sense of a new role in the changing political system. As the highest legislative body, it claimed an interventionist role in the creation of the new polity. It has to be remembered that in the Soviet system, while the effective leader of the country was the Party's General Secretary, it was the Chair of the Supreme Soviet who was the formal head of state, and a practice had developed whereby the General Secretary took over the latter post. With the Party gone, with the Russian presidency a creation of little over a year's standing, and with the whole of political life in movement, Khasbulatov's claim that parliament had primacy over the presidency was not surprising.

Other issues entered into the confrontation, such as the principles that should underlie the structure of the Federation, but it was these two – the nature and pace of economic change on the one hand, and what should be the power relationship between parliament and the presidency on the other – that stoked the fires of confrontation. The fact that confrontation led to crisis, however, had much to do with the personalisation of the confrontation around the figures of Yeltsin and Khasbulatov, and with the political style of Yeltsin himself.

From confrontation to conflict

During the course of 1992 and up to September 1993, these tensions played themselves out. The shock therapy measures of Gaidar launched in January 1992 met with public dismay as prices rocketed. Proposals were made in the Congress to counter their effect in industry by requiring the State Bank to continue to issue credits to failing firms, which it was the reformers' aim to close. This set President and Congress on a collision course, with the latter refusing to accept the former's draft of a new constitution and then, in March, attempting to impeach the President. The attempt failed, and the Congress set about drafting a new impeachment law, whose provisions would give a second attempt a better chance. In September 1993, anticipating the passing of this law, Yeltsin dismissed the Congress. The deputies thereupon barricaded themselves in the White House, declaring as President Alexander Rutskoi, Yeltsin's Vice-President, and appealing to the public for support.

A few thousand supporters answered the Congress's call and moved to take control of the Ostankino television centre in the north of Moscow. There they were confronted by forces of the Ministry of Internal Affairs and were repelled after several hours of gun fighting. The army up to this point had stayed determinedly neutral, but Yeltsin finally persuaded it to take action. The White House was stormed, and Khasbulatov and Rutskoi, among others, were arrested.

It was a moment full of meaning for the process of change in Russia. Polarised confrontation had seen off the last institutional hold of the Soviet Union, and had seen in the market in the aggressive form in which Yeltsin presented it. It had handsomely enhanced the power of the President, since a historically strong executive power – having survived both the Russian revolution of 1917 and the Gorbachev reforms – was now being reinforced. It illustrated also a less obvious facet of Russia's historical political patterns, in the way in which the military showed no inclination to intervene on its own initiative in the state's internal affairs, even at a moment of crisis as severe as this. It did not bring an immediate stabilisation to eight years of political turbulence; there were further convulsions to come. But it set the arrows pointing towards change.

At the same time, the storming of the White House did not elicit strong support in the population: polls showed that over 50 per cent were opposed to it while less than a quarter were in favour. If this was the birth of a new Russia, it bore some of the marks of its authoritarian paternity.

The constitution of 1993

The scene was now set for Yeltsin to present a new constitution and to install the new institutions that it prescribed. The constitution was approved by a referendum held on 12 December 1993. It established a dual executive, with the President clearly dominant over the government. It provided also for a parliamentary structure – the Federal Assembly, which comprises two houses, the State Duma and the Federation Council. It bore the marks of a Soviet heritage in including substantial sections devoted to guarantees of social welfare.

The constitution could not of itself shape the way in which its provisions would be interpreted and developed. However, the Russian tradition favouring strong rulers, together with the continuing uncertainties of the transition from communism, meant that its presidential nature would be confirmed and strengthened. The other side of the coin was that the provisions framed to establish the accountability of the executive, already limited in the constitution, had no tradition whatsoever to rest on and were not to be supported by later developments. On the contrary, the recent experience with the final Supreme Soviet (the elections to which had been partially free) could at the time be seen by its opponents as a warning against giving an elected legislature too much power.

The constitution was federal, maintaining the administrative divisions of the Russian Republic in Soviet times. It was in this sphere that the constitution was to have its first major test, in a determined move by the Chechen Republic to achieve independence. No other major challenge was mounted, but Yeltsin's policies had allowed (even encouraged) the regions to take a substantial degree of autonomy, and this was in fact weakening the state by the time of his resignation. Centrifugal regional tendencies, together with the appropriation of a large portion of the country's wealth by a few financial speculators, were the heritage of Yeltsin's period as President that Putin, coming after, was most concerned to put right.

Yeltsin himself suffered from increasingly bad health during this period, though he made an extraordinary rally to run an energetic and successful campaign in the presidential election of 1996, when he won 35 per cent of the vote in the first round and 54 per cent in the second. But thereafter he leaned ever more heavily on an entourage of close advisers. They were years marked by extensive corruption. In August 1999, one year after a dramatic economic crisis had led to a devaluation of the rouble and the loss to the population of a great part of their savings, Yeltsin presented Vladimir Putin to the country as his latest nominee as Prime Minister, and made clear that he was his personal choice as successor. Then, on 31 December, he resigned as President. A deal had been done whereby Yeltsin's anointing of Putin as his successor would give Yeltsin and his family protection against prosecution for the cases of corruption for which they were generally held responsible, at the same time as protecting the reform programme.

Yeltsin's personal style

Yeltsin had burst upon the scene by calling for a speeding up of the reform process in 1987, and had been evicted from the higher organs of power as a result. His confrontation with the parliament elected in Soviet days can be read

17

as a simple struggle between those crying 'Forward!' and those crying 'Back!'
It was very much a part of his personality to wish to drive things forward, and
he had the personal capacity to exercise that kind of leadership. But other
aspects of his attributes and behaviour fuelled opposition to him, despite his
immense popularity with the general population. In particular, exception was
taken to his choice of advisers and to the advantage they took of that role. The
interventions in matters of state of the head of the Presidential Guard and a
former general, Alexander Korzhakov, became legendary, as did Korzhakov's
prominence as boon companion in the President's boisterous private life.
Yeltsin's daughter Tanya and her chosen friends were also closely involved in
policy matters, and indeed the 'Family' was to become a prominent feature of
Russian political life.

The legacy to Vladimir Putin

Putin inherited a state of affairs that could reasonably be described as chaotic.
Yeltsin's one great achievement had been to ensure the shift from a planned
to a market economy, but the way in which he had done this created major
problems for his successor. By the mid-1990s the Russian state was unable to
perform the functions that the modern state is normally attributed. It could
not enforce the law across the territory, collect taxes or maintain social services. It could not pay people in public service, including the military – indeed,
the economy had become demonetised, with firms settling accounts through
barter and regions issuing promissory notes as currency. By the time Putin
entered on his second term as President, in 2004, it could be seen that a pendulum had swung twice. The first swing, under Gorbachev, had taken Soviet
society away from many of its familiar underpinnings. Under Yeltsin this
swing continued, as the economic reform completely disoriented an already
perplexed population. With Putin the pendulum has swung back towards
authoritarian central power. However, as pendulums do, it has slowed and has
not returned to the point at which it was when Gorbachev set it swinging. The
strong support for Putin and the political party that supported him in elections
for the Duma in 2003 and for the presidency in 2004 may spell popular relief
from the disruptions of the recent past. It may equally well represent the fruit
of political manipulations inherited from a Soviet past. Proponents of democracy within and outside Russia inevitably, and very reasonably, see it in terms
of the latter.

It is important to note, finally, that, with Gorbachev's policies of glasnost
and perestroika, political reform and economic reform were undertaken
simultaneously. In this respect, Russia has differed from the other giant
state emerging from communism – China. There, economic reform was
embarked on after the death of Mao Zedong, while the authoritarian rule of
the Communist Party was firmly maintained. The return to Soviet political

norms – but not economic ones – that this book records may well constitute, in part, an acknowledgement that to proceed on both fronts simultaneously gave a considerable hostage to fortune.

Further reading

R. Service, *Russia: Experiment with a People* (Basingstoke: Macmillan, 2002).

G. Gill, *Russia's Stillborn Democracy? From Gorbachev to Yeltsin* (Oxford: Oxford University Press, 2000).

D. R. Herspring (ed.), *Putin's Russia: Past Imperfect, Future Uncertain* (Lanham, MD: Rowman and Littlefield, 2002).

M. McAuley, *Russia's Politics of Uncertainty* (Cambridge: Cambridge University Press, 1997).

M. McFaul, *Russia's Unfinished Revolution* (Ithaca, NY: Cornell University Press, 2001).

R. Daniels, *Russia's Transformation: Snapshots of a Crumbling System* (Princeton, NJ: Princeton University Press, 1997).

J. Lowenhardt, *The Reincarnation of Russia* (London: Longman, 1995).

Part II

The state

2

The presidency

At 10.00 a.m. on weekday mornings the busy traffic on Kutuzovsky Prospekt, the long broad avenue leading to the heart of Moscow, mysteriously disappears. For a time there is an unusual silence. Then, at breakneck speed, a motorcade with armed outriders hurtles down the avenue and itself disappears in the direction of the Kremlin. This is Vladimir Putin, President of the Russian Federation, going to work in his office. The traffic then gradually returns to the avenue. This impressive daily event is symbolic of the power that the President wields in the Federation's political life. It is a power that is not afraid to proclaim itself, and clearly either is not concerned with public reactions or can choose to ignore them.

Background

History and circumstances have combined to endow the Russian political system with a strong executive with a single dominant figure at its apex. Historically, the autocratic rule of the Russian tsar had remained unchecked until 1906, when the creation of a parliament – the Duma, elected on a franchise repeatedly narrowed by the tsar – constituted a minimal restriction on his power. The power that Vladimir Ilich Lenin wielded after the revolution in 1917 was based on his accepted authority as leader of the Bolshevik Party and as head of the revolutionary government but, after a brief interregnum, the dictatorial power that Joseph Stalin accumulated as Party leader rested more and more on political policing. When he died, the Party leadership denounced his 'cult of personality', but the collective leadership that they instituted retained the post of General Secretary of the Bolshevik (later renamed Communist) Party, whose power was constrained only by the factional balance within the Party's Politburo. Once he dominated that, he dominated the political system and was accepted in that role.

Even when real reform of the Stalinist system came, it was introduced from above, by Mikhail Gorbachev as General Secretary of the Communist Party. The reforms were not so much an attack on the tradition of strong executive leadership as an attempt to build up countervailing institutions of democratic accountability. He was successful to the extent that he established the principle of free electoral choice, but the overall effect of his reforming policies was to create a turbulence that favoured the self-assertion of ambitious personalities.

The Yeltsin presidency

Chapter 1 has recorded the main features of Boris Yeltsin's presidency, the first of the new-born Russian Federation. From that account it is helpful to carry forward certain items into this chapter:

- The informal network of counsellors with whom Yeltsin surrounded himself was more than a team of political advisers. It was a clan-like structure with tentacles in both political and economic life. It brought wealth to many of its prominent members, including Yeltsin's family. The influence of the 'Family' lived on into and through Putin's first presidency.
- The emergence of a group of phenomenally rich financial speculators whose wealth stemmed from the way in which the privatisation process had been conducted was also to be an important factor in Putin's choice of priorities in his first presidency.
- Partly through Yeltsin's policies, and partly through the open texture of politics in the late Gorbachev period and during his own presidency, the regions had acquired a degree of autonomy which, coupled with the Chechens' outright demand for independence, was weakening the new Federation at the moment when consolidation was required.

Yeltsin could claim two major accomplishments by the time he resigned the presidency in 1999: he had turned the economy decisively to the market; and he had overcome the risk of a communist restoration. His success in the latter achievement was marked by the adoption of the 1993 constitution, at a time of defeat for the restorationist cause, and by his victory over Gennadi Zyuganov, leader of the Communist Party of the Russian Federation, in the 1996 presidential election. His record in guaranteeing the future of the new Federation, however, was less impressive. Taking the brunt of the turbulence caused by Gorbachev's policies and the revolutionary fervour that they had generated, he failed to deal with many of their negative results. It was of equal importance that, though a strong personality, he lacked the statesmanship required to achieve a synthesis between the forward movement of change and the cultural landscape in which those buffeted by the process of change sought to find their bearings.

Yet however negatively Yeltsin is judged as a President, nothing he did diminished the authority of the office of the presidency itself. Rather, he maintained its image by the ebullience of his personality, which conformed to the traditional Russian respect for the *khozyain* – a boss-figure capable of keeping order in his domain.

Enter Putin

As former head of the Federal Security Service (FSB, successor to the Committee of State Security, or KGB), Putin had the background appropriate for the task of stabilising society after the turbulence that Gorbachev's stewardship had created and Yeltsin's presidency had deepened. He was young and he was healthy (unlike Yeltsin during his own presidency). He was also much more methodical than Yeltsin. With Putin, the Russian tradition of strong central power came together with a need to restore order. The pages of this book show how, with limited but real concessions to constitutionality, Putin has preserved at the apex of the political system a presidency that dominates the executive, legislative and judicial functions of government. That domination, built up during his first presidency, was substantially reinforced during the second, in the aftermath of the Beslan tragedy (see Box 2.1).

Box 2.1 Beslan

On 1 September 2004, a 32-strong armed group occupied School No. 1 in the North Ossetian town of Beslan in the Caucasus and took hostage at least 1,156 pupils, parents and teachers. They demanded the withdrawal of Russian armed forces from Chechnya. The apparently accidental explosion two days later of one of their bombs destroyed the roof of the gymnasium where most of the hostages were held, putting an end to negotiation and leading to the storming of the building. The uncoordinated action of a number of government forces, coupled with the spontaneous participation of gun-carrying local residents and a failure to isolate the building, led to the death of 335 people, including all but one of the hostage-takers.

This event, apart from the local trauma that it caused, led to a series of political changes that constituted a sharp return to Soviet norms. They had been foreshadowed by earlier proposals, and could in part be held to be justified by clear weaknesses in the operation of the new democratic processes. Nevertheless, Beslan is likely to feature as a major landmark in the Federation's history and as the determining moment when Soviet political norms were revived in Russia in their main essentials. Ironically, some of the main planks of Soviet social protection, which had to some extent compensated for Soviet political authoritarianism, had only shortly before Beslan been severely watered down (see Chapter 11).

The President

The President is elected for a term of four years and cannot serve more than two consecutive terms. He or she must be at least 35 years old and must have lived in Russia continually for the preceding 10 years. Candidates must be nominated by at least 500 people and then gather two million signatures in support of their candidacy, unless they are proposed by a party or electoral bloc that attracted more than 7 per cent of the total vote in the most recent federal parliamentary election.

Table 2.1 *Presidential election in the Russian Federation, June 1996 (percentages of poll)*

Candidates obtaining over 1 per cent of first-round votes	First round	Second round
Boris Yeltsin	35.3	53.8
Gennadi Zyuganov	32.0	40.3
Alexander Lebed	14.5	–
Grigori Yavlinsky	7.3	–
Vladimir Zhirinovsky	5.7	–
Others	2.2	–
Against all candidates[a]	1.5	4.8
Invalid ballots	1.4	1.0

[a] An option presented on the ballot paper (see Chapter 8).
Source: Central Electoral Commission.

Table 2.2 *Presidential election in the Russian Federation, March 2000 (percentages of poll)*

Candidate	First round[a]
Vladimir Putin	52.9
Gennadi Zyuganov	29.2
Grigori Yavlinsky	5.8
Aman-Geldy Tuleev	3.0
Vladimir Zhirinovsky	2.7
Konstantin Titov	1.5
Ella Pamfilova	1.0
Others	2.0
Against all candidates[b]	1.9

[a] No second round was necessary, the winner of the first round having attracted over 50 per cent of the poll.
[b] An option presented on the ballot paper (see Chapter 8).
Source: Central Electoral Commission.

Table 2.3 *Presidential election in the Russian Federation, March 2004 (percentages of poll)*

Candidate	Party/public function	First round[a]
Vladimir Putin	No party affiliation; incumbent President	71.2
Nikolai Kharitonov	Communist Party of the Russian Federation (KPRF)	13.7
Sergei Glazev	Motherland–People's Patriotic Movement	4.1
Irina Khakamada	Union of Right Forces (former co-leader)	3.8
Oleg Malyshkin	Liberal Democratic Party of Russia (LDPR)	2.0
Sergei Mironov	Party of Russia's Rebirth/Party of Life; speaker of the Federation Council	0.8
Against all candidates[b]		3.5

[a] No second round was necessary, the winner of the first round having attracted over 50 per cent of the poll.
[b] An option presented on the ballot paper (see Chapter 8).
Source: Central Electoral Commission.

Presidential elections

At the time of writing there have been three presidential elections in the Russian Federation, one of them (in 1996) returning Yeltsin as President and two Putin (in 2000 and 2004). The 1996 election was of particular importance in setting Russia's course away from a communist restoration (see Tables 2.1 to 2.3).

To be elected a candidate must attract over 50 per cent of the poll. If no candidate succeeds, there is a run-off election between the two leading candidates from the first round.

The presidential function

There are six key roles that the President performs in the Russian political system:

Guardian of the state

First, the President is the guardian of the state. He guarantees the constitution of the Russian Federation, adopting measures to safeguard the state's independence and integrity. He is constitutionally head of the armed forces, he chairs the Security Council, and he 'approves the military doctrine'. These are functions and powers of the kind normally accorded to any head of state. However, there are reasons for this aspect of the President's role to have

---

Box 2.2 Vladimir Putin

Vladimir Vladimirovich Putin was born in Leningrad (later to be renamed St Petersburg) on 7 October 1952, the only child of a factory worker and his wife. It was while he was still at school that he conceived the ambition of serving in the security forces. He tells in his autobiography how at an early age he was struck by a film – *The Sword and the Shield* – which depicted the heroic deeds of a Soviet double agent in Nazi Germany. He tells also how, at the age of 16 years, he went to the KGB offices to ask if he could join the organisation. This was in 1968, at the time of the Prague Spring and of what, in Soviet eyes, was a threat to 'the gains of socialism'. He was advised first to take a university course. He accordingly completed a degree in law at the Leningrad State University, where one of his teachers was Anatoli Sobchak, who was to have an important influence on his later career.

On graduation he joined the KGB. There he worked in counter-intelligence and then foreign intelligence. In that role he was sent to the German Democratic Republic (GDR) and he was there when the GDR's communist regime collapsed and the wall between east and west Berlin fell.

Returning to Leningrad from Germany, Putin became an aide to the vice-president of the Leningrad State University, in charge of international issues, though remaining in the KGB. He left the KGB's employ in 1991, when Sobchak was elected mayor of Leningrad, and until 1996 he served as an adviser to Sobchak while working in the Leningrad administration, again dealing with its international affairs. For his last two years in St Petersburg he held the posts of first deputy chairman of the city government and chairman of the committee for external relations.

The contacts he had made by this time gave him entry to the hub of Russia's politics, in Moscow. He moved there and made rapid progress, first serving as deputy head of the Administration of the President's Affairs, then taking responsibility for relations between the President and the heads of regional

---

acquired a particular salience under Putin's presidency. First, the Federation had only recently been founded, and then in circumstances of a turbulence bordering on the revolutionary. This laid a particular responsibility on the Federation's first Presidents, who would be shaping its future. Rather more than simply guarding the state was involved. Second, under Yeltsin the effectiveness of the state had been considerably reduced as a result of the turn to the market (difficulties in organising a taxation regime, for example, reduced the state's ability to pay its employees, including the military). A third and final reason why Putin could be expected to take this responsibility especially seriously was his own personal background in the security forces. His childhood's ambition

governments. In July 1998 he was appointed head of the FSB, thus achieving the ambition of his youth. For a period he combined this with service as the Security Council's secretary. Then, in August 1999, Yeltsin appointed him Prime Minister, with the State Duma's willing approval. It was a strategic choice. Yeltsin needed a Prime Minister whom he could trust to protect him from prosecution on laying down the presidential office. This service Putin duly performed.

At this point Putin was little known by the public, but a series of terrorist bombings in Moscow and other cities gave him the chance to show his decisiveness. Already committed to the cause of bringing Chechnya's bid for independence to a close, he launched energetic military operations in that republic, which brought him swift acclaim. It also placed him well for the presidential election of 2000, for which he prepared by identifying himself with the Unity electoral bloc in the preceding State Duma elections. The partnership paid off handsomely. Both Unity and Putin personally were successful in their respective elections.

Putin said on Russian Public Television (ORT, 21 September 2003) that the Soviet Union was a complicated page in Russian history – 'heroic, creative, and tragic, but it is closed'. At the same time, there is no doubt about his intention to give Russia back stability by restoring features of the past. Equally, it is highly likely that there are many who are grateful for the comfort that this revival of the familiar has brought. During his presidencies a cult of Putin has developed. Not merely do portraits and statuettes of him adorn bureaucrats' desks across Russia, but essays about him are collected for publication in school textbooks, and a textile mill in Kostroma has been producing tapestries featuring his portrait, with plans to start manufacturing bed linen with the same design. This appears, however, to be a matter of limited and local enthusiasms. A national survey of 1,591 respondents by the Yuri Leveda Analytical Centre (reported in *Nezavisimaya gazeta*, 25 May 2004) showed that 11 per cent of respondents owned or would like to own a bust or portrait of Putin, against 81 per cent who lacked this inclination, and another 81 per cent evincing no desire to see a monument to Putin erected in their town.

having been to serve in those forces, undertaking this aspect of the presidential role was in a sense a culmination of that ambition (see Box 2.2).

The constitution gives the President two special powers in this area. In the event of an attack against the Federation he can introduce martial law; and he can declare a state of emergency on the territory of the Federation. In both cases he must notify the Federation Council and the State Duma (see Chapter 3), and the Federation Council must confirm the decision for it to be valid.

A further article of the constitution (article 85) gives the President a particular responsibility in assuring the internal integrity of the multinational Federation. In the event of disputes between Moscow and the federating units, and among those units, he can use processes of conciliation. If these fail he can have recourse to the courts. Pending their decision he is empowered to 'suspend the operation' of enactments of executive bodies of the subjects of the Federation if they conflict with the Federation's constitution ('subjects of the Federation' is the term the constitution uses for the various federal units). Here again, events have far overtaken a formal provision in the constitution. The challenge to the integrity of the state thrown down by the Chechen movement for independence, and the heavy-handed way in which the Russian armed forces have countered it, have completely eclipsed constitutional niceties framed for regulating a stable state of affairs.

In the less stressful matter of curbing the power that the regions had succeeded in arrogating to themselves during the Yeltsin period, Putin has used firm methods that do not strain his constitutional competence.

Head of the executive

Second, the President is head of the executive. Constitutionally, the Russian President is responsible for policy making, while 'executive power' is in the hands of the government (the subject of Chapter 3). But this stretches the meaning of executive power as it is understood in democratic systems, based on a tripartite separation of powers among executive, legislative and judicial functions. On that tripartite basis the presidency and the government jointly perform the executive function in the Russian Federation. That is, as in France, there is a dual executive. Unlike in France, however, in Russia the relationship between President and government is not open to negotiation and adjustment according to the outcome of elections. The government is permanently the junior partner and is an extension of the presidency. The wording of the constitution makes this clear, in that it gives the President the power to 'determine the guidelines of the internal and foreign policies of the state', while the government is assigned the task of carrying out those policies. Also, the President is not only the chief source of policy but he also appoints the government; thus the government has no other source of authority, since its composition is not determined by the elected parliament. Moreover, the boundary between the Administration of the President's Affairs and the government is in any case blurred, with a number of strategic government ministries being subordinated directly to the President (Chapter 3).

Legislative role

Third, the President plays a key role in legislation. While it is for the Federal Assembly to discuss and pass laws, the President is given wide powers in the legislative field, and both Yeltsin and Putin have taken full advantage of them.

• He is empowered to submit draft laws to the parliament.

- The constitution states that 'The President of the Russian Federation issues decrees and directives'. These do not require confirmation by the Assembly, though they cannot contravene the federal constitution. Yeltsin made full use of this power of issuing decrees and Putin has followed suit. This means that the making of law can follow two different channels, in one of which the President has sole initiative.
- The President has the constitutional power to initiate referendums. This power was used in 2003, when the current constitution was approved by referendum.

Patronage

Fourth, the President has wide powers in making political appointments. The more routine of these are listed in the constitution. Subject to approval by the Federation Council, he appoints judges in the Supreme Court, the Constitutional Court and the High Court of Arbitration. He nominates also, on the same basis, the judges of other federal courts. On his own he appoints the members of the Security Council, and those of his own extensive and powerful Administration. Subject to ratification by the State Duma, he appoints the chair of the State Bank.

Putin has extended the patronage powers of the presidency far beyond these constitutional provisions, frequently using his power to issue presidential decrees for the purpose. It was on this basis that he created a new post of President's Envoy (see below) and appoints the seven holders of it. He and his Administration have made sweeping personnel decisions deep into the regional structure, for example reorganising the police in five regions in July 2003. Again using his powers of decree, he dismissed the interior minister of the Ingush Republic and also the head of the Ministry of Internal Affairs' directorate in the Rostov region in the same year.

This power of patronage has enabled Putin to build up a team of people he trusts, many of whom have worked with him in the past, during his years in the regional administration in St Petersburg and, later, as head of the FSB. Given this activity in the sphere of personnel, it seems likely that the Administration of the President's Affairs is beginning to play a role akin to the Communist Party's *nomenklatura* of Soviet days. This is borne out by cases where Putin has used his powers of patronage to resettle in a new position prominent political figures who for one reason or another have found themselves robbed of their niche, as when he appointed to head the State Fisheries Commission the ex-governor of Primorye territory, Evgeni Nazdratenko, who had been forced from office through his disastrous administrative record (in a further relocation he was made a deputy secretary to the Security Council in May 2003). Later, he appointed Vladimir Yakovlev to head a new Commission of Housing and Communal Services in 2003 when that dignitary left office as governor of St Petersburg, and then to the post of President's Envoy in the Southern Federal

District. The fact that Yakovlev had been no friend of the President has been seen as evidence that in these personnel matters there may be cross-cutting clientelist networks inside the Administration of the President's Affairs.

Representing Russia

Fifth, the President represents Russia on the world stage. Since the collapse of the Soviet Union, Russia can no longer claim the status of a superpower, but it remains a major player in international relations, now being enrolled in the club of the world's major industrial states, making the G7 the G8. The Federation still has a military nuclear capacity and, despite the present weakness of the economy, its natural resources are immense.

Both Yeltsin and Putin have been dynamic in their interventions on the world scene. Putin in particular has been adept in turning world events to his country's advantage. We shall see in Chapter 14 how, in the aftermath of the destruction of the World Trade Center's twin towers in September 2001, he joined George W. Bush in the latter's war on terrorism, and in so doing gained a degree of acquiescence from the West to the way in which the Russian Federation's own internal war against the Chechens was being waged. He was able to employ the same strategy in his response to the hostage-taking crisis in Beslan in September 2004.

This is an area where the character of the Russian presidency coincides with current trends. Today's circumstances of instant communications and the growth in summitry have promoted presidential executive styles in many advanced industrial countries. Even in parliamentary systems that have functioned traditionally on cabinet principles, the constant need for an authoritative spokesperson at major international gatherings has been one of the factors forcing a prime minister into a presidential role.[1]

Focal point of politics

Finally, the President is the focal point of the Federation's politics. The centralising power of Moscow has for centuries been confronted with a wide range of competing loyalties in Russia – ethnic, religious and regional – over a huge geographical and cultural space, but there has always been at the centre of it all a point of focus, whether the tsar as autocrat, or the collective leadership of the Communist Party with its own personal focus in its General Secretary.

Acting as the focal point of society has been to a great extent a matter of imposing central rule, by ruthless means if necessary, but it has had a mythic aspect. The tsar's rule was rationalised in terms of its three pillars of autocracy, Orthodoxy and the collective consciousness of the 'people'. The Communist Party in Soviet days based its centralising rule on 'the unbreakable bond between Party and people' and the doctrine of the Party's historic role as the vanguard of the working class. Putin has been able to attract loyalty to himself by insisting on a firm hand at the centre after a period of turbulence and has come close to making what he terms the 'power vertical' the mythic basis of his claim to lead the nation. Indeed, part of the function of the 'power vertical' has been to remove or weaken other claimants to a role as focal points in Russia's political life, except perhaps the security forces, with which in any case he is himself identified.

History and circumstances are together sufficient to account for the President's role as focus of the Russian Federation's political life, but to them may also be added other, more concrete factors. Above all, Putin's control of the media (see Chapter 12) has given him the instrument he needs to project an image of himself as the nation's leader, an image that is reflected in his approval ratings, which throughout his first presidency and into his second hovered around 70 per cent (though they dipped to 66 per cent in the aftermath of the Beslan crisis in September 2004). Control of the media ensures extravagant coverage of his meetings in the international arena, where he can be seen acting as Russia's spokesman in the wider world.

In conformity with this aspect of his role, Putin has made a point of keeping people up to the mark, for example chiding his own Prime Minister (for instance in his address to the Assembly in May 2003), upbraiding the FSB, the Procurator-General and the Supreme Court chairman for lack of energy in catching and punishing terrorists after the bombing of a hospital in Mozdok in August 2003, and publicly castigating incompetence and venality in general.

Other roles

Apart from these major political roles, the constitution assigns the President a series of responsibilities that are normally assumed by heads of state. They include:

- accrediting foreign ambassadors;
- appointing Russia's ambassadors;
- awarding honours;
- the right of pardon for criminal offences.

The Administration of the President's Affairs

To aid him in discharging these various functions, the President has a substantial staff working directly for him and independent of the government, formally entitled the Administration of the President's Affairs. The number of officials that constitute the Administration has been put at around 2,000. Its head is a figure of immense political power, reckoned to have a political influence second only to that of the President.

The head of the Administration of the President's Affairs

From the start of Putin's first presidency until November 2003, the post of head of the Administration was held by Alexander Voloshin. It would be hard to exaggerate the role that Voloshin played in Russian politics during those years, though he was largely hidden from public view. Already a powerful figure in the Yeltsin 'Family', he played a key role, first, in preventing a proposed and potentially highly disruptive impeachment of President Yeltsin from succeeding and, second, in ensuring a smooth transfer of power from Yeltsin to Putin. In the following years the respected independent newspaper *Nezavisimaya gazeta*, in its annual ratings of personal political influence in the Russian Federation, regularly ranked Voloshin second, directly after Putin and ahead of the entire governmental team and all party leaders.

In the diplomatic sphere he chaired meetings devoted to reviewing the draft power-sharing treaty between Chechnya and the federal centre in 2003, and in the Iraq crisis in the same year it was he who went to Washington on 24 February to discuss the implications of the crisis for future relations between Russia and the United States. When Condoleezza Rice returned the visit in April, her main meeting was reported to have been with Voloshin. He paid visits to Armenia and Ukraine at crisis points in their relations with Russia. He also played a key role in economic affairs, serving as chairman of the electricity monopoly United Energy Systems.

When the head of the Yukos oil company, Mikhail Khodorkovsky, was arrested in October 2003, and the issue of the post-Soviet privatisations was re-opened (see Box 11.3, p. 208), Voloshin found himself in an exposed position. As a member of the Family he was connected to many of the 'oligarchs', who, like Khodorkovsky, had made vast fortunes as a result of the privatisations of the 1990s, and he was opposed to the reopening of the privatisation issue that the Yukos affair portended. He was effectively forced from office in November and was replaced by his deputy, Dmitri Medvedev, a lawyer who had worked in the St Petersburg administration and in industry.

Medvedev had followed Putin to Moscow, and had become chairman of the gas monopoly Gazprom in June 2000. He was appointed first deputy head of the Administration of the President's Affairs in December 1999. When he became its head, his post as first deputy head passed to Dmitri Kozak, also a lawyer, who had followed the same itinerary from the St Petersburg administration to Putin's team in Moscow, where he was given the job of working out a project for the strategic development of Russia to the year 2010, before being appointed head of the government administration in the reorganisation of March 2004 – that is, carrying responsibility for organising the work of the government itself. In this role he was not a member of the government – he was the President's man, overseeing its administration. He was later despatched by the President to head a Federal Commission for the North Caucasus as part of Putin's response to the hostage-taking crisis in Beslan in 2004.

The deputy heads of the Administration of the President's Affairs

At the close of Putin's first presidency there were eight deputy heads of the Administration, each of them discharging particular duties. Viktor Ivanov, for example, carried the political appointments brief, Vladislav Surkov oversaw relations with the Duma and served as the United Russia Party's electoral strategist in 2003 (though Putin himself has scrupulously avoided formal affiliation with this or any other political party), while Igor Sechin had charge of the President's office, organising his business. In the split that became visible within the Administration over the Yukos affair, Ivanov and Sechin emerged as advocates of taking a hard line against Khodorkovsky and other grand gainers from the privatisation process. Voloshin, Surkov, Medvedev and Kozak were seen as opposing the arrests made by the law-enforcement agencies.[2]

On being re-elected to the presidency in March 2004, Putin reorganised the Administration of the President's Affairs. Only Sechin and Surkov kept their posts as deputy heads supporting Medvedev, without a first deputy head (that post was left vacant at the time). On 21 April Medvedev presented the new distribution of responsibilities among them. He himself would cover organisational and analytical work on major policy issues, and the preparation of documents for the President. Sechin was to second him on these tasks as well as overseeing the chancellery and the Kremlin information department, and dealing with state secrets. Surkov would oversee regional and federal policies, while taking responsibility for relations with the Federal Assembly, political parties, public organisations and trade unions. The President's press service would also fall within his care. The remaining former deputy heads became presidential assistants, also in many cases keeping their former briefs. A new directorate was created within the Administration as part of the reorganisation, to oversee the reform of the governmental bureaucracy, the State Service.

Aides and advisers

President Putin has some 20 aides and advisers covering key areas. Ivanov, since the reorganisation a presidential aide, continued to carry responsibility for personnel matters, judicial appointments and state awards. The March 2004 reorganisation of the Administration left in office a number of incumbent advisers, such as Andrei Illarionov, Putin's chief adviser on the economy, Sergei Samoilov, who covered regional affairs, and Gennadi Troshev, who dealt with Chechen affairs, and Cossack affairs in addition. Advisers draft documents and reports for the President, and can ask federal ministries and agencies for information that they need in order to fulfil their function. An Experts Department is responsible for preparing analytical reports for the President.

Putin also appoints Envoys for specific purposes. At the start of his second presidency Alexander Kotenkov was serving as his emissary to the Federation

Council, and Alexander Kosopkin to the State Duma. There was a press officer, a press service and a head of protocol. In October 2004 Putin appointed Anatoli Safonov presidential Envoy for international cooperation in the battle against terrorism and organised crime.

President, presidency and the Administration of the President's Affairs

The President and his Administration together form a team, with complex relationships within it. They have been treated separately here partly because of the high prominence of the office of President in the political system and partly because the constitution treats them separately, stating that the President 'forms the Administration of the President of the Russian Federation'. The reason why it is important to note that they form a single unit within the executive is that Putin has made a good deal of political capital out of staying personally aloof from decisions and developments for which he is in fact responsible. He can, in this way, hide behind his Administration.

However, it may not always be a matter of using the Administration as a cover and there may, in some cases, be good reasons for really keeping his distance. The President appoints his Administration, but the appointees are likely to be powerful figures. Once appointed, they do not necessarily see eye to eye with their patron. They may form clientelist relationships of their own, within or outside the Administration. This process appears to have been at work as Putin's first term neared its end, and evidence of it surfaced in the Yukos affair (see above). Lilia Shevtsova points out that there is a general paradox, according to which the more power a leader has, the more he has to share it with his entourage, and the more he shares it, the weaker he becomes.[3] All the more important is it, therefore, to strive to discern where responsibility for a given decision or policy lies, though this is often not easy. It is worth noting that:

- factional relationships of this sort were common in the Communist Party's Politburo in Soviet times;
- there are other clear resemblances between the Administration of the President's Affairs and the former Politburo;
- in any political system, when democratic procedures are missing or weak they tend to be replaced by factionalism and personal relationships;
- tensions of this kind exist in the president's administration in any presidential system, but they are exacerbated in Russia because the power of the President has weakened all other sources of authority. The President is, as it were, closeted with his Administration at the apex of a steep pyramid. This means that the question 'Who is Putin?' has bedevilled all analysis of Russian politics during his presidencies.

The President's Envoys

One of Putin's earliest steps on assuming the presidency was to create a new layer of government, accountable to the President, between the federal institutions in Moscow and the regions. In May 2000 he designated seven 'federal districts', using the boundaries of the seven military districts for the purpose, and he appointed a President's Envoy to each of them. Each district was to incorporate several component units ('subjects') of the Federation (Table 2.4).[4] In the context of the time, these Envoys were seen primarily as a means whereby Putin could ensure that the process of aligning the constitutions of national-minority republics with that of the Federation was being energetically addressed, but it was clear that they were also to serve a wider purpose.

This new layer of government was created by presidential decree, and fell within the President's power to form his administration, though many held that it effectively modified the constitution. Once in being, it immediately acquired a key political role – as well as a substantial administration, with a salaried staff and a deliberative council. The Procurator-General's Office established branches at that level, and the activity of federal inspectors based in the districts soon gave an indication of at least one aspect of the Envoys' function. The Ministry of Internal Affairs also has directorates at this level. Putin's own view of the Envoys' function is that they should unite efforts for managing crises, such as those caused by immigration, but also should ensure that there is effective planning and the promotion of joint social projects. But the Envoys also have an important security role, Putin having made it clear that they should closely coordinate their work with the directors of district security structures – the Ministry of Internal Affairs, the FSB and the regional procurator's office.[5] This security role was underlined by the fact that no fewer than six out of seven of the first Envoys appointed had backgrounds in the security forces.

A restructuring of the Far Eastern Federal District in May 2004 revealed that Konstantin Pulikovsky had until then had seven deputy Envoys (he thereafter had two) and five assistants. The district retained its 10 federal inspectors

Table 2.4 *The federal districts and President's Envoys (at September 2004)*

Federal district	Capital	President's Envoy
Central	Moscow	Georgi Poltavchenko
North-western	St Petersburg	Ilya Klebanov
Southern	Rostov-on-Don	Vladimir Kozak
Volga	Nizhni Novgorod	Sergei Kirienko
Ural	Yekaterinburg	Petr Latyshev
Siberian	Novosibirsk	Anatoli Kvashnin
Far Eastern	Khabarovsk	Konstantin Pulikovsky

for its 10 regions. The resulting total number of personnel in Pulikovsky's apparatus was 75.[6]

What was not clear at the start was how long the new institution was to remain in existence. In an interview with *Nezavisimaya gazeta* in October 2000, the Envoy to the Volga Federal District, Sergei Kirienko, said the position of the President's Envoy was not at all permanent and that once regional laws had been made to conform to federal laws (one of the Envoys' main tasks) the office could be abolished.[7] Only a little later, however, he noted that challenges to harmonisation would recur. In fact, the change from popular election to effective appointment by the President for the post of regional governor (or republican president) in the aftermath of the Beslan tragedy has given the President a means of direct control of the regions, which is likely to lead to the demise of the President's Envoy.

As noted, another result of Beslan was that a special Federal Commission for the North Caucasus was created within the Southern Federal District. Its first head was Vladimir Kozak, one of Putin's most trusted lieutenants, who at the same time replaced Vladimir Yakovlev as President's Envoy for the district.

Deliberative bodies

Through the Security Council, the State Council and the Council of Legislators, the Russian President has come to be surrounded with a wide range of deliberative bodies supporting him in his policy-making role.

The Security Council

Of all the agencies depending directly on the President, the Security Council is of far and away the greatest political importance. According to the constitution, the President 'forms and heads the Security Council'. On 24 April 2004 Putin signed a decree approving its membership for the start of his second presidency. It was to include the Prime Minister, the speakers of both houses of the Federal Assembly, the Minister of International Affairs, the head of the Foreign Intelligence Service, the director of the Federal Security Service, the Minister of Internal Affairs, the head of the Administration of the President's Affairs, the head of the Russian Academy of Sciences and the President's Envoys to the seven federal districts.

It has a secretary, supported by a number of deputy secretaries. An indication of the importance of the post of secretary is the high profile of its incumbents. Vladimir Rushailo, who was secretary to the Council in Putin's first term, had immediately before that been Minister of Internal Affairs, and Putin himself held the post briefly in 1999. As with the Administration of the President's Affairs, the deputy secretaries of the Security Council carry particular briefs. Thus Valentin Stepankov told the press on his appointment in April 2003 that his new responsibilities would include working with the staffs of the President's Envoys.[8] A later appointment as deputy secretary, Evgeni Nazdratenko, was to oversee ecological security and the preservation of bio-resources.

The Security Council has commissions attached to it, which make recommendations to the President. The Council's role is advisory; it has no executive role. It is none the less of the greatest strategic importance.

The State Council

Two bodies advisory to the President – the State Council and the Council of Legislators (see below) – were created by Putin to construct a new relationship between the presidency and the regions.

The State Council, created in September 2000, brings together the presidents of the republics and the governors of the oblasts (regions – see Chapter 4) and of the autonomous districts of the Federation. It sometimes meets in enlarged session in preparation for crucial strategic decisions – for example, those concerning nuclear arms reductions and relations with the North Atlantic Treaty Organisation. On these occasions the session can include leaders of the Duma's parties and fractions, the heads of the foreign affairs committees of both chambers of the Federal Assembly, the Security Council secretary, the Defence and International Affairs Ministers and other leading politicians.

The State Council has a presidium which deals with business between plenary sessions. Since May 2003 this has been chosen on a rotating basis, with seven regional leaders, one from each of Russia's federal districts, serving on the presidium for a six-month term.

The Council of Legislators

A consultative group – the Council of Legislators – was set up on 21 May 2002 to include the heads of regional legislatures and members of the Federation Council. The Council of Legislators meets quarterly at the Federation Council and once every six months at the Kremlin, with the President in the chair. It, too, has a presidium, to which 11 members are elected.

Other agencies subordinated to the presidency

The 'power structures'

Not strictly part of the Administration of the President's Affairs, but none the less responsible to the President and not to the government, is a group of ministries, services and agencies known as the 'power structures'. After a governmental reorganisation in March 2004 these were as follows.

- The five key strategically most important ministries, with a number of services (and one agency) attached to them:
  - the **Ministry of Internal Affairs**, with the Federal Migration Service;
  - the **Ministry for Civil Defence, Emergency Situations and Disaster Relief**;
  - the **Ministry for Foreign Affairs**;
  - the **Ministry of Defence**, with the Federal Service for Military–Technical Cooperation, the Federal Service for Defence Contracts, the Federal Service for Technical and Export Controls and the Federal Agency for Special Construction;
  - the **Ministry of Justice**, with the Federal Corrections Service and the Federal Service of Marshals of the Court.

- Five free-standing federal services:
  - the **State Courier Service**;
  - the **Foreign Intelligence Service**;
  - the **Federal Security Service**;
  - the **Federal Service for Control of Narcotics and Psychotropic Substances**;
  - the **Federal Protection Service** (which provides bodyguards).

- Two free-standing federal agencies:
  - the **Chief Administration for the President's Special Programmes**;
  - the **President's Administrative Office**.

The fact that these bodies are directly responsible to the President is of the greatest significance in demonstrating his exceptional power. Their role will be treated further in Chapter 3.

The Council for Combating Corruption and other bodies

Comprising the Prime Minister, the speakers of both chambers of parliament, the heads of the Constitutional, Supreme, and Arbitration Courts, and other officials, the Council for Combating Corruption was set up by presidential decree on 24 November 2003 to tackle one of the Federation's gravest and most deeply rooted problems. The main goal of the Council, which is a consultative body, is to help the President determine state priorities in fighting corruption. It includes a commission dedicated to resolving conflicts of interest. The work of the commission is to include the delicate task of working out the ground rules to cover cases where a senior public servant, through appointment to a new post, is in a position to profit from information gained in the earlier function.

There are numerous other committees and commissions that report directly to the President, as opposed to the government. Many of these are concerned with economic or technical matters, such as the presidential Committee on

Natural Resources. Others have a social brief, as with the presidential Human Rights Commission, headed in Putin's first term and into the second by Ella Pamfilova.

Constraints on the President's power

Despite the undoubted dominance of the presidency within the Russian political system, there are certain constraints on his power, some constitutional, others less formal.

There are two major constitutional constraints, beyond electoral considerations of ensuring re-election. The first is the provision in the constitution that allows for the President to be removed from office by impeachment. The procedure is that a motion to impeach is debated and voted on in the State Duma. If the vote is successful, the Supreme Court must ratify the motion as to its substance, and the Constitutional Court has to approve the procedures followed. The proposal then goes to the Federation Council for the final decision, which requires a two-thirds majority vote. The impeachment procedure was put to the test in May 1999, when, at the instigation of the Communist Party, a proposal to impeach Yeltsin on five charges failed. The charges were: that he had waged an illegal war in Chechnya; that he was responsible for the dismemberment of the Soviet Union in 1991 without a legal basis; that his coup against the Supreme Soviet of 1993, in the storming of the White House (see Chapter 1), was equally illegal; that he had destroyed the Russian military; and that his economic policies were tantamount to genocide of the Russian people. The vote on impeachment failed. The Duma emerged from the affair much weakened and the presidency strengthened.[9]

Second, the 1993 constitution established a Constitutional Court, which is competent to rule against the President if he exceeds his powers in a particular decision.

There is also the informal constraint that, although the President appoints his Administration, he has to stay on top of any factional divisions that arise. Once factional differences crystallise, it is difficult to dismiss individuals, and a large-scale dismissal involves high political risks. The need to accommodate and negotiate within the presidential team acts as a further constraint on the President's freedom of action.

Putin as President

On being elected President, Putin launched a series of major initiatives that illustrated fully the dominance of the presidency in the Russian political system (Figure 2.1) and the role that he clearly saw it should play in bringing about orderly change. His immediate objectives were:

- To bring to an end the dispute over Chechnya's demand for independence. In fact he embarked on this as Prime Minister (before being elected President) but it took until almost the end of his first presidency for a settlement to emerge, which in the event proved unstable.
- To curb the power of the 'oligarchs'. These financial adventurers had made fabulous gains from the privatisation process and had acquired considerable political leverage.
- To rein in the decentralised power that the regions had managed to arrogate to themselves in the Yeltsin years.
- To ensure the passing of the extensive legislation consequent on the reforms of the Yeltsin period, including laws to govern the operation of political parties and the electoral process.

The people he appointed to spearhead the work involved in addressing these priority tasks were drawn to a great extent from the security structures and the armed forces. As with the majority of the new President's Envoys to the federal districts, many of the heads of the 'power structures' had military or security backgrounds.

Second, he used the Administration of the President's Affairs either to undertake directly, or to coordinate, the execution of these policies. The reining in of the regions provides the clearest example of this. A wide-ranging programme,

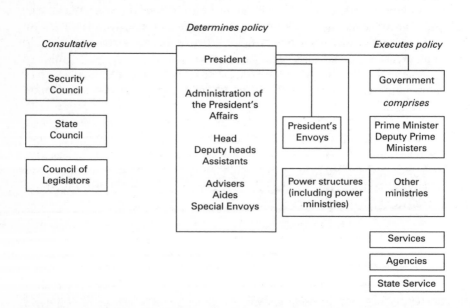

Figure 2.1 *The executive of the Russian Federation.*

which included aligning regional constitutions and charters with the federal constitution, together with the complete reorganisation of local government, was put in the hands of Dmitri Kozak, at the time one of the deputy heads of the Administration of the President's Affairs.

Putin's style

Putin's record has confirmed and indeed strengthened the dominant role of the President within the political system, but the style that he adopted in performing his role has shown a political subtlety that was entirely absent from the ebullient and forthright style of his predecessor.

It has been a style of indirect action. Personally, he has remained detached from controversial issues, while at the same time clearly pursuing his proclaimed priorities. Never putting himself directly at the head of a political party, he none the less indirectly encouraged the fortunes first of the Unity party and then of United Russia. His control of the media was also secured largely through indirect means, by allowing or encouraging media organisations to collapse from financial or other failings. From his detached vantage point in the presidency, he was able to criticise the government without making himself responsible for its failures (in fact, however, as Mikhail Kasyanov emphasised when he was Prime Minister, the President's powers in economic matters are limited). Putting himself above party and above sectional interests, Putin has been able to present himself as the people's President, aware of a popular belief in a strong hand at the centre (Box 2.3), and aware also of a popular mistrust of political parties and concupiscent business people determined to appropriate portions of the common patrimony.

Behind his style of indirect action has been an insistence on the 'power vertical'. The power vertical can be seen at work in his assertion of central power against the regions, in his acquisition and use for his purposes of a near total monopoly of the television network and a good part of the printed media, in the emasculation of the State Duma, and through selective use of the law-enforcement agencies to keep powerful holders of economic power in a state of fear.

Box 2.3 Putin on the state

'For Russians a strong state is not an anomaly that should be got rid of. Quite on the contrary, they see it as a source and guarantor of order, and the initiator and main driving force of any change.... I am not calling for totalitarianism.... A strong state power in Russia is a democratic, law-based, workable federal state.'

(Vladimir Putin, 'Russia on the threshold of the millennium', *Rossiiskaya gazeta*, 30 December 1999)

Figure 2.2 Vladimir Putin (by Zlatovsky, courtesy of Courrier International*).*

At the end of his first term in office it was difficult to make a clear assessment of Putin as President. Two contradictory interpretations of his actions and policies could be sustained. One version highlighted his past in the security organs, his appointing of numerous officials in his own likeness from the same source and his use of the law-enforcement agencies to wield an arbitrary stick with which to reduce areas of independent or critical action. On this view, his claim to be working towards a democratic order was spurious. The other, more positive view emphasised the urgent need to restore order after the Yeltsin presidency. It credited him, and his notion of 'guided democracy', with giving the nation a sense of stability through a return to at least some of the familiar landmarks of the Soviet order, while laying down the juridical basis for movement towards democracy that had been necessarily postponed.

Russians, however, are jaundiced about claims by their leaders that good times lie ahead.

There is no doubt that Putin has gained from not being expressly associated with any particular party and from an indirect style of political action that allows others or circumstances to produce the results he favours. It has enabled him to sustain high approval ratings at home. It has brought him dividends abroad, too, as it has allowed him to appear to foreign observers as more cosmopolitan than his own officials and the Russian political class. That said, his high ratings could have a downside to them, in postponing to an indefinite future the establishment of a democratic order, especially since it appears that a large part of public opinion is not favourable to democracy anyway – at least not in the form that it is presented to them today, with its associations of Western cultural and economic imperialism.

Assessment

There are at present no plural checks on the power of the Russian President. This accords with Putin's emphasis on the 'power vertical' and with his concept of 'guided democracy'. The presidency has succeeded in overwhelming such challenges as business interests and the regions have presented, and has subordinated to itself the potentially countervailing power of the media.

To concentrate on checks to the President's power or lack of them, however, gives only a partial perspective on the President's role in Russian politics. The powerful presidency controls, but at the same time it attracts. It acts as a political magnet. Since that is where real power and influence lie, and since that is the source of jobs, funding and favours, even the most headstrong political figures will rationally prefer to align themselves with the presidency than to oppose it.

Two major factors have led to this dominance: the Russian political culture and the turbulence of the change of regime. The relationship between them is complex. On the one hand, the political and economic changes ushered in by Gorbachev's policies conflicted with established values and practices.[10] On the other, the circumstances of uncertainty and change invited strong individual leadership at the centre, thus accentuating an existing tradition. This paradox was most evident under Yeltsin, who, though a President in the authoritarian mould, allowed the reform movement to weaken the Russian state by giving increased autonomy to the regions and by putting considerable economic power in the hands of a new speculative business elite. Under Putin both these challenges to the state have been checked, in a more general return to the values and practices with which Russian society, for better or worse, is more comfortable. In this way, the pressure of circumstances, Putin's personality and Russian political culture have come together to endorse a dominant presidency at the heart of the Federation's politics.

The tasks that the contemporary President faces are in many cases new. Now that Russia is open to the world, the President's role in international affairs has changed radically, even though many of the parameters of foreign policy follow from abiding geopolitical realities. A partly privatised economy has brought into being powerful forces, whose interests will ultimately require accommodation if continuity from the Soviet past is not to overtake completely the shift from plan to market. The same proviso affects the subordinate role into which Putin has corralled the media. It was to a great extent the blocking of the channels of communication that brought about the Soviet Union's downfall.

Given the authoritarian tradition in Russian and Soviet politics, it is hard to see from what source today a realistic challenge to the President's power might come. The popularity that Putin maintained throughout his first presidency and into his second, sustained by a good performance of the economy and a steep rise in incomes, seems to confirm the Russian people's willingness to accept a new version of the ancient image of the tsar as the little father of the people. 'In Russia, a President is more than a President', said Putin at his investiture. In his first presidency he showed what this might mean, going beyond the President's powers as given in the constitution and exercising a power exceeding the norm in presidential systems of the liberal-democratic world. But the key to the meaning of his elliptic phrase may lie more in the words 'in Russia', expressing an intention to fulfil a role consecrated by the political culture of himself and his people, and by needs imposed by the conjuncture in which he found himself.

Further reading

G. Easter, 'Preferences for presidentialism', *World Politics*, 49:2 (1997), 184–211.

E. Huskey, *Presidential Power in Russia* (Armonk, NY: M. E. Sharpe, 1999).

M. S. Fish, 'The executive deception: superpresidentialism and the degradation of Russian politics', in V. Sperling (ed.), *Building the Russian State: Institutional Crisis and the Quest for Democratic Governance* (Boulder, CO: Westview Press, 2000).

A. Brown, *The Gorbachev Factor* (Oxford: Oxford University Press, 1996).

A. Brown and L. Shevtsova (eds), *Gorbachev, Yeltsin, and Putin: Political Leadership in Russia's Transition* (Washington, DC: Carnegie Endowment for International Peace, 2001).

G. W. Breslauer, 'Boris Yeltsin as patriarch', *Post-Soviet Affairs*, 15:2 (1999), 186–200.

E. Huskey, 'Overcoming the Yeltsin legacy: Vladimir Putin and Russian political reform', in A. Brown (ed.), *Contemporary Russian Politics: A Reader* (Oxford: Oxford University Press, 2001).

Autobiographies

B. Yeltsin, *The Struggle for Russia* (New York: Random House, 1994).

V. V. Putin, with N. Gevorkyan, N. Timakova and A. Kolesnikov, *First Person: An Astonishingly Frank Self-portrait by Russia's President*, translation by Catherine A. Fitzpatrick (New York: Public Affairs, 2000).

Website

The presidential website is at www.president.kremlin.ru.

Notes

1   G. Easter, 'Preferences for presidentialism', *World Politics*, 49:2 (1997), 184–211.
2   Viktor Loshak, editor in chief of *Moskovskie novosti*, writing in no. 27, July 2003.
3   See L. Shevtsova, 'Enough of providential men!', *Izvestiya*, 25 February 2004.
4   M. Hyde, 'Putin's federal reforms and their implications for presidential power in Russia', *Europe–Asia Studies*, 53:5 (2001), 719–43.
5   Interfax news agency, 17 May 2002.
6   *RosBalt*, 11 May 2004; *RFE/RL Newsline*, 13 May 2004.
7   *RFE/RL Russian Federation Report*, 25 October 2000.
8   *Izvestiya*, 14 April 2003; *Zavtra*, 15 April 2003 .
9   *East European Constitutional Review*, 8:3 (1999), 29.
10 I. Klyamkin and L. Shevtsova, 'The tactical origins of Russia's new political institutions', in A. Brown (ed.), *Contemporary Russian Politics: A Reader* (Oxford: Oxford University Press, 2001).

3

The government

Background

In the Soviet Union the government was a mammoth organisation with a massive task, which included administering the economic plan. The means of production, distribution and exchange, with the partial exception of agriculture, were the property of the state, and it fell to the government to organise not only public services and the maintenance of law and order, but the whole of industry as well. In these circumstances it was rational for the industrial and extractive ministries to concentrate production in a few large, in some cases gigantic, enterprises. When the economy was restructured with the fall of the Soviet Union, the industrial ministries were either broken up or simply detached from the government's direct control. The government's role was reduced, though still substantial. Beyond it now lay a number of huge state-owned but semi-independent concerns exercising a monopoly in certain key areas (the energy-producing giant United Energy Systems, for example) and a number of substantial privatised enterprises likewise often exercising an effective monopoly. The government was thus transformed in size, but also in its function, since it now had to deal with a private sector and with large companies that were either entirely or partially state owned, but did not form part of the government's ministerial structure.

One feature of the Soviet government, however, partially survived – its subordination to a higher authority. The Communist Party's leading bodies – the Politburo and the Central Committee's Secretariat – were responsible for providing policy guidelines for the government, and for supervising and facilitating its work, respectively. This involved an active role in appointments to strategically important posts. Today the President is expressly charged by the constitution with laying down policy guidelines. The Communist Party's territorial committees with their powerful secretaries have gone, but the Administration of the President's Affairs and the President's Envoys perform many of the functions carried out earlier by the Communist Party's apparatus. As with so many facets of the politics of the Russian Federation, the government's role is therefore a mixture of the old and the new. But its subordination to a higher body outside itself remains, and this has not been affected by the existence now of a legislature filled through formally free elections.

The federal government

The constitution states that 'executive power in the Russian Federation is exercised by the government of the Russian Federation', which consists of the head of government of the Russian Federation (that is, the Prime Minister), a deputy and the federal ministries. A fuller picture of the executive function in the Russian Federation (as distinct from the legislative and judicial functions) would require a broader formulation (see also Figure 2.1, p. 42).

First, the powers of the President and of the Administration of the President's Affairs encroach substantially on those of the government itself. The spheres of internal security, defence, justice and foreign policy form a presidential domain and, as noted in Chapter 2, the ministers and officials charged with those briefs are directly subordinated to the presidency.

Second, the government's ministerial structure covers only one part of the state's administrative responsibilities. Beyond it a host of agencies and organisations carry out governmental and quasi-governmental functions, while yet further removed from the formal government lie a number of state-owned, or partially state-owned, companies on whose services the government relies for the performance of its public function. Official sources usually restrict the term 'government' to the actual ministries (16 of them since Putin reduced their number after his re-election in 2004), but it is used less formally to designate all those bodies (over 50 of them) that exercise governmental functions. When the presidential domain and quasi-governmental organisations are removed from the state's executive responsibilities, the government's chief executive responsibilities are reduced to:

- drafting the annual budget and implementing it;
- generating and implementing policy in culture, science, education, health, social security and the environment;
- ensuring public order and the prevention of crime (a function shared with the presidency).

The government also plays an important role in legislation, first by itself presenting bills to the State Duma, including the annual budget. It also has the prerogative of prior scrutiny of any bill presented to the Duma that has financial implications. Its primary role, however, is one of implementation, and in this executive capacity its various ministries issue administrative orders and regulations.

What gives the Russian government its particular character is partly its dependence on the presidency and partly – which is the other side of the same coin – its lack of accountability to the people through their elected representatives in the parliament in any but the most formal sense. We shall see that the parliament is able to exercise a number of checks on the government, but government policies have not so far been determined by parliament through party programmes, nor is the government's composition determined by the relative strengths of political parties in a competitive party system. The result is that the government has a strongly bureaucratic nature.

The federal government building is familiarly known as the 'White House'. It was here that the struggle between Boris Yeltsin and the Supreme Soviet of the last Congress of People's Deputies came to a head in September 1993, when Yeltsin staged what was effectively a coup, sending in troops to storm that building and evicting the Supreme Soviet from it. The new legislature that thereafter came into being – the State Duma – was to be housed elsewhere, and the White House has since then been the seat of the government.

The federal government comprises the Prime Minister (the title is strictly chair of the Council of Ministers), a deputy Prime Minister, the ministers, a series of services, agencies and commissions, and a government administration, which organises the government's business. On 12 May 2004, the State Duma gave its approval to Putin's proposal of Mikhail Fradkov as Prime Minister; this promotion took him from his post as Russia's representative to the European Union (see Box 3.1). In February Fradkov's predecessor, Mikhail Kasyanov, had been dismissed in an evident move by Putin to prepare the way for his own second presidency. Between the proposal of Fradkov for the post of Prime Minister and the Duma's vote of approval, Putin had appointed one of his most trusted lieutenants, Dmitri Kozak, to head the government administration. It was assumed that Putin's intention in placing Kozak in this post was to ensure that the government under Fradkov would be less inclined to adopt an independent stance than the previous government, under Kasyanov, had been. It was also a marker of the seriousness of Putin's intention to undertake seriously a reform of the Federation's overall administration.

The governmental structure is staffed by the State Service, which is internally arranged in a strictly graded hierarchy, whose members are known familiarly as *chinovniki* (*chin* being the Russian word for official rank and the term used in pre-revolutionary Russia for the government service).

The Prime Minister's relationship with the presidency

Despite the power that he wields as head of the government, the Prime Minister is clearly in a subordinate position in relation to the President. First, as noted, the respective roles assigned them in the constitution as policy maker against executant give the more important function to the President.

Second, framed as it was to give the new order a clear figurehead at a time of political stress, the constitution also gave the President the power both to appoint and to dismiss the Prime Minister. The procedure is that the President

Box 3.1 A Prime Minister's career

Mikhail Efimovich Fradkov was born on 1 September 1950, and 22 years later qualified as an engineer in the Moscow Machine-Tool Institute. From 1972 to 1998 he held various posts in the foreign trade field, including two years as economics counsellor in the Russian embassy in India and a year at the talks on the General Agreement on Tariffs and Trade (GATT) in Geneva. In 1997–98, after a year heading an insurance company he was reappointed Minister of Foreign Trade in, first, Sergei Stepanov's government and then in that of Putin. After briefly holding posts concerned with military and technical matters in the Administration of the President's Affairs and in government he became first deputy secretary of the Security Council, and then in 2001 was put in charge of the Federal Tax Police Service. In March 2003 he was despatched to Brussels as representative of the Russian Federation at the European Union (EU). In March 2004 he was appointed Prime Minister.

An article in *Moskovskie novosti* (no. 8, February 2004) entitled 'A compromise of all with all' lists five compromises that Fradkov's appointment involved:

- Between Putin's appointees from the security structures and the 'liberals', Fradkov being equidistant from both. The latter could be relieved that the Prime Minister would not be wearing epaulettes, while Fradkov's past in the Security Council and foreign economic trade spelled at least a past connection with the security agencies.
- Between the factions in the Kremlin. He was well in both with the conservatives such as Viktor Ivanov and Igor Sechin because of these past security links, and with the liberals, through mutual connections with the financial concern Alfa-Group.
- Between the 'Russian statists' and the 'Westernisers'. He had worked in the State Service for 30 years, which might have been badly perceived in the West, were it not for the international posts that he had held, including that of Russia's representative to the EU.
- Between administrative manipulation and compromising factors. Fradkov had held three posts at ministerial level, but mysteriously his departure from each post was accompanied by the demise of the ministry or agency he headed. On the other hand, there were two financial scandals that he could be associated with if the Kremlin wanted to be sure that Fradkov would remain cooperative.
- Between the President and the electorate. When sacking Kasyanov, Putin promised to appoint someone who would personify a specific course of development for the country. But this would mean that Putin's ratings would suffer – either the liberals or the nationalists would be alienated. With Fradkov no one would be disappointed. Who, then, would determine the course of development? Obviously the President himself.

The newspaper ended by pointing out that among the voices urging that the Federal Tax Police Service (which had been headed by Fradkov) be abolished were those of the oligarchs, including Mikhail Khodorkovsky, the head of the Yukos oil company at the time. That oligarch could expect less sympathy from Fradkov than from Kasyanov.

proposes a name to the State Duma, which has one week in which either to accept or to reject it. If it rejects the nomination the President makes a further one. If the Duma rejects three nominations, the President dismisses the government and calls fresh elections. The procedure did not, however, prevent Yeltsin, as President, from changing Prime Ministers at will, the rhythm of change mounting as uncertainties about his succession increased from 1996. Indeed, the year from August 1997 saw no fewer than four changes of Prime Minister.

Third, in the case of ministerial appointments, the Prime Minister has only the power to propose names for the President to approve, which puts the entire government within the President's patronage. This presidential power of patronage can take a more proactive form; for example, in May 2003, Putin dismissed the head of the government administration at the time, Igor Shuvalov – in order to put him in charge of a unit in the President's own jurisdiction and one, moreover, with the brief of addressing 'strategic goals', which could not but encroach on the government's sphere of action.

Fourth, the five key 'power' ministries (Internal Affairs, Emergency Situations, Justice, Defence and International Affairs) are, as noted in Chapter 2, subordinated directly to the President (though the Prime Minister coordinates their work with that of the government). It is worth noting also that the President can and does chair meetings of the cabinet, in addition to the routine weekly meetings that Putin instituted between himself and the Prime Minister, sometimes with the top cabinet ministers.

Furthermore, as ultimate guardian of the national interest, and without the responsibilities of day-to-day administration, the President can make demands that the government is not necessarily able to fulfil. He can in this way wrong-foot the Prime Minister and the government and increase his own stature. In his annual address to the State Duma in mid-2002, Putin called on the government to increase the speed of economic growth, effectively charging it with dragging its feet. This met with a cool response from the Prime Minister at the time, Kasyanov, who stated publicly that the 6–8 per cent annual growth that Putin called for could not be achieved without major structural reforms, which would take time to put in place. In making this claim he was defending his autonomy in relation to the President. Moreover, in effectively accusing the President of voluntarism he could not but remind Russians of Soviet days, when the Communist Party, under its General Secretary, would summon the people, and particularly those in responsible positions, to aim beyond realisable targets ('There is no fortress Bolshevism cannot storm', originally a political slogan of the Stalin years, had become a sardonic joke by the time the Soviet Union collapsed). In the event, however, Kasyanov's sally rebounded, and he was removed from his post in 2004.

Yet the Prime Minister's position does offer important political advantages. In particular, its incumbent is one of the few figures in the political system capable of building up a national constituency of support, second only to the

President in this regard. Thus, even though the President can appoint and dismiss the Prime Minister, and even though, therefore, the latter will agree with the President's general policy, the premiership has the potential to become a potential launching pad for a bid for the presidency. No doubt it was partly considerations of this kind that led Putin to dismiss Kasyanov and his government on 24 January 2004, shortly before the presidential elections of March. Another consideration, however, was that Kasyanov was a member of the Family. It was clear by this time that Putin was taking steps to get conditions right for a second presidency, and in matters of personnel the effective dismissal of Alexander Voloshin from his post as head of the Administration of the President's Affairs in November 2003 had already shown that Putin would be shedding members of Yeltsin's clientele.

The deputy Prime Minister

At the close of Putin's first presidency there were no fewer than six deputy Prime Ministers. Each of them had supervised a group of ministries and government agencies (as indeed did the Prime Minister himself) and in a few cases headed a ministry of particular importance. It was, therefore, a major innovation when, on his appointment as Prime Minister, Fradkov announced that henceforth there would be only a single deputy Prime Minister, reducing that post to what its name suggests – someone who stands in for the Prime Minister should the need arise. The single deputy Prime Minister appointed in March 2004 was Alexander Zhukov, who had been chairman of the State Duma's Budget Committee in the second and third Dumas. He studied economics at Moscow State University and in 1991 spent five months at Harvard University Business School. Before March 2004 the deputy Prime Ministers, with the Prime Minister, formed a small cabinet, which held regular meetings and was serviced by a staff of its own. This is no longer the case. The reduction in the number of deputy Prime Ministers to one was in keeping with Putin's appointment of his most trusted officials, first Dmitri Kozak and then, from September 2004, Sergei Naryshkin, to head the administration of the government: it reduced the profile of the government in relation to the presidency.

Ministries, services and agencies

Government ministers are usually drawn from within the state bureaucracy and are appointed by the President on the proposal of the Prime Minister. Until October 2004, they were debarred by law from membership of a political party while in office. This, however, did not prevent Boris Gryzlov, the Minister of Internal Affairs, from accepting in November 2002 the leadership of the United Russia party, which was forming in support of the President. (Gryzlov's claim that he was first and foremost the Minister of Internal Affairs and that in his free time he was a supporter of United Russia, though not actually a member of that party, brought wry smiles to the faces of political commentators.) On 13 October 2004 the Duma legislated to allow government ministers to join political parties and hold leadership posts within them.

While each of the 88 regional 'subjects' of the Federation (see Chapter 4) has its own government, the regional ministries covering the most strategically important areas of public life – such as finance – function as branches of the federal ministries. At times this subordination has been used to rein in what the federal government sees as regional waywardness. Thus *Kommersant-Daily* reported that the federal Minister of Taxation, Gennadi Bukaev, had appointed as director of the Ministry of Taxation of the Bashkortostan Republic a figure who told the newspaper that in his post he would 'struggle for the supremacy of Russian financial laws in Bashkortostan'.[1] The republic's waywardness was the subject of a further intervention by a federal minister later in that year. This time it was the federal Minister of Internal Affairs, Gryzlov, who chided his subordinate, the republican interior minister, for negligence in carrying out his duties, and charged him and his deputies with directing their activities at fulfilling orders from the republican authorities that often contradicted federal legislation.[2]

The 2004 reorganisation

During Putin's first presidency a deputy Prime Minister, Boris Aleshin, had been put in charge of a working party to examine ways of streamlining the governmental structure of the Federation. Proposals were made for a reduction in the number of ministries from the existing 24. The Russian Union of Industrialists and Entrepreneurs proposed a reduction to eight (finance; internal affairs; defence; international affairs; economic development and trade; justice; labour, social insurance and health; and science, education and culture), the other existing ministries being distributed among the categories of federal agencies.[3] At the same time, federal ministries had themselves been reviewing their functions and cutting out superfluous ones, in accordance with an administrative-reform plan drawn up by the Economic Development and Trade Ministry.[4] That ministry foresaw measures that would require government departments to justify all their functions.

On 9 March 2004, shortly after Fradkov's appointment as Prime Minister, Putin announced that the government was to be reorganised. The number of ministries was reduced from 24 to 15 (though increased at the end of May 2004 to 16), in addition to the posts of Prime Minister and deputy Prime Minister. A three-tier structure was created. The first tier now comprises the government ministries, whose job it is to generate policy in their sphere of competence and to issue normative orders. The second layer consists of 18 federal services in charge of implementation and compliance. Their role is

Table 3.1 *The government of the Russian Federation (at September 2004)*

Post	Holder
Prime Minister	Mikhail Fradkov
Deputy Prime Minister	Alexander Zhukov
Agriculture	Alexei Gordeev
Economic Development and Trade	Herman Gref
Health and Social Development	Mikhail Zurabov
Defence	Sergei Ivanov
Head of the government administration and minister	Sergei Naryshkin
Finance	Alexei Kudrin
International Affairs	Sergei Lavrov
Transport	Igor Levitin
Information Technologies and Communications	Leonid Reiman
Internal Affairs	Rashid Nurgaliev
Culture and Mass Communications	Alexander Sokolov
Natural Resources	Yuri Trutnev
Education and Science	Andrei Fursenko
Industry and Energy	Viktor Khristenko
Justice	Yuri Chaika
Civil Defence, Emergency Situations and Disaster Relief	Sergei Shoigu
Nationalities (created in the aftermath of the Beslan tragedy in 2004)	Vladimir Yakovlev

purely executive. The third tier is made up of some 25 federal agencies, which discharge state services to the population.

The reorganisation was accompanied by a substantial reduction in personnel and a wholesale redistribution of government posts. A number of the key ministers of Putin's first presidency retained their portfolios (Table 3.1): Sergei Ivanov at Defence, Alexei Kudrin at Finance, Herman Gref at Economic Development and Trade, Alexei Gordeev at Agriculture, Sergei Shoigu at Emergency Situations and Yuri Chaika at Justice. New appointments that were clearly going to be important in his second presidency included that of Sergei Lavrov as Minister of International Affairs and Rashid Nurgaliev as Minister of Internal Affairs. A new ministry, of Industry and Energy, was created and Viktor Khristenko was put in charge of it.

Staff reductions

No sooner had Kozak been installed as head of the government administration than he began to require the ministries to make sweeping reductions in their staffs. Many, indeed, had already started reducing their personnel in anticipation of this requirement. At the end of March a maximum of two deputy ministers for each ministry was laid down. The effect of this may be gauged by the fact that Gref's Ministry of Economic Development and Trade had up to that point had 12 deputy ministers and three first deputy ministers, while the equivalent figures for Kudrin's Finance Ministry were nine and three. On 1 April 2004 Kozak announced that the overall number of deputy ministers would be reduced from 250 to 18. As with their ministerial chiefs, heads of department were to be limited to two deputies apiece. *Vedomosti* of 27 April 2004 reported Kozak as saying that the governmental reorganisation would reduce the ministerial staffs from 1,017 to 240, and cut the number of departments from 23 to 12 (the many empty offices were to be sealed to save money on their upkeep). The extent of the cuts made by Kozak raised questions about the Prime Minister's own field of competence in relation to that of Kozak. It was noted that by the end of April some of the dismissed ministers had returned as assistants to Fradkov.

As part of this reorganisation, Fradkov also addressed the overexpansion in the number of government commissions. He abolished 146 of them, and put those remaining under the purview of himself, his deputy Prime Minister (Zhukov) and the head of the government administration.

The distinction between government ministries and various services, agencies and commissions had, before the reorganisation, always been somewhat vague. *Rosaviakom*, the Russian Aviation and Space Agency, had control of the Baikonur space centre, but it was the Defence Ministry that controlled two important cosmodromes, at Plesetsk and Svobodny. Again, political expediency at times resulted in the same task being passed between the categories, as when charge of security operations in Chechnya was transferred from the Federal Security Service (FSB) to the Ministry of Internal Affairs in 2003.

Ministries in very many cases created quasi-governmental organisations within their own structure. Before the governmental reorganisation of March 2004 the Federal Atomic Energy Agency, *Rosenergoatom*, was part of the Nuclear Energy Ministry, and created within itself a Unified Generating Company to rival the electricity generating monopoly, United Energy Systems (EES), which is itself beyond ministerial control. Many of the new services and agencies are headed by people of considerable clout, for example former ministers.

The reorganisation of the services, agencies and commissions

It will be recalled (Chapter 2) that a number of ministries are subordinated directly to the President and that a number of services and agencies were attached to three of them (the Ministries of Internal Affairs, Defence and Justice) as part of the governmental reorganisation of 2004. The remaining ministries – those not answering directly to the President – likewise had a series of services and agencies attached to them. Examples are presented in Table 3.2.

Table 3.2 *Examples of federal services and agencies attached to ministries*

Ministry	Service/agency
Industry and Energy	Nuclear Oversight Service Service for Technical Regulation and Measurement Service for Technical Oversight Atomic Energy Agency Space Agency Agency for Industry Agency for Construction, Housing and Utilities Energy Agency
Finance	Taxation Service Insurance Oversight Service Financial and Budgetary Oversight Service Financial Monitoring Service Federal Treasury Service
Economic Development and Trade	State Statistical Service Customs Service Tariffs Service Government Reserves Agency Land Register Agency Agency for the Management of Federal Property
Health and Social Development	Oversight Service for Consumer Rights and Human Welfare Oversight Service for Health and Social Development Labour and Employment Service Health and Social Development Agency Physical Culture, Sport and Tourism Agency
Culture and Mass Media	Archives Agency Culture and Cinematography Agency Agency for the Press and Mass Media
Agriculture	Veterinary and Plant Disease Oversight Service Fisheries Agency Agriculture Agency
Education and Science	Intellectual Property, Patents and Trademarks Service Service for Oversight of Education and Science Science Agency Education Agency

The power structures and the government

Federal ministries vary in their degree of strategic importance. Some have had particular political prominence as a result of their strategic role in the process of transformation from a planned to a market economy, such as the former Ministry of Property Relations and the Ministry for Anti-monopoly Policy and Support of Entrepreneurial Activity (neither still extant), or the Ministry of Economic Development and Trade (which survives). But, however important the role of these ministries is in the process of economic reform, they occupy a secondary place in Russia's ministerial system. Pride of place is given to the five ministries listed in Chapter 2 among the 'power structures' – the Ministries of the Interior, Defence, International Affairs, Emergency Situations and Justice. These, as noted, are subordinated directly to the President, together with a series of services and agencies that also form part of the power structures and are likewise listed in Chapter 2. The term 'power structure' does not appear in the constitution, nor in official listings of the government, where all the ministries normally appear without that distinction being made. In Russian political discourse, however, and in the public's awareness, the existence of the power structures and the special status that they enjoy are fully acknowledged. In such contexts they are regularly associated with the 'power vertical' – another informal term that is recognised as connoting a key feature of Russian politics. The power structures, therefore, have to be treated as a part both of the presidency and of the government.

This is an arrangement that reflects many features of Russian politics. First, it attests the primacy of the presidency; a governing cabinet that does not control the key ministries concerned with defence and public order is clearly in a subordinate position. Second, it is in part a product of Putin's determination to put the political house in order after the turmoil unleashed by the perestroika period and the subsequent disorganisation of political life caused by the way in which the Yeltsin presidency addressed its reform programme. But, third, it reflects also an obsession with security that was so strong a feature of the Soviet period, and which in fact reaches back into the tsarist order. In Putin's Russia security has been not so much a part of government as an extra dimension to government. We return in greater detail to this theme in Chapter 5.

For the moment it is to be noted that the special status of the power structures blurs the borderline between the presidency and the government, very much to the advantage of the presidency. It is an arrangement that can work only as long as the government is effectively subordinated to the presidency. Should the development of the party system lead to true party competition and to the formation of stable party loyalties based on clearly defined programmatic cleavages, the position could arise where President and government derive their authority from competing constituencies. In such circumstances it is doubtful whether any form of cohabitation could be found that would tolerate so important a part of government business being run from the Kremlin. But such considerations remain abstract for the moment, since there is a connection between the Kremlin's reliance on the power structures and the present weakness of the institutions of civil society. The question of whether the promotion of democracy by means of the power structures offers a way out of this vicious circle is one of the continuing themes of this book.

One of the power structures has a brief extending so deeply into more general social affairs that its work merits particular attention here – the Ministry of Internal Affairs (MVD).

The Ministry of Internal Affairs

The MVD has had an unfortunate history in that its predecessor – the People's Commissariat of Internal Affairs (NKVD) – had charge of the labour camps of the gulag in the Stalinist period. From 1956 it was freed from this economic role and many of its functions in political policing were given to the Committee of State Security (the KGB). It retained its role in civil and criminal policing. Now, in the new Russian Federation, it has had to deal with the myriad forms of illegal and semi-legal behaviour created by the opening of the economy to market forces, and to other novel problems stemming from the change of regime, such as a greater mobility of the population within and across the borders of the Federation. The key factors in this last case have been the wars of independence in Chechnya (see Chapter 4), the movement of people into the Federation from the former, now independent, republics of the Soviet Union, and the importance given by the Kremlin to fighting terrorism.

In the case of economic crime, the MVD has developed an important investigative role. The scale of this work is illustrated by a report in August 2002 from General Boris Gavrilov, deputy chief of the MVD's investigative committee, that over 10 million tons – some 60 million barrels – of oil were being stolen each year as a result of illicit dealings. In 2001 his committee had closed down 395 local pipelines that were illegally diverting oil from the state network, Transneft, and 158 people were arrested.[5] The Ministry's fight against economic crime was given an added dimension after March 2003, when the previously independent Federal Tax Police Service was abolished and its role transferred to the MVD. The fact that the Ministry has a special Economic Crime Directorate devoted to Moscow alone is a marker both of its importance in the fight against deviance and of the extent to which economic crime is concentrated in the federal capital.

On 23 June 2003 the MVD's Internal Affairs Directorate, in conjunction with the FSB and the Procurator-General's Office, arrested a number of Moscow police officers on a charge of running a criminal gang. The group included three colonels and three lieutenant colonels from no less a quarter than the Criminal Investigations Department of the MVD's Moscow Directorate (high officials of the MVD all bear military ranks). The officers were accused of planting guns, narcotics and ammunition on citizens with a view to blackmailing them and of fabricating 'hundreds' of criminal cases in order to extort bribes.[6] The targets for protection money were Moscow casinos, shopping centres and restaurants. It then emerged that the group had equipped themselves with a lavish complex of houses on an extensive estate with a tennis court and a floodlit football pitch. Worse than this provision of healthy sporting facilities was the discovery on the premises of over $3 million in cash, two kilograms of gold, antiques, a 'substantial quantity' of roubles, plastic explosives and material for packaging heroin.[7] Two months later further, but apparently unconnected, arrests of MVD officials took place, including that of a department head in the Ministry's Moscow Economic Crimes Directorate and the acting head of the MVD's Moscow Ecological Department. Once again, blackmail and extortion were involved. It was pointed out at the time that these two bodies cover areas – business and pollution-creating production – that are particularly open to bribery.

In September 2004 the MVD was charged with a particularly important mission. One week after the hostage-taking crisis in Beslan that month (see Box 2.1, p. 25) – the inadequate governmental response to which was blamed on a lack of coordination among the security forces – it was announced that operational groups would be formed within each of the federal subjects of the Southern Federal District. These were to be headed by senior MVD officers and were to coordinate the operations of all the anti-terrorism forces, including the special units of the FSB, the Ministries of Defence and of Emergency Situations, and of the MVD itself. This was a revival of tsarist imperial policy in the Caucasus, when military, policing and civil authority was unified and placed under a single command.

The State Service

In the Soviet Union all employees beyond certain categories in agriculture were on the payroll of the state. There is now a significant private sector in the Russian Federation, but the number of public-sector workers remains huge. In the Russian Federation the staff of the various government or quasi-governmental departments form the State Service. The remaining workers on the state's payroll – teachers, health and social workers, for example – are usually referred to by the informal term *byudzhetniki* ('budgetniks').

The total number given for the State Service at federal, regional and municipal level by the State Statistics Service in May 2004 was 1,300,500. This did not include personnel from the Ministry of Defence, the MVD and other law-enforcement agencies. Between 1 January 2003 and 1 January 2004 it had grown by 48,100.[8] The State Service is frequently presented as being too highly staffed and as parasitic. These charges stem probably from instances of inefficiency, the prevalence of corruption and suspicions of submissiveness to the presidential office. In fact, however, in comparative terms the State Service is not large. It has been estimated as forming 0.8 per cent of the population (against 4.4 per cent in the United States).[9] Furthermore, inefficient and venal or not, for centuries the state bureaucracy has been the backbone of the Russian state, and the Russian state is one of the most ancient in Europe. In particular, it played a key role in easing the reforms into place after the fall of communism and in preventing them, in the most adverse circumstances, from destabilising the country.

At the time of writing, an administrative reform is in progress, and the details given here are subject to revision when that reform is completed. The reform is apparently intended to cover also the Administration of the President's Affairs.[10] A bill introduced by the President into the Duma in the spring of 2003 was aimed at the creation of clear mechanisms for making and implementing decisions, for determining what information should be in the public domain, and for determining the functions of state servants. The bill also established a State Service for the Federation's component regions, and increased the number of posts that would fall within the category of State Service.

Meanwhile, on 13 August 2003 Putin signed a decree setting out 16 general principles for the conduct of state servants. The ITAR-TASS news agency reported that the decree called on state servants to perform their official duties professionally and 'to carry out their activities within the bounds of the competence of state bodies as defined by the law'. State servants were to observe 'political neutrality', avoid conflicts of interest and refrain from making public statements going beyond their official competence. The presidency later introduced a further law on the State Service, according to which: state servants cannot be appointed to posts where they would be related by blood or marriage to their immediate supervisors; they cannot hold office in local self-government organs or trade unions; and they must not engage in entrepreneurial activities. On leaving their post, state servants will be prevented from accepting posts in areas over which they had had official oversight. Finally, they are to make annual declarations of their income and property and are forbidden to accept gifts, except under special, legally stipulated circumstances.[11]

A further aspect of the reforms concerned the structure of the State Service. State servants were to be grouped into four functional classes – leading personnel, assistants (councillors), specialists and supporting specialists. They were to be divided further into five groups – higher, main, leading, senior and junior – each of these containing categories one, two and three.

Officials are to be obliged to refuse to carry out commands if they are illegal, even in the case of a written order. State servants should present declarations about any share certificates that they have, and these must be transferred into the trust department of a designated state body. Emoluments for state service will be calculated according to a precise scheme, with increments for length of service and bonuses for work connected with state secrets and for carrying out particularly important and complex tasks.[12] In view of the extensive corruption in Russian administrative life, these provisions must be taken as expressing aspirations for the future, which may be difficult to realise.

Assessment

The government of the Russian Federation – the ministries, services and agencies that carry out governmental functions – is clearly subordinate to the presidency. Its autonomy is restricted by the President's powers of appointment and dismissal. The key ministries and agencies are subordinated directly and explicitly to the President. Furthermore, the accountability of government to parliament has, under Putin, been shown to be vestigial. The members of the government are not drawn from the political parties in the Duma, while the question of whether the electorate can call the government to account through its elected parliament has been rendered void by the presidency's control of the media and of the electoral process.

In terms of the potential for the democratic development of Russian politics, it might be asked whether this subordination of government to the presidency is of central importance, any more than it is in the case of the USA, where the President is likewise responsible for the entire executive structure. The point, however, is that in Russia there is a lack of effective and independent countervailing powers in the legislative and judicial spheres. The President can set his own agenda, and has the means to prevent it favourably to the virtual exclusion of alternatives. Having no independent sources of representation, the government's actions are determined solely by the President's priorities.

In terms of the relationship of change to continuity, this chapter offers little of interest. Today's position resembles, in all important details, the relationship of the government to the Communist Party leadership in the Soviet political system, the chief difference being that the hands-on running of the economy has been transferred from government ministries to quasi-governmental organisations and private companies.

In today's Russian Federation the bureaucracy has gained from the disappearance of the territorial apparatus of the Communist Party of the Soviet Union, to which it was effectively subordinated, but it has retained the over-regulated character of its Soviet days. The reforms created a need for new regulations and also gave rise to new demands from the population. The result is that long-standing structural failures, the lack of the time needed to overcome them, the shortage of public funding and the burden of new tasks requiring a new regulatory framework place real pressures on the bureaucracy. These are eased to a great extent by corruption. This, in the present circumstances, relieves the state of expenses that it would otherwise incur through the provision of social services.[13]

On entering his second term as President, Putin made clear his intention to give reform of the Federation's administration a high priority. It is a mammoth task, but until it is confronted the public service will remain the weak link in the Russian executive.

Further reading

L. Shevtsova, 'The problem of executive power in Russia', *Journal of Democracy*, 11:1 (2000), 32–9.

E. Huskey, 'Political leadership and the centre–periphery struggle: Putin's administrative reforms', in A. Brown and L. Shevtsova (eds), *Gorbachev, Yeltsin and Putin: Political Leadership in Russia's Transition* (Washington, DC: Carnegie Endowment of International Peace, 2001).

M. McFaul, *Unfinished Revolution: Political Change from Gorbachev to Putin* (Ithaca, NY: Cornell University Press, 2001) (especially ch. 6).

L. Shevtsova, *Putin's Russia* (Washington, DC: Carnegie Endowment for International Peace, 2004).

K. W. Ryavec, *Russian Bureaucracy: Power and Pathology* (Lanham, MD: Rowman and Littlefield, 2003).

V. Sperling (ed.), *Building the Russian State: Institutional Crisis and the Quest for Democratic Governance* (Boulder, CO: Westview Press, 2000).

Website

Government website: www.government.ru.

Notes

1 *Kommersant-Daily*, 28 June 2003.
2 RFE/RL (Tatar-Bashkir Service), 11 August 2003.
3 *Nezavisimaya gazeta*, 17 April 2003.
4 *Izvestiya*, 21 August 2003.
5 *RFE/RL Newsline*, 13 August 2002, citing RIA-Novosti news agency.
6 ITAR-TASS news agency, 23 June 2003; *Izvestiya*, 22 August 2003.
7 www.newsru.com, 23–25 June 2003.
8 *RFER/RL Newsline*, 14 May 2004, citing Interfax.
9 M. Mendras, *Comment fonctionne la Russie?* (Paris: Autrement, 2003), p. 21.
10 *Nezavisimaya gazeta*, 26 March 2003.
11 *RFE/RL Newsline*, 26 September 2003, citing RIA-Novosti news agency.
12 *Nezavisimaya gazeta*, 18 March 2003.
13 A. Ledeneva, *Russia's Economy of Favours* (Cambridge: Cambridge University Press, 1998); and see Chapter 13.

4

Governing the regions

Background

The territory that Russia occupies is enormous, extending over 11 time zones and reaching in the east to within 100 kilometres of the coast of the United States in Alaska. Nine of these time zones lie to the east of the Ural Mountains, which conventionally form the border between Europe and Asia. It was in 1579 that a Cossack commander, Yermak, crossed the Urals and began the gradual extension of Russia's frontier eastwards to the Pacific over what is now known as Siberia. This expansion eastwards took in many indigenous ethnic groups but brought Russian settlement with it, so that the major towns of Siberia are Russian, and Siberia has come to have a special place in the Russian consciousness. To the south, wars against the Turks brought the Russian empire to the Caucasus and added further ethnic groups to it, this time Muslim.

But Russia was already multi-ethnic before the major expansions to the east and the south. There were Finnic peoples settled since the earliest times in the wooded territories of the early princes of Muscovy – today's Mari and Komi, for example. Then from the Mongol invasion of the thirteenth century Russia inherited substantial Turkic populations, most prominently the Bashkirs and the Tatars on the middle Volga, both Muslim peoples.

Russia is thus exceptional both in its size and in the complexity of its ethnic and cultural composition, even without the added complexity of the 14 republics that became independent when the Soviet Union collapsed. The way in which the Communist Party of the Soviet Union ruled that vast and varied society through a centralised political control qualified by cultural autonomy has been noted in Chapter 1.

With the fall of the communist regime, and with the drafting of a new constitution, the question arose of how the territory should be administratively divided. It was generally accepted that the form of government should be federal, though not everyone agreed – some thought that the time had come to put an end to the privilege that the ethnic minorities enjoyed of having their own territory bearing their name. But if federal, then on what basis should it be?[1]

It was decided to maintain the existing administrative categories of autonomous republic, autonomous region and national district for the minority areas,
alongside the Russian-populated 'regions' (oblasts) and 'territories' (krais), but
that the term 'autonomous' should be dropped from the title of the republics.
It was decided also that in the new order all these units would be equally 'subjects of the Federation'. Thus the former Autonomous Soviet Socialist Republic
of Tatarstan became simply the Republic of Tatarstan, and was put on the
same footing as, for example, the oblast of Murmansk and the city of Moscow,
which, with St Petersburg, was given the status of 'city of direct federal subordination'. As a result there are today 88 subjects of the Russian Federation.
The republics, however, have retained certain privileges. They can adopt their
own constitution, provided that it does not conflict with the federal constitution, and can maintain some of the symbols of nationhood – flags and coats of
arms, for example.

Although the subjects of the Federation display a confusing array of titles,
they are more uniform in terms of their status than was the case before 1993,
but also they all emerged initially in a stronger position in relation to the administrative centre in Moscow than in the previous order, circumstances having
conspired to put a good deal of power in their hands. The break-up of the Soviet
system was of itself bound to lead to a draining of power downwards to regional
level, at least temporarily, but it was given a helping hand by two factors.

The first was the rivalry between Mikhail Gorbachev and Boris Yeltsin
and its repercussions. When, in 1991, Gorbachev, as President of the Soviet
Union, was painstakingly drafting a new treaty to accommodate demands for
autonomy voiced by components of the Soviet Union, Yeltsin – then President
of the Russian Republic – muddied the waters by telling the autonomous
republics in his fiefdom to 'take as much power as you can swallow'. This led
to adventurous steps being taken in some quarters. In particular, the Chechen
Republic made an outright bid for independence. The leadership of the Tatar
Autonomous Soviet Socialist Republic, which was embedded within the
Federation and could not aspire to total independence, none the less claimed
statehood for 'Tatarstan' and with it control of the Republic's considerable
resources, which included oil. In 1994 a Russia–Tatarstan power-sharing
treaty was signed which the Tatarstan leadership saw as a treaty between
sovereign states. This was still in effect when Vladimir Putin came to power.

The extent to which demands for independence were associated with claims
for control over economic resources, as in Tatarstan, is illustrated also by
the case of the Siberian Accord (a regional interest group – see Chapter 10).
Siberia contains a large part of Russia's very substantial natural wealth, and in
1990 the leaderships of a number of the Siberian regions came together as the
Accord to explore ways in which they could collectively assert their regional
interests, including control over their natural resources.[2]

The confrontation between Yeltsin and the Congress of People's Deputies
in 1993 had an immediate effect on the movements for regional autonomy.

Many of their leading figures had been supporters of the discredited Congress rebels and now found themselves in a weak position. The Siberian Accord at once trimmed its demands. Tatarstan, on the other hand, was far less affected by the new turn of events. Its leader, Mintimer Shaimiev, a shrewd ex-member of the Soviet *nomenklatura*, had sided with the putschists in 1991 and had survived that bad choice. He now moved to protect himself and as much of his decentralising policy as he could by organising support for Yeltsin in the 1996 presidential election. By that time the differing deals that Yelsin had done with the republican leaderships in order to buy them off in his rivalry with Gorbachev had affected the nature of the new Russian Federation, yielding an asymmetric structure.

The second factor leading to an increase in regional power in the wake of the break-up of the Soviet Union was that perestroika brought to an end the system of central command planning, and with it the state monopoly of foreign trade. All goods entering and leaving the Soviet Union had required the approval of the Office of External Trade. By adjusting orders to changing world prices, this Office had been able to prevent fluctuations in the latter from disrupting planned output. The abandoning of both these bureaucratic mechanisms decentralised economic decision making, which gave more freedom to interests in the regions – firms, individuals and the regional authorities themselves. Furthermore, one aim of those conducting the economic reform was to find a way of breaking up the economic monolith inherited from the Soviet period. This met with initiatives from below, an early sign of the latter being the establishment of links between individual firms and a foreign market.

Putin calls the regions to order

One of Putin's priorities was to rein in these centrifugal forces that the Yeltsin period had unleashed. The practical steps that he took in order to do so were in line with his concept of the 'power vertical'.

- First, as noted (Chapter 2), he appointed seven special President's Envoys to act as his lieutenants, and divided the Federation into seven federal districts for this purpose, building on the existing military districts (see Table 2.4, p. 37, and below).
- Second, he got the Federal Assembly to approve a law that allowed him to recall regional leaders who broke federal laws and who governed according to their own constitutions. On the other hand, he approved a law passed by the Duma that gave some of the more controversial regional leaders the right to stand for a third term in office, whereas the federal constitution specified a limit of two terms.
- Third, he changed the system by which the Federation Council, the Federal Assembly's upper chamber, was appointed. Up to that point, regional governors and republican presidents had held a seat in the Council *ex*

officio. Putin replaced this system with one in which a representative was sent to the Council from each regional executive and each legislature. The new State Council, in which the governors now sat, held only occasional meetings and had no direct legislative function.

- Finally, he set about bringing the constitutions of the republics into alignment with the federal constitution. This grew into an extensive programme involving the whole range of centre–periphery relations, including a re-organisation of local government.

Administrative organisation

According to the 2002 census, the Russian Federation's population of 145.16 million comprises some 160 ethnic groups, although fewer than a quarter of them number over 100,000 (see Tables 4.1 and 4.2).

As noted, the areas of settlement of the more numerous ethnic groups were given constitutional status in the Soviet Union and have retained it in today's

Table 4.1 *Major ethnic groups with home territory in the Russian Federation (2002 census)*

Ethnic group	Number (millions)	Percentage of total population
Russians	115.87	79.8
Tatars	5.56	3.8
Bashkirs	1.67	1.2
Chuvash	1.64	1.1
Chechens[a]	1.36	0.9
Mordvinians	0.84	0.6
Avars	0.76	0.5
Udmurts	0.64	0.4
Mari	0.60	0.4

[a] The Chechen figure has been greeted with some scepticism, given the losses in the wars and the difficulties of conducting a census in a war-ravaged territory.

Table 4.2 *Major national groups within the Russian Federation with home territory outside it (2002 census)*

National group	Number (millions)	Percentage of total population
Ukrainians	2.94	2.0
Armenians	1.13	0.8
Belarusians	0.81	0.6
Kazakhs	0.66	0.5
Azerbaijanis	0.62	0.4

Box 4.1 The 'subjects' of the Russian Federation

- 2 cities directly subordinated to the Federation (Moscow and St Petersburg);
- 21 republics;
- 7 krais (often translated as 'territories');
- 48 oblasts (often translated as 'regions');
- 1 autonomous oblast;
- 9 autonomous districts (henceforth ADs).

Notes
- All these 88 units are termed in Russian 'subjects' of the Federation (*sub'yekty*).
- The two Russian terms krai and oblast are used untranslated in this book to avoid the ambiguities that arise with the terms 'territory' and 'region'. This enables the 88 subjects of the federation to be referred to collectively as 'the regions'.
- The creation of Perm krai from a merger of Perm oblast with Komi-Permyak AD, finally decided in 2004, has been included in these figures.
- These numbers are due to change as the result of mergers that have been proposed. They are correct as at December 2004.

Some facts
- In the constitution the ADs are said to 'form part of' either a krai or an oblast. This means that the krai or oblast shares constitutional oversight of the AD with the federal centre.
- There is no distinction between a krai and an oblast apart from that title; a krai is really just a big oblast.
- The titular nationality constitutes a majority of the population in only 7 of the 32 national-minority entities (republics and ADs).
- Of the 88 regions, 46 lie on the Federation's border.

Russian Federation, with varying titles depending chiefly on the size of the ethnic group (Box 4.1). The Cossacks constitute a special case (Box 4.2).

Each region is equipped with legislative, executive and judicial bodies reproducing those of the Federation. According to the federal constitution, the subjects of the Federation are 'bodies of state power'. Article 5.2 states that 'The Republic (State) has its own constitution and laws' while other subjects of the Federation have a 'charter'. Note that the election law requires that each subject of the Federation must have at least one single-member mandate for the State Duma.

Box 4.2 The Cossacks – a special case

The Cossacks descend from the communal military brotherhoods of Russians and Ukrainians of the south and south-west of Russia in the fifteenth to the nineteenth centuries, often fugitive serfs, each 'force' led by a *hetman*. The military role that the Cossacks played historically in extending and protecting the troublesome southern border of the tsarist empire has led them to develop a particularly intense loyalty to Russian nationhood and its symbols, in which territory, ethnicity and religion are intermixed. 'We should not share our land with anyone', said Viktor Vodolatsky, the leader of the Great Force of the Don in an interview with *Nezavisimaya gazeta* (9 September 2002). He was concerned equally about the growth in the number of mosques, immigration into Russian ethnic areas from Dagestan and Chechnya, and about the presence in Russia of minorities such as the Meskhetian Turks (and the Rom), all amounting to a 'change in the ethnic map of southern Russia' and a threat to the 'ethnic identity of the Slav peoples'. Being a group given more to action that to words, the Cossacks have been offering their services, in their own uniform, to the regular forces of law and order, and at times embarking on public-order initiatives of their own – for example, rounding up drug smugglers and locating Chechen detachments in abandoned villages outside Chechnya (*Nezavisimaya gazeta*, 23 May 2003). In 1992 a detachment of Cossacks – wearing tsarist uniforms from the First World War – arrived to defend an enclave of Russians in the newly independent Moldova.

The federal districts

It will be recalled that one of Putin's first measures on assuming the presidency was to appoint a President's Envoy to each of seven 'federal districts'. The full details of the districts are set out in Table 4.3.

Proposals to merge 'subjects' of the Federation

There have been a number of proposals to diminish the number of subjects of the Federation by merging them with one or more others. The reasons advanced for this were, first, that enlargement is necessary from the point of view of internal and external security. Indeed, some of the power ministries have for some time been merging their departments in certain ADs with those of larger neighbouring krais and oblasts. A second reason is that it would simplify administration of the country, especially given the huge variation in territory and population. A third reason is simply that the present patchwork

Table 4.3 *The federal districts*

Federal district	Subjects of the Federation included	Capital
Central	Moscow city, Moscow oblast and the oblasts of Belgorod, Bryansk, Ivanovo, Kaluga, Kostroma, Kursk, Lipetsk, Orel, Ryazan, Smolensk, Tambov, Tula, Tver, Vladimir, Voronezh and Yaroslavl	Moscow
North-western	St Petersburg city, Karelian Rep., Komi Rep., Nenets AD, and the oblasts of Arkhangelsk, Kaliningrad, Leningrad, Murmansk, Novgorod, Pskov and Vologda	St Petersburg
Southern	Krasnodar krai, Stavropol krai, Adygeya Rep., Chechen Rep., Dagestan Rep., Ingush Rep., Kabardino-Balkar Rep., Kalmyk Rep., Karachaevo-Cherkess Rep., North Ossetia Rep., and the oblasts of Astrakhan, Rostov and Volgograd	Rostov-on-Don
Volga	Bashkortostan Rep., Chavash Rep., Mari-El Rep., Mordova Rep., Tatarstan Rep., Udmurt Rep., and the oblasts of Kirov, Nizhni Novgorod, Orenburg, Penza, Samara, Saratov and Ulyanovsk	Nizhni Novgorod
Ural	Perm krai, Khanty-Mansii AD – Yugra,[a] Yamalo-Nenets AD, and the oblasts of Chelyabinsk, Kurgan, Sverdlovsk and Tyumen	Yekaterinburg
Siberian	Altai krai, Krasnoyarsk krai, Buryat Rep., High-Altai Rep., Khakasiya Rep., Tuva Rep., Aginsky-Buryat AD, Evenk AD, Taimyr AD, Ust-Ordynsk AD, and the oblasts of Chita, Irkutsk, Kemerovo, Novosibirsk, Omsk and Tomsk	Novosibirsk
Far Eastern	Primorye krai, Khabarovsk krai, Sakha Rep., Chukot AD, Koryak AD, Jewish autonomous oblast, and the oblasts of Amur, Kamchatka, Magadan and Sakhalin	Khabarovsk

AD – autonomous district.
Rep. – Republic.
[a] Note that Khanty-Mansii AD changed its name to Khanty-Mansii AD – Yugra in 2003.
See also the map on pages xiv–xv.

came about as a result of many historical layers of administrative reorganisation and should be rationalised.

It is mostly the ADs that have been concerned – that is, mergers with each other or into a krai or oblast. In many cases the ethnic group around which these lesser units were originally formed has been strongly Russified.

Opposition to mergers has come chiefly from the leaders of well endowed oblasts in response to suggestions that they might merge with neighbouring oblasts (cases in point are Moscow city with Moscow oblast; Voronezh oblast with Lipetsk, Tambov and Kursk oblasts). Putin has expressed himself in favour of mergers if they help to solve economic problems, and his formal position is that no change should be imposed on the regions from above, any mergers being entirely a matter of an initiative from the regions concerned.

The first case to arise was a proposed merger of Perm oblast with Komi-Permyak AD, which had been discussed for 12 years but could not be realised until a law of 2002 laid the juridical groundwork for combining Federation subjects. This merger has now been approved and the new enlarged unit, to be called Perm krai, will come into being in 2005.[3]

A number of proposed mergers are under discussion at the time of writing:

- Taimyr and Evenk ADs with Krasnoyarsk krai (this was at an advanced stage at the time of writing, October 2004);
- Ust-Ordynsk Buryat AD with Irkutsk oblast;
- Krasnodar krai with Adygeya Republic;
- Altai krai with the Altai Republic;
- Nenets AD with the Komi Republic;
- Yamalo-Nenets AD with Tyumen oblast;
- Chelyabinsk, Sverdlovsk and Kurgan oblasts;

The organs of regional government

Despite Putin's moves to rein in the regions, they none the less retained a good deal of the autonomy that they had arrogated to themselves during the Yeltsin period. The Federation treaty drawn up by Yeltsin in 1994 had given them competences that could not easily be withdrawn and Putin showed himself to be respectful of the letter of the constitution. Seen in the context of the time, Putin was restricting the autonomy of the regions against the backdrop of a decreasing efficacy of the state, while at the same time accommodating a degree of tolerance in centre–periphery relations required by the move from a planned to a market economy and by the break-up of the monopoly power of the Communist Party.

Governors and republican presidents

At the head of the executive of each subject of the Federation is a governor (*gubernator*) or, in the case of the nationality republics, a president. Until the Beslan tragedy of September 2004 (see Box 2.1, p. 25) these posts were filled through open and free elections, though these were often subject to intense political, often underhand, manoeuvring. At the beginning of Putin's presidency a limit of two terms was placed on the length of tenure for governors, but a law passed in 2001 allowed them to be elected for a third or even a fourth term.

However, in the immediate aftermath of Beslan, Putin proposed that these posts should no longer be filled by direct election but that instead regional assemblies should endorse candidates recommended by the federal President. Should his nomination be rejected twice, he would have the power both to dissolve the assembly and to appoint an acting regional governor (or republican president). Incumbent governors were to serve out their current terms.

It was a landmark proposal. First, it was a major step in the return to Soviet practice. These regional chiefs would thenceforth be in almost the same relationship with the central leadership as had been the Communist Party first secretaries in the Soviet Union's republics, autonomous republics and oblasts, with no direct mandate from the people, and depending for their appointment on a central *nomenklatura*. Second, the centralisation that this step involved severely modified the federal character of the Russian constitution. Since September 2004 Russia has been federal in name only, as had been the case with the Soviet Union, the nominally federal units enjoying at best devolved powers.

In fact, this decision was the culmination of a process that had been under way since Putin came to power. A law of 2000 entitled the President to dismiss governors who had violated federal laws on more than one occasion, and under discussion had been the temporary suspension of governors if their region went bankrupt, or if bad management led to the breakdown of services in harsh winter conditions (the two major problems that had been occurring). The verticality of power, before September 2004 and after, has extended downwards, governors being empowered to dismiss heads of municipal administrations if they have failed to comply with federal laws or the judgement of a court. This power had been invoked, for example, at the end of March 2003 by the governor of Sverdlovsk oblast, Eduard Rossel, to warn the mayor of Yekaterinburg over his failure to implement a 2000 local-court decision requiring the indexation of wages for state-sector workers.

The governor or president appoints a government, and can also create commissions to deal with specific problems. But many of the departments of a regional administration are subordinated to a corresponding ministry at federal level, as their equivalents had been in the Soviet Union. Moreover, certain important institutions, such as the Procuracy, are federal.

Who are the governors and what was their previous experience?

When the Communist Party's territorial apparatus lost its control in the Soviet Union after the attempted coup in August 1991, Yeltsin, as President of the Russian Republic, began to make appointments of heads of administration in the regions, though he left in place the existing leaders in the ethnic republics and districts, since at the time he was wooing them in his struggle with Gorbachev. Soon the pre-revolutionary term 'governor' found its way back into

Table 4.4 *Governors and presidents in post in 1999 and their mode of achieving office*

Mode of achieving office	Number
By appointment	36
of whom Soviet-era regional heads	13
By election	53
of whom Soviet-era regional heads	7
Soviet-era senior military figures	6

Source: Derived from T. H. Rigby, 'Russia's provincial bosses: a collective career profile', *The Journal of Communist Studies and Transition Politics,* 17:4 (2001), 11.

use and at the same time pressures for a democratic process of recruitment led to election replacing appointment. It became the rule after the promulgation of the 1993 constitution. In many cases the newly elected governors were drawn from people who had held positions in the previous Soviet regional administration. The position at the time of Yeltsin's retirement as President at the end of 1999 is given in Table 4.4.

Table 4.5 *Candidates for the post of governor of Moscow and St Petersburg, 2003*

Candidate	Profession/employment
Moscow, 7 December	
Yuri Luzhkov	Incumbent governor (and winner)
Herman Sterlingov	Businessman
Alexander Lebedev	Head of the National Reserve Bank
Nikolai Lifanov	Director of the Progress construction firm
Alexander Krasnov	Former head of the Presnensky urban district administration
St Petersburg, 21 September/5 October	
Valentina Matvienko	President's Envoy to the North-western Federal District (and winner)
Anna Markova	Incumbent deputy governor
Petr Shelishch	State Duma deputy
Mikhail Amosov, Konstantin Sukhenko, Vadim Voitanovsky, Alexei Timofeev	All deputies of the St Petersburg assembly
Sergei Belyaev	Chair of St Petersburg's regional programmes
Sergei Pryanishnikov	Director of pornographic films
Viktor Efimov	Director of the First Pasta factory
Oleg Titov	Pulkovo airlines steward

This changed in a small but significant way when Putin assumed the presidency and certain oligarchs sought to protect themselves by gaining immunity through election as governor, often in outlying regions where lay the natural resources that provided their wealth. Celebrated cases were those of Roman Abramovich, who was elected governor of the Chukot AD on the very eastern tip of Siberia, and Alexander Khloponin, who exchanged his post at the head of Norilsk Nickel for the governorship of the Taimyr AD, in which his giant firm lay, before going on to be elected governor of the whole Krasnoyarsk krai in October 2002.

An impression of the background of the kind of people who were standing for the post of governor towards the end of Putin's first presidency can be gleaned by examining the list of candidates for two major regions. Table 4.5 shows the candidates standing for the governorships of Moscow and St Petersburg in 2003.

The winner of the St Petersburg post, Valentina Matvienko, had held Communist Party posts until the perestroika period, when she switched to a post in the St Petersburg administration. During Putin's first presidency she was, first, deputy Prime Minister in charge of social affairs and then President's Envoy in the North-western Federal District. The candidacy of Victor Efimov is significant as an example of the strong entry into the legislative and executive organs at federal and regional level of representatives of retailing and consumer production.

The regional legislative assemblies

Each region of the Federation elects an assembly. In some cases these have an upper and a lower house (in Sverdlovsk oblast, for example). The interval between elections varies, as does the size of the assemblies. The Moscow city Duma has 35 members, the Sakhalin assembly 28. Each region also adopts its own charter, or in the case of the republics its own constitution. Each sends a representative to the Federation Council.

There is the same problem of accountability at regional as at federal level. Strong presidents, governors and mayors find numerous ways of dominating, or even harassing, their assemblies, though the action of the mayor of Vladivostok, who in September 2003 turned off the electricity in the assembly building to stop it starting work, is doubtless exceptional. Executive dominance, however, can be the counterpart of legislative weakness. In this case in Vladivostok the city legislature had not even managed to elect itself a chair.[4]

Centre–periphery relations

The chief principle underlying the constitution's statements on the relative powers of the federal centre and the Federation's subjects is one of joint jurisdictions, though there is also a much weaker principle of residual powers. The constitution outlines a wide area where the Federation has sole powers, concerning chiefly issues of security, defence, the judicial system and foreign affairs, apart from such concerns as statistical records, state awards and honours, and the State Service. There is a substantial article on powers jointly held by the Federation and its components, where the emphasis is on social issues. Many of these clauses of the constitution deal with the ownership of land and other resources, and with the status and delimitation of powers of the Federation's subjects. The very little that is not provided for in these two substantial articles is catered for in article 73, which assigns 'state power in its entirety' over residual issues to the Federation's subjects. In cases of conflict between the powers of the Federation and its subjects, the Federation's powers take precedence.

The interpretation of these provisions was determined by practical politics. Just as certain of the republics had made extreme claims for regional autonomy when the centre was constrained by the pressures of the moment to cede powers to them, so Putin was firm in his resolution to regain the ground lost in the period of Yeltsin's presidency as far as was possible within the framework of a reformed economy.

The process of spontaneous decentralisation had indeed gone far. A celebrated example was what came to be known as the 'Tatarstan model'.[5] It will be recalled that in his rivalry with Gorbachev and his struggle with the parliament, Yeltsin had courted favour with the republican leaderships. The Tatarstan Republic set out to extract the maximum benefit from this opportunity. Full independence was ruled out by its position on the middle Volga, far from the Federation's boundary, but the republic's president, Mintimer Shaimiev, contrived to increase its autonomy by exploiting two potentially conflicting domestic factors. The first was a strong Tatar nationalist movement; the second was a regional economic interest based on considerable natural resources, which could draw support from the entire population – Russians, Tatars and the rest. The result was the 1994 power-sharing agreement, noted above.

Demarcating constitutional competences

To meet the challenge, Putin created a commission headed by Dmitri Kozak, then a deputy head of the Administration of the President's Affairs, to make proposals on 'the demarcation of the objects of jurisdiction and competence between the organs of governmental power of the federation and the organs of governmental power of its subjects'. The commission's work was to develop into a massive programme covering not only the relations between Moscow and the regions but the whole area of local government in addition.

There was at first resistance from many quarters. In Sakha, deputies in the legislative assembly blocked amendments proposed by Sakha's president aimed at bringing the republic's constitution into line with the Kremlin's interpretation of the federal constitution.[6] But Tatarstan and Bashkortostan were forced to give up some of the provisions of the constitutions that they had adopted in the 1990s. By the end of 2000, the speaker of the Federation Council could claim that legislative conformity with the federal constitution had been achieved in 60 of the Federation's then 89 subjects (now 88). In January 2003, a bill was introduced into the State Duma by Putin that would amend the law on the way in which regional legislatures and executive organs were organised. The bill clarified the status of the so-called power-sharing agreements between the federal centre and the regions, requiring that they be confirmed by federal law. The bill also established the basic principles for administering and distributing state property in the regions. A major step had been taken in the direction of recentralisation. Foot-dragging continued, none the less, in the more refractory republics. As late as November 2003 Tatarstan's demand to be able to use the Roman script in writing its 'state language' was being ruled out by amendments passed by the Duma in favour of a uniform use of Cyrillic.

The distribution of financial resources

A key question in centre–periphery relations is the distribution of resources, particularly financial. What expenditures are to fall on which levels of government? How is taxation to be organised? To what extent is the centre to redistribute resources from rich regions to poor? The share of regional and local budgets in the income of the consolidated budget (the federal centre accounting for the balance) from 1998 to 2003 is given in Table 4.6, which shows a turn towards centralisation after Putin's accession to power, the figures spelling increasing financial power in the hands of the federal centre. The trend has been for the centre to take the income directly and then channel it back to the regions. The result is that over 80 per cent of income from taxation going into regional budgets takes the form of allocations from the centre, with stipulations on what the money is to be spent on, so that the funds come to the regions as subsidies and grants in aid. Among the centre's chief aims is getting the regions to pay more to their public-service workers, and to reduce existing subsidies for household utilities and services, to which we return Chapter 11.[7]

The centre follows a policy of redistributing wealth to some extent between rich and poor regions. In March 2002 Anatoli Lisitsyn, the governor of Yaroslavl oblast, complained that the budget code stated that the income gathered on regional territory should be divided equally between centre and region, but that in Yaroslavl, a donor region, the centre took 53 per cent in 2001 and 61 per cent in 2002, with further increases in view. He pointed out that the centre organises the structure of taxation in such a way that the regions are assigned taxes that are hard to collect in relation to the return.[8]

The central government is prepared to assert its authority in cases of bad administration leading to insolvency. In August 2003 the State Duma passed a

Table 4.6 *Percentage share of regional and local budgets in the income of the consolidated budget*

1998	1999	2000	2001	2002	2003
52.3	48.9	47.3	40.9	36.8	39.8

Source: Ministry of Finance of the Russian Federation, given in *Nezavisimaya gazeta*, 14 February 2003.

law that provided for the running of any region with debts of over 30 per cent of annual revenue to be brought under the supervision of federal financial commissioners. The State Duma would be authorised to impose the scheme if the region failed to adopt it.

Reform of local government

A further outcome of the work of the Kozak commission was a bill to reform local government, which was signed into law by the President on 6 October 2003. It specified the competences of the three levels of government – federal, regional and local. Its details were hotly contested, particularly their financial provisions, and it was made to stipulate that unfunded mandates from higher levels of government to lower would be prohibited. The countryside was to be reorganised into some 20,000 new village and municipal entities, each of them requiring its own budget, but Kozak told reporters that neither the total number of state officials nor the burden on taxpayers would increase.[9]

Chechnya

The single case where the Russian Federation has been put to the test by an internal military challenge to its territorial integrity is that of the republic of Chechnya.

Once the constituent republics of the Soviet Union raised the banner of revolt during Gorbachev's period in office, the future of the Russian Republic, with its patchwork of ethnic minorities, became a major preoccupation. It is in many ways surprising that Chechnya was the only territory that claimed outright independence when the Soviet Union collapsed.

Chechnya lies on the northern buttresses of the Caucasus (see Figure 4.1). Its southern part extends into the mountains, but in the north it stretches into a plain where the capital, Grozny, is situated. In the 1989 census, which counted Chechnya and neighbouring Ingushetia together, 23 per cent of the population was Russian. The Chechens are a Muslim people, though the independence movement was at first political in nature. Historically they have

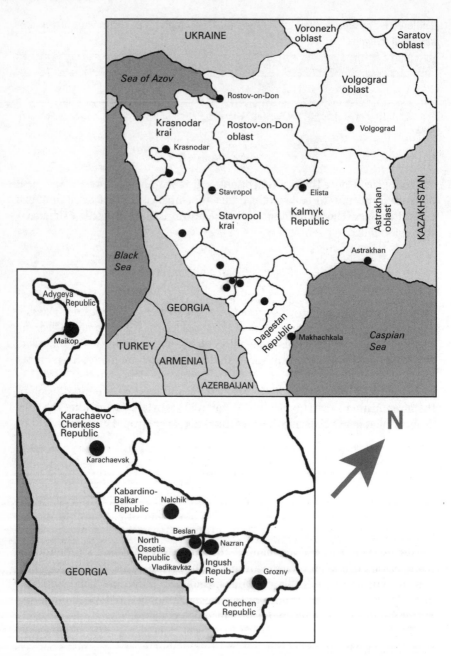

Figure 4.1 *The Caucasus.*

prided themselves on being a warrior people, one of the emblems of which is the knife that they have traditionally carried – the *kinzhal.*

Of great importance also is the fact that tension between the Chechens and Moscow is not new. The tsarist army never succeeded in warring down a determined movement for independence in the nineteenth century, led by Shamil, and years of warfare were concluded only when Shamil accepted a settlement which effectively bought him off. There was therefore some justification for Stalin's suspicion of possible Chechen treachery, which led him to exile the entire population, together with the neighbouring Ingush, to Central Asia during the Second World War (the Great Patriotic War in Russian historiography). The Chechens were reinstated in their homeland in 1957.

In 1991, with the election of Dzhokar Dudayev as Chechen president, independence was proclaimed, and a constitution for a Republic of Ichkeria was drafted. At first Yeltsin refused to negotiate, which inflamed the situation. In 1994 Russian troops entered Chechnya. The fighting was to continue for two years, with the outright ineptitude of the Russian military and the very heavy casualties having a traumatic effect on Russian society.[10] To the misery of parents who had lost their sons was added the apprehension of mothers whose sons were approaching the age for military service, and whose protest took organisational form.

The Kasavyurt agreement – essentially a defeat for Moscow – brought a temporary end to the fighting in 1996. Then in September 1999 there was a series of explosions in residential tower blocks in Moscow and Volgodonsk. The bomb attacks were attributed to Chechen separatists and Putin's determined response in reopening the war (he was Prime Minister at the time) was the crucial factor in his success in the subsequent presidential election. From the date of the explosions rumours circulated that they were staged to promote Putin's chances in the election campaign. It was an issue that was not to go away throughout Putin's first period in office.

The performance of the Russian military was an improvement on the disasters of the first war, the army having to some extent recovered from the disorganisation it had suffered as a result of Yeltsin's economic policies. But it was soon to get bogged down; there were reports of fearful atrocities committed against the Chechens and of the almost total destruction of Grozny. The elected Chechen president, Aslan Maskhadov, was outlawed, and Moscow put its own man in his place, Akhmed Kadyrov. All attempts to press for a political settlement (by, among others, Evgeni Primakov, the doyen of Soviet and Russian foreign affairs) were rejected by Putin.

Soon such sympathy as there had been for the Chechens in the rest of Russia had dissipated or turned to downright hostility and there were moves to expel people of a Caucasian appearance from Moscow. Further terrorist attacks took place. Particularly massive in its impact was the taking hostage of a theatre audience in Moscow's inner suburbs in October 2002 by a band of young Chechen militants. (Details of this and other terrorist attacks are given in Chapter 5.) By this time elections to the State Duma, and also for the federal presidency, were looming, and Putin forced the pace by proposing the adoption in Chechnya of a new constitution and the election of a new president of the republic.

A referendum on the new constitution, and on the laws preparing the way for presidential and parliamentary elections, was held in Chechnya on 23 March 2003. The text stated unequivocally that Chechnya was 'an integral part of the Russian Federation'. Ninety-six per cent of those who could be persuaded to turn out voted 'yes'. The figure was greeted by observers and commentators with extreme scepticism, but far greater opprobrium was attracted by the way in which the list of contenders for the presidency was whittled down. Kadyrov was elected and the Chechen question was declared closed. On 6 February 2004, an explosion in the Moscow metro, attributed to Chechen terrorists, killed over 40 people.

Then, on 9 May 2004, a bomb blast at a stadium in Grozny during celebrations to mark victory in 1945 killed six people, including Kadyrov himself. The 40 people injured in the explosion included many other members of the Chechen leadership, among them prime minister Sergei Abramov. It was a severe setback for Putin and his Chechen policy. It continued to be pursued, however, and a further manipulated election replaced Kadyrov with Alu Alkhanov as president on 29 August 2004. There followed the hostage-taking crisis in Beslan in September 2004 (see Box 2.1), which had a momentous effect on Russian politics, sharply promoting Putin's move towards centralisation and extending the existing return to Soviet political norms.

The impact of the Chechen conflict on Russia's politics since 1994, but particularly since October 2002, cannot be overestimated. It has generated, through the demonisation of the Chechen people, a wave of racism in other parts of the Federation. It has been a focal point for dissident opposition to the regime – and less radical but more sharply targeted demonstrations of anger from organisations such as the Committees of Soldiers' Mothers (see Chapters 5 and 13). Putin's policies and strategies in many areas have turned on the Chechen question. In particular, it provided him with a spectacularly successful bridge to a relationship with the United States in a joint struggle against terrorism.

But the Russian determination to prevent a Chechen secession is only partly to shore up the dam against further separatist movements. At stake also is the route the pipelines are to take in conveying oil from the Caspian to the Mediterranean, and control of any pipeline passing through the north Caucasus. This is treated Chapter 14.

Assessment

The regions constitute a sphere of the Russian Federation's politics where change has been inevitable. While the fall of the Soviet Union was not caused by demands for independence from its constituent republics, it was certainly precipitated by them. The process of disintegration stopped at that point, with the crucially important exception of Chechnya's struggle for independence, but the degree of autonomy that certain regions had acquired during the Yeltsin presidency meant that, in the short term at least, Moscow's relations with them would have to accommodate strongly expressed regional interests. These Putin set out to rein in. In his autobiography Putin was quite categorical in his views on the matter: 'From the very beginning, Russia was created as a super-centralised state. That's practically laid down in its genetic code, its traditions, and the mentality of its people'.[11] Yet some form of decentralisation was generally regarded as being essential to the reform programme, and it is equally assumed that the Russian state will retain its federal character in some form.

It must be remembered that the Soviet Union had styled itself a federation, though the constitutional powers of the federating units were completely eclipsed by the central monopoly of the Communist Party. Today, the control of regional affairs by central ministries, the structure and reach of the law-enforcement agencies, and the merely vestigial residual powers reserved to the regions in the constitution, not to mention the probable fallout from Chechnya's bid for independence, suggest that the Russian Federation will continue to be marked by a traditional centralism. It remains to be seen to what extent countervailing tendencies, of the kind that have led to the development of regional governance in many Western European countries, will affect the vastly larger Russian Federation.

The steps that Putin has taken in relation to the regions can be seen as a rationalisation of structures within an increasingly centralised, though still formally federal, state. The rationalisation can be seen in the proposed amalgamations of ADs with each other or with a neighbouring oblast, which reflect the centre's interest in promoting security and administrative efficiency through the creation of larger units. It can be seen also in the energetic measures taken to ensure alignment of the republican constitutions with that of the Federation, which have qualified the 'asymmetric' federalism that resulted from Yeltsin's separate deals done with the republics in order to secure their support.[12]

The events in Beslan in September 2004 were a watershed in the federal relationship, with a marked turn to centralisation, as the Kremlin's response to the crisis brought central nomination for election in the appointment of republican presidents and regional governors. The consequent clustering of regional leaders in the United Russia party was a further step in the resuscitation of the Soviet relationship between a central power in Moscow and a network of appointed regional leaders in a vertical pyramid of power, the whole encapsulated in a single dominant party. At the same time, it has to be granted that the way in which the centre–periphery relationship was working in the new Federation up to that point was allowing republican presidents and regional governors to develop an authoritarian role in their own bailiwicks, while drawing them towards the Kremlin for favours and support. It was, however, a relationship that, whatever its faults, did at least offer a possible ground for the eventual development of a regional democratic politics.

Further reading

V. Gelman, *et al.*, *Making and Breaking Democratic Transitions: The Comparative Politics of Russia's Regions* (Lanham, MD: Rowman and Littlefield, 2003).

R. W. Orttung, D. N. Lussier and A. Paretskaya (eds), *The Republics and Regions of the Russian Federation: A Guide to Politics, Policies and Leaders* (Armonk, NY: M. E. Sharpe, 2000).

G. Lapidus, *The New Russia: Troubled Transformation* (Boulder, CO: Westview Press, 1994).

J. M. Ostrow, 'Conflict management in Russia's federal institutions', *Post-Soviet Affairs*, 18:1 (2002), 49–70.

H. E. Hale and R. Taagpera, 'Russia: consolidation or collapse?', *Europe–Asia Studies*, 54:7 (2002), 1101–25.

M. Mendras, 'How regional elites preserve their power', *Post-Soviet Affairs*, 15:1 (1999), 291–307.

D. Hutcheson, *Political Parties in the Russian Regions* (London: RoutledgeCurzon, 2003).

Notes

1 See J. Kahn, 'What is the new Russian federalism?', in A. Brown (ed.), *Contemporary Russian Politics: A Reader* (Oxford: Oxford University Press, 2001).

2 V. Gelman, 'Regime transformation, uncertainty and prospects for democratisation: the politics of Russia's regions in comparative perspective', *Europe–Asia Studies*, 51:6 (1999), 939–56.

3 *Kommersant-Daily*, 10 March 2004.

4 *Kommersant-Daily*, 27 September 2003.

5 G. Sharafutdinova, 'Paradiplomacy in the Russian regions: Tatarstan's search for statehood', *Europe–Asia Studies*, 55:4 (2003), 613–29.

6 'Constitutional watch', *East European Constitutional Review*, 10:2/3 (2001), 40.

7 *Financial Times*, 10 June 2003.

8 *Nezavisimaya gazeta*, 20 March 2002.

9 For more on local government, see T. Lankina, 'Local government and ethnic and social activism in Russia', in A. Brown (ed.), *Contemporary Russian Politics: A Reader* (Oxford: Oxford University Press, 2001).

10 For the first Chechen war, see A. Lieven, *Chechnya: Tombstone of Russian Power* (New Haven, CT: Yale University Press, 1998).

11 V. V. Putin, with N. Gevorkyan, N. Timakova and A. Kolesnikov, *First Person: An Astonishingly Frank Self-portrait by Russia's President*, translation by Catherine A. Fitzpatrick (New York: Public Affairs, 2000), 51.

12 J. Hughes and G. Sasse (eds), *Ethnicity and Territory in the Former Soviet Union* (London: Frank Cass, 2002).

5

Security and defence

Background

For a number of reasons, defence and security have a particular importance in Russian politics. First, while Russia is no longer a superpower it remains none the less an exceptionally powerful state, with a nuclear capacity, an immense territory and extensive resources. Russia has, indeed, been referred to as a 'genetic' superpower, in the sense that its present relative weakness, caused by the turbulence of communism's collapse, does not match the potential that its resources are capable of realising, and the current weakness may not be of long duration. But, however temporary, the weakness has come about through deep changes that have affected the fields of defence and security as much as they have affected other fields that this book examines, if not more.

Second, Russian government has historically been obsessed with secrecy and security concerns. This has stemmed partly from Russia's sense of lagging behind an economically and militarily more developed West and, internally, from pathological suspicions of internal dissent – a product of the autocratic nature of Russian government over the centuries. This obsession and suspicious-ness reached an apogee in the Soviet period. The strategy for economic development adopted by the Bolsheviks required a sealing of the border so as to defend the planned economy from the uncertainties of world prices and also from messages that might undermine the Bolshevik leadership's doctrines. On the basis of this radical policy, paranoia developed in the Stalin period – and was indeed promoted by a leadership which could constantly claim that the enemy was at the gates. Fears of both external and internal enemies fed an anxiety about spies and led to an extensive apparatus of counter-espionage.

A third reason for the prominence of the security forces in Vladimir Putin's Russia is the choices Putin made in appointing people to responsible posts in government and in his own Administration. Once in power he turned to two sources for these appointments. One was the contacts made during his period in the administration of Leningrad/St Petersburg from 1990 to 1996. The second was the security and military structures. Putin's chief career back-ground was in the Committee of State Security – the KGB – where he worked from 1975 to 1990. Later, for a year and a half from July 1998, he was chief of the Federal Security Service (FSB), the KGB's successor. These experiences provided him with a pool of people he could trust to fill the key political posts in his Administration and to help him meet his priority tasks – controlling the power of the 'oligarchs', gathering taxes, tackling crime and curbing the autonomy that the regions had succeeded in arrogating to themselves.

His reliance on the security apparatus in making his appointments was of a far greater political significance than his use of the St Petersburg connection. Whatever Putin's origins had been, he would, like Leonid Brezhnev and Boris Yeltsin before him, have brought with him a clientele of trusted colleagues to hold key posts. Clientelism of this sort had been a characteristic of the Soviet period and the change of regime only served to promote it, by discrediting the existing *nomenklatura* elite. Bringing earlier contacts from St Petersburg served a general purpose, which did not in itself define the nature of the new elite. On the other hand, the appointment of people from the defence and security structures to key posts did make a significant contribution – first, in confirming in positions of power people drawn from the institutional props of the former regime and, second, in providing a bulwark against the assertion of a rival financial and business elite. In addition, it gave him access to the security networks that he needed in order to deal with his opponents and clear the way for the implementation of his policies.

Finally, as the governing group was seeking a successor to Yeltsin for the presidency in 1999, there was a model of what was needed in Yuri Andropov, who had succeeded Brezhnev as General Secretary of the Communist Party of the Soviet Union in November 1982, but who had died after only a little over a year in office. Andropov's career had been spent in the KGB, latterly as its head. On coming to office as the Party's General Secretary he had mounted a programme of reform, but did not have time to bring it to fruition before he died. Putin could be presented as in many ways Andropov's heir. It was an image of reform through the application of a strong hand – in fact, in view of the background that Putin shared with Andropov, of policing.

A number of factors thus conspired to make Putin's Russia effectively a police state, coexisting awkwardly with an attempt to develop democratic institutions in a context where they had no historical anchoring.

Putin and the security forces

It was noted in Chapter 2 that six out of seven of the President's Envoys appointed in 2000 had a background in the security or military structures. To this it can be added that no fewer than 70 per cent of the personnel in their administrations shared that background.[1] This is just one example of the way in which, during Putin's presidency, key posts in the state's higher administration have been staffed with people who have served in the security or military

Table 5.1 *Percentage of military personnel in the Russian higher elite groups, 1988–2002*

Date	Country's top leadership (Politburo of CPSU central committee, or Security Council of RF)	Government
1988	4.8	5.4
1993	33.3	11.4
1999	46.4	22.0
2002	58.3	32.8

Source: 'Khaki power': interview with Olga Kryshtanovskaya, in *Nezavismaya gazeta*, 19 August 2003.

Table 5.2 *Proportion of military and security personnel in Putin's first presidency*

Institution	Percentage
State Duma	9
Regional elite	10
Federation Council	15
Federal government	33
Security Council	58

Source: Adapted from O. Kryshtanovskaya and S. White, 'Putin's militocracy', *Post-Soviet Affairs*, 19:4 (2003), 289–306.

structures. The informal term *siloviki* has come into common parlance in Russia to connote them (from *sila*, the Russian word for 'force'). In the extensive studies that she has made of the matter, the sociologist Olga Kryshtanovskaya has claimed that the siloviki have established a network of representatives at all levels of power (Tables 5.1 and 5.2).

The prominence of the security factor in Russian politics is not just a matter of what kind of person is in what kind of job. It affects directly the way in which the law is administered. In terms of constitutionality, the Russian Federation has made marked advances on a low baseline in the Soviet Union, and in his first term as President, Putin laid down a framework of law in a number of areas where order was lacking. However, Russian political life is still subject to arbitrary action on the part of the law-enforcement agencies. The law is not ignored – indeed, it is constantly affirmed – but it is selectively applied. The people who embody the state stand ready to intervene if the law is not yielding the results they would wish. This leads to sudden and abrupt 'snatch squad' actions on the part of the security forces.[2] It is a manner of acting that creates fear and uncertainty in society in general. So dominant is this pattern of behaviour in Putin's Russia that it can be held to characterise the entire political system.

Those who have studied this phenomenon have pointed out that security in the Russian Federation today is not simply one function of government among many. A concern for security affects all spheres of government and gives each an added dimension. Prominent cases that are mentioned in this chapter and in Chapter 13 are migration and academic research – two areas that have primarily a social importance but which have often attracted the attention of the security forces. The term 'securitisation' has been put forward to connote this extra dimension of security that is added to every sphere of governmental activity.[3]

While it is from both the armed forces and the internal security services that Putin has drawn the personnel to support him in pursuing his policies, the latter are naturally of the greater prominence in developing this added security dimension of politics in Russia. It is to them that we now turn.

The internal security forces

Of the security agencies concerned with internal security, the Federal Security Service (FSB) and the Ministry of Internal Affairs (MVD) tower above the others, with the Ministry for Emergency Situations playing an important role.

The MVD has been treated in Chapter 2 as a key civilian government ministry, but it also has a substantial force of armed troops under its command, and has had since as far back as 1811. This force played a leading role in the suppression of movements against the Soviet order in the Baltic states and western Ukraine in the 1980s. Moreover, there has been a constant transfer of functions between the FSB and the MVD, normally depending on the political concerns of the moment. Thus, responsibility for security operations in Chechnya (not the military operations, over which the armed forces retained command) was moved from the FSB to the MVD in 2003 when the republic was given a new constitution and a fresh presidential election was planned. As noted, the staff of the MVD carry military ranks.

The Ministry for Emergency Situations is also highly militarised. In October 2003 the minister, Sergei Shoigu, said that his ministry had been reformed. Its personnel had been reduced, salaries increased and qualified new specialists attracted. In the reforms, ministry troops were cut by some 75 per cent, which meant dismantling 16 regiments and six brigades. Even after that, the ministry still employed 371,000 people, including 86 generals – one-third the number of generals that the Ministry of Defence contains.[4]

The FSB is the heir to the Soviet KGB. The KGB was strongly affected by the decline in the Communist Party's own authority and also by the bad odour into which it had fallen as a result of the processes of glasnost and democratisation. The removal of the statue of Felix Dzerzhinsky, the founder of the Soviet Union's first political police (the Cheka), from its place on the square near the KGB's headquarters in Moscow was a symbol of the unpopularity that the 'organs' had accumulated. The KGB was accordingly broken up and its functions transferred to a number of separate bodies, the most important of which were the FSB (which received the KGB's central policing function), the Foreign Intelligence Service, the Federal Agency of Government Communication and Information (FAPSI), the Federal Border Guard Service and the Federal Tax Police Service.

On assuming the presidency Putin reversed a number of the steps taken during the Yeltsin period. One of these reversals was a partial restoration of the KGB, though without that title. With a series of presidential decrees issued on 11 March 2003, he disbanded FAPSI and the Federal Border Guard Service, and gave the bulk of the former's extensive functions and all of the latter's to the FSB. The Border Guard Service had been a mammoth organisation, with a budget twice as large as that of the FSB, and with three times as many employees and 10 times as many generals.[5] Bringing it into the FSB would make considerable savings.

The Federal Tax Police Service was also abolished and its functions were transferred to the MVD, which took on 14,000 former Tax Police employees, who were to work alongside personnel from the Economic Crimes Department in a new agency that the MVD was forming.[6] Putin further appointed the North-western Federal District's former President's Envoy Viktor Cherkesov to head a new State Committee on Narcotics Trafficking, which became one of the power structures (under a changed name – see Chapter 2).

On 12 August 2003 Putin completed the reorganisation of the security services by signing a decree that gave the FSB departments of analysis and strategic planning, counter-intelligence, protection of the constitutional order and military counter-intelligence, together, as noted, with the Federal Border Guard Service. The FSB was to be given a 19-member collegium to act as its highest administrative body.

The armed forces

Adjusting to the end of the cold war

Despite the Soviet Union's ultimate arrival at nuclear parity with the United States, the price that was paid for it was massive, and the Soviet Union's military prowess cloaked an overall economic weakness in comparison with the capitalist economies of the West. The proportion of the economy that was assigned to the military budget had been kept high by a ruling party whose political monopoly enabled it to silence other claims on the country's resources. The result was a dual economy, in which a disproportionate amount of the skilled workforce and material resources were devoted to the defence industries. The fall of the Soviet Union saw the beginning of the end of this imbalance as the economy was civilianised, but the process has been gradual. Conversion of plant and resources to new production took time and while this civilianisation of the economy could preserve some benefits inherited from the Soviet system, such as a high place for armaments in Russian exports, the armed forces overall suffered a loss.

The collapse of the Soviet Union led to a severe problem of morale. The Communist Party had devoted exaggerated attention to impressing on military personnel the Party's view of a national mission based on hostility to a capitalist West. In practical terms, the military had had to suffer the loss of the Soviet Union's control of Eastern Europe in the 1980s and, more grievous still, the disintegration of the Soviet state itself. This left considerable military resources outside the territory of the new Federation – in Transdniestria (the eastern strip of a now independent Moldova) and in Ukraine, where the entire Black Sea fleet was based at the Ukrainian port of Sevastopol. These blows to military pride came on top of the failed intervention in Afghanistan from 1979 to 1989, and further setbacks in Chechnya, where a fragile agreement signed at Kasavyurt in 1996 cloaked a dismal performance by the Federation's forces. The economic chaos of the Yeltsin presidency played its part in undermining the viability and morale of the military, which was unable to meet its salaries bill.

Developments in the Russian armed forces since the fall of communism must be seen against the shift from a foreign policy of willing cooperation with the West in the Yeltsin period, conducted by the Minister for International Affairs, Andrei Kozyrev, to a far more guarded policy under Putin. This in turn reflects Putin's moves to strengthen the state, which had a natural counterpart in a stiffening of Russia's attitude to competitors and an attention to morale in the armed forces.

The account given here does not deal with military hardware, but concentrates on policy issues. It connects with a good deal of the material of Chapter 14, on Russia and the wider world.

Military doctrine and military reform

Under Putin the armed forces have been able in some measure to rebuild the esteem that they have normally always had in Russia. Even before his formal accession to the presidency, a new 'Federal Security Concept' and 'Military Doctrine' were adopted, in December 1999 and January 2000, respectively. The former justified 'the use of all available means and forces, including nuclear weapons ... in case of need to repel an armed aggression when all other means of settling the crisis situation have been exhausted or proved ineffective'. In relation to the previous text, of 1997, this was taken by commentators to have lowered the threshold for the threat of using, or the actual use of, nuclear weapons, though it did not to any great extent alarm the US defence authorities, even with its suggestion of first use of the nuclear option. The forthright statement can be seen as one of Putin's general moves to reverse the weakening of the state and its defences during the Yeltsin presidency, but it was produced with other considerations in mind. A theme running through both documents is the growing Russian apprehensions at the expansion of the North Atlantic Treaty Organisation (NATO) to take in new states, some of them former Soviet satellites.[7]

At the same time Putin launched a reform of the structure of the armed forces and of their armaments. The measures taken involved:

- reducing the numerical strength of the armed forces – in fact cutting them by more than half;
- bringing back into service a series of mothballed large strategic nuclear missiles inherited from the Soviet era but capable of meeting any present risk;
- establishing a rapid-reaction force and completing the transformation from a part-conscript to a contract-based army (see below).

Later, in a further statement on military doctrine announced in October 2003 at an enlarged meeting of the military high command, the Defence Minister, Sergei Ivanov, reasserted that Russia was prepared to resort to nuclear weapons. Although Russia was not facing significant immediate threats, it was impossible to rule out the need to resort to pre-emptive action if Russia's interests, or those of its allies, required it. The firmness of these statements reflected, first, the increasing self-assertion of conservative forces in domestic politics at the time and, second, anxiety about the presence of the United States in Central Asia and the Caucasus, which could lead to an unstable situation developing within the Commonwealth of Independent States (the CIS, which comprises all but three of the former Soviet Union's constituent republics – see Chapter 14). This, in turn, could involve a direct threat to Russian citizens or ethnic Russians in the CIS.[8]

From conscription to contract

A central plank in the reform of the armed services during Putin's first term as President was a decision to run down conscription in favour of an increase in contract service. During his address to the Federal Assembly on 16 May 2003, the President had included in his list of priorities the modernisation of the armed forces and had given 2007 as the date by which the shift from conscription to contract service should be completed. He added that people from the former Soviet republics might be enrolled as volunteers, and that this might earn them Russian citizenship after a certain period of service.

Debate on the subject had started before his speech and had crystallised around two rival proposals, one from the Defence Ministry and the other from the Union of Right Forces (SPS) in the Duma, in collaboration with the Institute of the Economy, run by the former Prime Minister Yegor Gaidar. The differences centred on cost and on the balance to be struck between regular and conscript forces. The Defence Ministry's version proposed a transfer of only some 15 per cent of the armed forces overall to a volunteer basis between

2004 and 2007. After six months in a training centre, conscripts would be able either to sign a contract for three years' regular service or to complete the standard conscription period (of two years) on the present purely nominal rates of pay. Cynics pointed out that the military might be loath to forego the effectively unpaid labour that conscripts provide, from simple agricultural tasks to helping build dachas for senior officers.[9]

The version put forward by the SPS questioned the Defence Ministry's financial figures and proposed that a far larger proportion of the military should be attributed to contract service. This version would have reduced conscription to six months in a military training establishment. Behind this recommendation lay concerns about the large number of conscript suicides induced by bullying and maltreatment (see below), and also about the bribery that arranging for deferments and desired postings attracted. The SPS maintained also that the Ministry's version would create tensions between privileged and less privileged categories in the armed services.

In July 2003 the cabinet approved the Defence Ministry's version. According to the proposal, service by contract would account for approximately half the armed forces by 2007. Conditions of service would be improved, with higher salaries. At the same time, service for conscripts would be reduced from two years to one, though from a later date.

The reaction of senior military figures to the proposed reorganisation was not enthusiastic. At a roundtable in June fears were expressed about the reforms in general, which included reductions in the strategic missile forces. It was proposed at the conference that the transition to a larger regular army begin not in the army but in the Federal Border Guard Service and the MVD's troops.[10] Clearly, nobody wanted to be the guinea pig.

Military service

Maltreatment of recruits and its effects

A major current problem is the bullying and maltreatment of conscripts. According to the Union of Committees of Soldiers' Mothers and the SPS, some 2,000 service people die each year as a result of criminal maltreatment, suicide or other incidents. The number for 2002 was put at 531 by the Defence Ministry, but whatever the precise figure it is certain that bullying and initiation ceremonies account for many conscript deaths. It is accepted to be a problem, and has involved a number of high-profile cases (including in the elite regiment that guards the Kremlin and the President).[11]

Actual deaths are the tip of an iceberg. It was reported that more than 40,000 soldiers appealed to the Union of Committees of Soldiers' Mothers in 2002 for help because of alleged maltreatment by officers and other service personnel.[12] This leads in turn to a high number of desertions and a high rate of draft avoidance. The problem for the military authorities can be illustrated from a no doubt extreme case in Balakovo in Saratov oblast, where, out of 4,500 conscription-age youths, 80 per cent had obtained deferment and many of the rest had been ruled unfit for service. Of the under 300 who remained, 150 had failed to report for duty. The proposed penalties were not drastic, at least in the first instance – public shaming in the press or, if that failed, a fine of R500 ($14 at the time).[13]

Alternative service

On 25 July 2002 a law was signed that enabled young men of conscription age to undertake civilian instead of military service. It was passed with amendments proposed by the General Staff, which were in turn strongly opposed by liberal deputies and human rights activists. One amendment ruled out the possibility of fulfilling alternative service near the conscript's home. Another denied conscripts the right to choose whether to do their alternative service at a civilian or a military institution. The board judging whether or not a potential recruit's beliefs allowed him to take up arms was to be composed of military officers, which was a cause for concern for the bill's opponents, as was the fact that the alternative service would last longer than the standard military stint. On the other hand, the four-year period proposed at first by the military for alternative service was rejected in favour of a maximum term of three and a half years if the service was to be performed in civilian organisations, and three years if in the armed forces as civilian personnel. Then, on 8 October 2003, the State Duma passed in its first reading a further bill that would after all enable young men to perform their alternative military service near their homes. The original 2002 law came into force on 1 January 2004.

The Minister of Labour, Alexander Pochinok, whose ministry was given responsibility for administering the alternative service, did not expect the take-up for it to be high, given that those who opted for it would be given heavy manual labour, such as working for polar expeditions or doing sanitation work.[14]

Combating terrorism

The primary domestic source of terrorist activity has been the movement for Chechen independence, years of regular warfare within the republic (1994–96 and from 1999) having been accompanied by terrorist actions beyond its confines. Three cases have had a particularly marked effect on Russian politics. First, in September 1999, bombs exploded in apartment buildings in Moscow and in Volgodonsk, causing 50 deaths. The second case occurred in October 2002, when a suicide squad of 41 Chechens, men and women, occupied the Dubrovka theatre in suburban Moscow and took the audience hostage. The siege ended with the authorities pumping an opiate gas into the theatre, immobilising the hostage-takers and enabling the theatre to be stormed by the FSB's anti-terrorist forces. The death toll among the audience, from the gas and the storming, amounted to 128. The way in which the crisis had been handled caused considerable public indignation. The third case, which caused an even greater trauma in Russian politics, was the further hostage-taking in Beslan in September 2004 (see Box 2.1, p. 25), where, again, the impact of the terrorist event was heightened by the clumsy manner in which it was dealt with by the authorities.

Apart from these major cases of terrorism stemming from the long-standing conflict over the status of Chechnya, there have been a number of bomb explosions outside Chechnya in which Chechens have been implicated, most of them in Moscow. A significant number of them have been carried out by women. Two women, believed to be Chechen fighters, detonated explosives attached to their bodies near the entrance to an open-air rock concert at Tushino in Moscow on 5 July 2003, killing themselves along with 13 others, and a similar suicide attack in Moscow on 31 August 2004 killed nine people. A woman from Chechnya was arrested on 9 July 2003 near the Kremlin after she tried to detonate a bomb hidden in her bag. More successful were two Chechen women who detonated explosives almost simultaneously on two passenger jets on 24 August 2004, causing the deaths of 89 passengers and crew members. Cases such as these have suggested that the Chechen war has created a category of terrorists from among the widows that the fighting has produced. The destruction of the twin towers of the World Trade Center in New York on 11 September 2001 gave Putin the opportunity to claim that the Chechens' struggle for independence was part of a world terrorist phenomenon, and to use that argument to further his relations with the United States. But however opportunist his strategy, the actions that Chechen separatists have carried out in the Federation beyond their borders are clearly cases of terrorist tactics.

They have also led the security forces to suspect of terrorism the Muslim fundamentalist Hizb ut-Tahrir network. This originated in Central Asia but has been active also in the north Caucasus. A joint operation by the FSB and MVD in Moscow on 6 June 2003 led to the arrest of 121 activists.

The FSB, the MVD and the army all have special detachments for meeting the terrorist challenge. The storming of the theatre in the hostage-taking of October 2002 was carried out by two of the FSB's special forces – the Alfa and the Vympel groups. The Alfa anti-terrorism force is a carry-over from the Soviet-era KGB, in which capacity it played a prominent role in the war in Afghanistan. Vympel was originally formed in 1981 within the KGB's first main directorate, with the mission of carrying out covert operations abroad. When the KGB was broken up from October 1993 Vympel was transferred to the MVD, the name Vympel being abandoned. The FSB subsequently created a new anti-terrorism unit under that title. The MVD deploys the 'military detachments for special assignments' (OMON), which have been widely used in Chechnya. For special activities reaching far beyond combating terrorism, the Russian army uses Spetsnaz ('special purposes'), whose function has been concentrated in recent history on reconnaissance and sabotage. Spetsnaz is controlled by the General Staff's Main Intelligence Directorate.

Counter-intelligence and spies

No description of security in today's Russia would be complete without some account of the counter-intelligence capability that, in Soviet days, formed so dramatic a part of Russia's image. However, with the end of the tensions of the cold war, a good deal of the drama has dissipated and the efforts of Russian counter-intelligence have moved away from catching spies to other areas of perceived insecurity. In view of what has been said in this chapter, it will not be surprising to hear that, with or without full justification, the law-enforcement agencies today frequently see a security threat in any actions or views critical of the government. The line between criticism and disloyalty, it must be admitted, is not always clear, particularly in relation to the passing of information on technical or partly technical matters. In such areas international journalists operating in a context of open information see things differently from Russian security officials with a traditional suspicion of the outside world.

Four cases have been given international prominence. The first is that of Alexander Nikitin, an environmental activist and former naval officer who was arrested and charged in 1996 with releasing (to a Norwegian environmental group) classified material about the illegal dumping of nuclear waste by the Russian northern fleet, based on the Kola Peninsula. The dangers posed by the disintegrating hulks of Russian nuclear submarines are generally known and widely acknowledged. None the less, to talk of them to the outside world was sufficient for a prosecution on a charge of treason for disclosing state secrets. The FSB had made sure that the prosecution would go ahead even after the Procurator-General's Office had found the case insubstantial in the early stages. The trial eventually ended in acquittal on 17 April 2000.

Meanwhile, a second case had arisen. In December 2001 Grigori Pasko, a military journalist, was sentenced to four years' imprisonment by a military court on a charge of passing classified information about the Russian Pacific fleet to Japanese journalists. His action, as in the case of Nikitin, had been taken because of his environmental concerns. He was released on 22 January 2003 after serving two years and eight months of his sentence, including his detention awaiting trial (he refused the offer of a state pardon, on the grounds that to accept it would be tantamount to admitting his guilt).

A third celebrated case was that of Anatoli Babkin, a scientist in his seventies who, in May 2000, was arrested and accused of handing over classified information about a rocket-propelled torpedo to a US naval specialist. On 18 February 2003 the Moscow municipal court convicted him of spying for the United States and delivered an eight-year suspended sentence, in addition to five years' probation.[15] He was banned from conducting research for three years, barred from holding any administrative posts at his research centre and stripped of his academic honours. According to his lawyers, Babkin merely authorised the transfer of certain scientific papers to an American university under the terms of an approved contract. However, the Procurator-General's Office saw things differently and appealed against the sentence on the grounds that it was too mild.

Igor Sutyagin, a former researcher at the Russian Academy of Science's USA and Canada Institute, was arrested in 27 October 1999 on suspicion of passing classified information to a British consulting firm, and remained in jail for four years despite a ruling in October 2002 that his imprisonment was illegal. Commenting on his case, the chair of the Moscow Helsinki Group (a human rights organisation), Lyudmila Alekseeva, claimed that Sutyagin never had access to classified information and obtained all his information from open sources. He was sentenced on 7 April 2004 to 15 years' imprisonment. The European Court of Human Rights is reviewing the case.

Assessment

One of the most prominent features of the Russian Federation's political system today is an exaggerated preoccupation with security, at a time when the pressures of the cold war are no longer present. The reasons for the persistence of this preoccupation are partly historical, extending back into tsarist times, but reaching a high point in the Soviet Union when the closed frontier, coupled with the ruling party's concern to secure itself in power, generated a phobia of external influences strong enough to survive beyond the end of the cold war.

These historical reasons, however, do not provide a complete explanation. To achieve that, factors stemming from the way in which the transition from communism unfolded must be added, and two in particular. The first is Putin's drive to stabilise Russia after the disorder that resulted from Yeltsin's management of the reform process and from the latter's permissive style. This must be seen against the element of libertarianism that the collapse of the highly authoritarian Soviet system was bound to cause. Circumstances invited the intervention of a personality prepared to impose stern policing. The fact that Putin had a background in the security forces suited him for the task, but brought the risk that the promotion of stability would suppress the first shoots of pluralist politics. The risk was increased by Putin's bringing personnel with a background in the security structures and the armed forces into his administration on a large scale.

The second factor stemming from the transition from communism is the struggle among the social forces striving for influence after the collapse of the monolithic Soviet elite. Discredited finally by the attempted putsch of August 1991, and then banned by Yeltsin in the Russian Republic, the Communist

Party of the Soviet Union fell from power as a structure. Its leading members, however, still populated the political space. On assuming the presidency, Putin prevented a power vacuum from forming as a result of the departure of the Communist Party's civilian apparatus of rule by replacing it with the military and paramilitary structures that had been the Party's supports. This was tantamount to a restoration of the Soviet elite and it meant that the conduct of the reforms would remain in its hands. They and he, however, could expect challenges from new social forces brought onto the scene by the change in property relations that the reform entailed.

A major potential challenge was based in the economy, and in areas of it that were internationally oriented – finance and marketable energy sources. The fact that a group of financial speculators managed to acquire a significant portion of the country's wealth in those sectors made the challenge real. The details of the emergence of that confrontation are matters for later chapters, but to this chapter belong the steps that Putin took to place in positions of power people whose background marked them out as defenders of a statist position against this new elite with financial and international underpinnings.

The ability of the military and security forces to continue to dictate the pace and nature of social change is uncertain. Their stranglehold on the means of communication spells corruption and insecure decision making. There is doubt, in any case, whether they are capable of exercising power in realms that require flexibility and imagination. Finally, their intervention in Russian politics has revived practices that contributed to the very crisis that led to the introduction of reform in the 1980s in the first place.

Further reading

Y. Albats, *KGB: State within a State: The Secret Police and its Hold on Russia's Past, Present and Future* (London: I. B. Tauris, 1995).

A. C. Aldis and R. N. McDermott, *Russian Military Reform, 1992–2002* (London: Frank Cass, 2003).

B. Buzan, O. Waever and J. de Wilde, *Security: A New Framework for Analysis* (Boulder, CO: Lynne Rienner, 1998).

O. Kryshtanovskaya and S. White, 'Putin's militocracy', *Post-Soviet Affairs*, 19:4 (2003), 289–306.

B. Parrott (ed.), *State Building and Military Power in Russia and the New States of Eurasia* (New York: M. E. Sharpe, 1995).

J. M. Waller, *Secret Empire: The KGB in Russia Today* (Boulder, CO: Westview Press, 1994).

Notes

1 'Khaki power': interview with Olga Kryshtanovskaya, in *Nezavismaya gazeta*, 19 August 2003, p. 2

2 'Snatch squad' is Edwin Bacon's term. See his 'Conceptualising contemporary Russia', *Slavonic and East European Review*, 81:2 (2003), 293–301.

3 See B. Buzan, O. Waever and J. de Wilde, *Security: A New Framework for Analysis* (Boulder, CO: Lynne Rienner, 1998).

4 *RFE/RL Newsline*, 16 October 2003, citing *Izvestiya*.

5 *RFE/RL Newsline*, 17 March 2003.

6 *RFE/RL Newsline*, 14 May 2003.

7 The texts are available at www.da.mod.uk/CSRC/documents/Russian/OB77 (Military Doctrine) and www.fas.org/nuke/guide/russia/doctrine (Security Concept).

8 'In the interests of security', *Izvestiya*, 3 October 2003.

9 'Ivanov is ready to bury the military reform', *Nezavasimya gazeta*, 23 April 2003.

10 *RFE/RL Newsline*, 28 May 2003, citing the RIA-Novosti news agency.

11 *RFE/RL Newsline*, 3 June 2003, citing *Izvestiya* and RTR.

12 *Nezavisimaya gazeta*, 26 February 2003

13 *RFE/RL Newsline*, 7 April 2003, citing the newspaper *Vremya-MN*.

14 Interview with Alexander Pochinok, the Minister of Labour, *Izvestiya*, 22 July 2003.

15 'A sort of spy', *Izvestiya*, 19 February 2003.

6

The state and the law

Background

In the thaw that followed Joseph Stalin's death in 1953, Western experts who visited the Soviet Union were surprised to find a fully articulated legal system in place. This contrasted with the cases of arbitrary action on the part of the state's officials that were evidently still occurring. Later, when the prison camps of the gulag were being emptied, it was often said that nobody had been sent to the gulag without a fully documented conviction, however spurious. Throughout the years of Stalin's terror a legal tradition remained in place, while those holding political power operated largely outside it. Like the Soviet constitution of 1936, which remained in force until 1977, the juridical order was there but it did not bind the holders of power.

In a commentary on Soviet law published in 1963, when the legal order was in most fields able to apply its traditional principles, Harold Berman described how a Soviet jurisprudence was functioning in a systematic way that corresponded to the social and ideological underpinnings of the Soviet state.[1] He termed it 'parental law'. Later, other commentators described the Soviet Union as a 'patrimonial' system.[2] Behind both terms lay the Communist Party's claim to be guarding a patrimony acquired in the revolution, to be husbanded and directed towards a doctrinally enshrined goal. In the power structure the Party had created, that goal justified an authoritarian power akin to parental care.

One feature of this patrimonial rule was a degree of informality in political relationships, which acted as a brake on the development of the rule of law in Russia. It has allowed the holders of power to make arbitrary personal decisions in the name of the common good or of the state (the two tending to coalesce). But behind this informality the Soviet state preserved a juridical and a constitutional order, a framework of rules laid down by the state for the orderly running of the state. An example of the paradox that this involved was the planning mechanism. The plan, organised by the State Planning Commission, had the force of law. It could not, however, have worked without a host of informal economic deals which were in fact illegal but which provided a form of lubrication for the mechanism.

The question that still confronts the Russian Federation is whether a patrimonial system based on a strong state is compatible with the economic reforms that have been undertaken, not to mention the political aspirations that Mikhail Gorbachev's policies gave rise to.

The constitution

As political events unfolded in the Gorbachev years, constitutionalism could be said to have marked its emergence when the Baltic republics of the Soviet Union found that they could base their demand for independence on the constitution, with some chance of it being respected, if not necessarily accepted. This was one of the fruits of the policy of glasnost and of Gorbachev's emphasis on laying down a consistent foundation of constitutional, civil and criminal law. This was some years before the first post-Soviet constitution was promulgated, in 1993. By that point the tensions engendered by Gorbachev's policies had sharpened. The attempted coup of August 1991 had polarised opinions and finally discredited the Communist Party. There followed the dissolution of the Union, but without previous constitutional discussion as to how its successor was to be governed. The struggle that developed in the emerging Russian Federation between a communist-dominated Congress of People's Deputies, elected in 1990, on the one hand, and, on the other, President Boris Yeltsin and the reformers who espoused the cause of market-oriented policies, was about power – the power to make one of those views of the future prevail. For neither camp, not even the reformers at that point, was it primarily a fight to establish constitutional rules. The final drafting of the 1993 constitution followed a physical confrontation in September of that year between the Congress and Yeltsin's civilian supporters and troops loyal to him. Constitutionalism was a victim of these struggles.

One result was that the constitution provided for a strong executive, with a powerful presidency at its head. Another result was that both Yeltsin, and then Vladimir Putin after him, treated the constitution as an instrument of power. They both took full advantage of the powers given to the presidency and came close to making it the embodiment of the law, in the sense that the constitutional rights of citizens were eclipsed by the use that both Presidents, but particularly Putin, made of the law-enforcement agencies. In the circumstances the strong presidency weakened the development of constitutionalism.

Two further features of the constitution have been mentioned in the fore-going. The first is that it provides for a dual executive (Chapter 3). The second is its federal nature. One of the aims of its drafters was to bring order into the piecemeal deals that the 'subjects' of the Federation had made with Moscow since the early years of the Gorbachev period, or simply the differing degrees of autonomy that they had achieved in the Yeltsin years of central weakness. In the constitution as it was finally drafted the powers reserved to the federating units after the prerogatives of the centre had been enumerated were exceedingly small. Putin's presidency has confirmed the dominance of the centre, but has given the centre–periphery relationship clearer contours, which amount to a form of deconcentration, or devolved government.

A final feature of the constitution is that it goes beyond political competences and rights to specify in detail the social rights of citizens. This stems in part from an acknowledgement that the advanced social-security policies of the Soviet period should be maintained, and partly from the Continental tradition favouring a codifying of the law.

Is the constitution observed?

The constitutional position in the Russian Federation comes near to reproducing that in the Soviet Union. The Soviet constitution scrupulously set out procedures and competences, which were largely adhered to, but there was an external source of political power that transcended the constitution and was given only passing mention in it – the Communist Party and its 'leading role'. In today's Russian Federation, that particular source of authority has gone, but there still remains a factor that has stretched its provisions – though falling short of transcending it as in Soviet days – the use that a powerful executive, with the President at its head, has made of the law-enforcement agencies.

The question of whether the constitution is observed in the Russian Federation cannot be answered with a clear 'yes' or 'no'. On the one hand, the public authorities perform their stipulated functions according to competences laid down in the constitution. On the other, the citizen has inadequate protection from the law-enforcement agencies, which are applying the policies of an effectively unaccountable executive. There are at present two impediments to constitutionalism (as opposed to simply the constitution) having a full impact on the governmental process in Russia. The first, just noted, is the lack of true accountability of an exceptionally strong executive. The second is that constitutionalism is a cultural matter. For it to develop and take root both the rulers and the ruled have to have a sense of the illegitimacy that constitutionalism imposes on arbitrary acts and personal decisions that ignore the impersonal nature of the rule of law.

Many graphic examples are given below, but an unsensational example is offered by Putin's creation of a layer of government between the presidency and the regions in 2000 – the federal districts presided over by the President's Envoys. This clearly modified the constitution and amounted to an amendment of it. On the other hand, the decision could be held to have fallen within his powers of decree. The point is, however, that he went ahead and took the decision without any public debate as to its desirability or constitutional implications; nor was there any likelihood that raising the question would have any effect whatsoever on his intention to take that step. Constitutionalism in this case was simply not an issue.

The Procuracy

The Russian Federation follows the European Continental legal tradition in having a branch of the judicial system – the Procuracy – dedicated to investigating apparent or alleged transgressions of the law and to bringing prosecutions before the courts if there is a case to be answered. It is headed by the Procurator-General, who is appointed by the Federation Council on the President's nomination. The structure of the Procuracy then extends downwards to the regional level, taking in the intermediate level of the federal districts, where it also has branches that deal, for example, with cases of abuse of office by ministers of republics or regions. There is a limit of 18 months on pre-trial detention. An attempt in January 2004 to have this limit reduced to a year failed. As in other countries, terrorism has led to a strengthening rather than a liberalisation of regulation in this field.

General European experience shows that the Procuracy as an institution can serve as an independent organ of justice, separating the police function of catching wrong-doers from the judicial function of laying charges. Its independence depends on a respect for a separation of powers and for the rule of law, while the respect in which it is itself held depends on the consistency that it shows, especially in politically important cases. Rather than showing consistency, the Russian Procuracy has frequently preferred to be selective. It must be allowed that circumstances have given it a political role that would in any case have tested its objectivity and independence to the utmost. In the 1990s, when in the privatisation process the executive was turning a blind eye to all manner of illegal or semi-legal deals, to apply the law strictly would have placed the Procuracy in a difficult political position. In the event, its complicity with the executive's wayward policies had the effect of leaving a great many financial speculators open to possible later prosecution. This could again have given the Procuracy political problems, faced with a President ready to play cat and mouse with the speculators, had it been minded to take an independent stand. In fact, it ranged itself with the President, and the Procurator-General during Putin's first presidency, Vladimir Ustinov, was an invaluable ally in restricting opposition to Putin's policies.

The Procuracy has a military wing, concerned with issues such as thefts of hardware from military and naval bases. Cases resulting from the military Procuracy's investigations are tried in military courts.

The judiciary

The judiciary of the Russian Federation has three branches:

- the Constitutional Court;
- the arbitration courts, heading up in the High Court of Arbitration;
- the courts of general jurisdiction, heading up in the Supreme Court.

The Constitutional Court

A law of 1991 set up a constitutional court, at a moment of political uncertainty, when rival draft versions of a new constitution were constantly succeeding one another. The adoption of the 1993 constitution provided a more secure environment for a new constitutional court to establish its authority.

It now comprises 19 judges, who are appointed by the Federation Council on the President's nomination. The composition of the first constitutional court after the adoption of the constitution took over a year to complete, since the Federation Council frequently refused to accept the President's nominations. The Court's chair at the time of writing (2004) was Valeri Zorkin, a judge of generally respected integrity, under whom the Constitutional Court became an independent player on Russia's legal and political scene.

The Constitutional Court has the following functions:

- it ensures that the enactments of legislatures and executives at all levels of the Federation conform to federal law;
- it resolves disputes over the competences of state bodies;
- it pronounces on cases of possible infringement of citizens' rights and freedoms;
- it provides interpretations of the constitution;
- it ensures that the proper procedures have been followed in the case of a decision to impeach the President.

An example of the Constitutional Court being called on to clarify the constitution arose in July 1999, when it ruled that if the President is temporarily incapacitated, the Prime Minister will carry out the President's duties, without the need for the President to lay down his office. In that case the Prime Minister cannot, however, dissolve parliament or amend the constitution, nor is required to call parliamentary elections.

The Constitutional Court under Zorkin pronounced on its own competences when it ruled on 18 July 2003 that it alone can consider legal disputes over whether regional legislation complies with federal laws. *Vremya-MN* commented that this would 'open a new page in the relationship between the federal centre and the regions'.[3] The case had been brought to the Constitutional Court by deputies in the assemblies of Tatarstan and Bashkortostan, who challenged the Procuracy's claim to be competent to rule on disputes of that kind. The Court's decision was expected to mean that certain local eccentricities would now be allowed, provided that the constitution did not expressly prohibit them. Moscow's exceptional provision for the election of a vice-mayor, for example, might under this ruling now be more likely to be accepted.

Another case calling for a pronouncement on competences arose over the question of whether banks could be required to disclose information about their clients' accounts when bailiffs were attempting to carry out court orders. Courts in a number of regions had been handing down contradictory rulings on this, and a city court in Khanty-Mansii autonomous district brought the issue before the Constitutional Court. The Court ruled that banks could allow court orders to be enforced and could if necessary reveal the required information, but not beyond the limit of the sum mentioned in the court order.

Tatarstan has been the source of many other cases involving centre–periphery relations. A republican constitution newly drafted to conform to that of the Federation was queried by the Procurator-General's Office, whereupon Tatarstan lodged a series of appeals with the Constitutional Court, causing a logjam of cases concerning that republic. In May 2003 the Court had to request Tatarstan's parliament to withhold a challenge to a federal law imposing the use of the Cyrillic alphabet until it had dealt with the earlier cases.

As a final example, in April 2003 journalists and over 100 deputies of the State Duma appealed to the Constitutional Court over the press law that had shortly before been passed by the Duma (see Chapter 12). The law imposed severe penalties on media outlets that permitted comments to be made on candidates for election by anyone other than the candidates themselves, which effectively ruled out any electoral debate through the media. It was a composite law and the Court overturned the sections containing that restriction.

The arbitration courts

The Russian Federation has a complete structure of courts to deal with arbitration. They are best seen as business and industrial courts. They are largely a heritage from the Soviet Union, when the abolition of the market had the effect of bureaucratising the whole of economic life. In those circumstances arbitration filled the role that is performed by litigation between juridical persons in Western market societies. Still today, firms tend to have recourse to the arbitration courts to sort out disputes, as it is a system with which they are familiar. The structure of the arbitration courts is a simple two-tier one, heading up to the High Court of Arbitration.

The preference for arbitration dies hard. When, in the reformed post-communist economy, enterprises found themselves in conflict with each other over matters that they preferred not to take to the arbitration courts of the state, a parallel structure of lower-level arbitration tribunals grew up, which were effectively informal arbitration courts. A law of July 2002 gave them a legislative framework. Their advantage over the state's arbitration courts is that they enable entrepreneurs to keep deals confidential and to retain relations of partnership with the other side in the dispute. They work speedily and the state arbitration has to accept their decisions. However, they are not numerous. There were in 2002 some 400 of them working, mostly attached to the Federation's trade and industry chambers, though there is a smaller number of local ones. In cases where these less formal courts are being used, the arbitration courts do not interfere.

The courts of general jurisdiction

The Russian Federation has a system of courts of general jurisdiction, containing within itself a three-tiered system of military courts. The basic level at which justice is delivered in the Russian Federation is the district court, presided over by justices of the peace, an office that was revived in 2000 from pre-Soviet times. District courts try all kinds of cases except those going before the arbitration courts. More than 90 per cent of all cases, civil and criminal, are handled by the district courts. The remaining, more serious cases are heard by courts at the oblast and krai level. Trials may take one of three forms, in that cases may be heard by:

- a professional judge sitting with two lay 'people's assessors';
- a panel of three professional judges;
- a single judge.

In 1993, it was decided to introduce trial by jury, but it has taken time to implement the decision over the whole territory of the Russian Federation. Ten years later jury trials were allowed in only nine of Russia's then 89 (now 88) regions. It has been one of Putin's aims to extend the jury system to the whole of the Federation. Only defendants accused of murder and a restricted number of other crimes may request them. Acquittals in trials by jury are rare.

The basic level of the structure of military courts is that of armies, fleets, garrisons and military formations. The middle tier comprises military courts of the branches of the armed forces at the level of the seven military districts. The system heads up in the Military Collegium of the Supreme Court. Normally, cases involving law-enforcement officers are heard by the military courts and these trials take place away from the public gaze. At times, however, the rule has been waived, if it is deemed expedient to give a particular case fuller publicity.

The Supreme Court

One of the Supreme Court's chief functions is to act as a court of appeal against decisions of the lower courts. Apart from this, it issues guidelines to the lower courts on juridical questions. Russian law is based on a series of codes (the criminal and labour codes, for example – see Box 6.1) and questions of interpretation turn on the application of these codes rather than, as in the Anglo-Saxon tradition, on case law. The Supreme Court's guidelines are binding not only on the lower courts but also on all agencies of the state whose work has a legal aspect.

The Supreme Court does not have powers of judicial review, which are the preserve of the Constitutional Court, but it may pronounce on the interpretation of laws, and its opinions carry a substantial authority. It can find, for example, that the actions of a state official have gone beyond a federal law, but it would be for the Constitutional Court to decide whether the federal law is constitutional. On a celebrated occasion the Supreme Court ruled, on appeal,

---

Box 6.1 Legal codes

Russian law functions on the application of codes, in the Continental European tradition of Roman law. During Putin's first presidency four major codes were adopted:

- the land code, which came into force in January 2003, and which is treated in Chapter 13;
- the labour code, which came into force on 1 February 2002, replacing the Soviet labour code adopted in 1971, and which is mentioned in Chapter 10;
- revised criminal and administrative law codes, which came into force at the end of June 2002.

A new housing code was drafted during Putin's second presidency. Examples of other major codes are the civil code, the criminal code, the criminal procedure code, the penal code, the tax code and the budget code.

---

against a decision of the Ministry of Internal Affairs to refuse Muslim women permission to have their passport photograph taken wearing a headscarf. But passport matters fall within the President's decree powers and, had the Ministry challenged the legal basis of the Supreme Court's decision, the case would have had to go to the Constitutional Court. The issue of headscarves is taken further in Chapter 13.[4]

The Audit Chamber

Not strictly speaking one of the law-enforcement agencies, the Audit Chamber has been useful to Putin in the steps he has taken to strengthen the state since assuming the presidency. There are three particular reasons for the high profile that the Chamber has acquired. The first is that, in their speculative activities in the privatisation process, the oligarchs frequently overstepped the bounds of strict legality and very often in fields, such as money laundering, where the Chamber had a legitimate interest. The Audit Chamber can audit only those companies in which the state has a stake, however. The second, connected, reason is that it was Putin's intention to claw back as much as possible of the huge sums that had been expatriated from Russia during the Yeltsin years. The third reason is that one of Putin's preferred ways of curbing challenges to his policies has been to allow individuals or organisations to incur debts or take risks and so become vulnerable to action through the courts as a result of inspections by the Audit Chamber. It was to a great extent through these means, for example, that he acquired control of the television network. Clearly, a cooperative Chamber would facilitate such moves.

Under Sergei Stepashin, a former Prime Minister with earlier experience in the security forces, the Audit Chamber became one of Putin's most valuable assets, pursuing cases of financial criminal activity in general and conducting investigations at the time of the Yukos affair in the late summer of 2003 (see Chapter 11). After Mikhail Khodorkovsky's incarceration, the Audit Chamber moved against Roman Abramovich, head of the Sibneft oil company, calling for a review of Sibneft's tax payments (Stepashin called the purchase of Britain's Chelsea Football Club by Abramovich an arrogant and demonstrative challenge to Russia).[5]

A particular service that Stepashin performed for Putin was to investigate the alleged diversion of more than R1 million ($32,000) intended for local road construction at the time of the tercentenary of the foundation of St Petersburg in June 2003. Apart from the purely accounting aspect of this enquiry, Putin was taking the opportunity to weaken an opponent, Vladimir Yakovlev, the governor of St Petersburg at that time. For good measure the Chamber launched a criminal case on 6 June against the former chairman of the city's election commission, Alexander Garusov, on suspicion of financial misdeeds between 2000 and 2002.[6]

It is not only the President who can call on the Audit Chamber's services. Duma deputies have very frequently requested an intervention. In these cases 90 signatures are required. The demand has been so great that Stepashin was led to suggest that a vote of the whole house should be required for the Chamber to act.[7]

The Audit Chamber may be dismissed before the end of its due term if over half the members of the Federation Council or State Duma favour dismissal.

Semi-judicial structures and practices

Among the new juridical institutions that the Russian Federation has adopted is that of the Commissioner for Human Rights. The first holder of the post, from 1993, was Sergei Kovalev, who had been active in the human rights movement in the Soviet Union since the mid-1960s, but he lost the position after his protest against the Russian invasion of Chechnya in 1994. Oleg Mironov held the post until April 2003, when he was replaced by Vladimir Lukin, deputy leader of the Yabloko party. The Commissioner is elected by the Duma.

There is also a separate Human Rights Commission in the Administration of the President's Affairs, headed since 2002 by Ella Pamfilova, a much respected spokesperson on matters of public welfare.

A law allowing for the establishment of an office for human rights in the regions was passed in 1997, though not all subjects of the Federation have availed themselves of it. Problems of immigration provide a good deal of work for a commissioner or a commission of this kind.

An attempt to set up a second form of semi-judicial activity was defeated in the Duma in the autumn of 2003. In the wake of the hostage-taking in the Moscow Dubrovka theatre in October 2002 and the crude way in which it was handled (see Chapter 5), deputies from the liberal parties proposed the creation of independent investigative commissions, with a view to giving both legislative chambers a mechanism for scrutinising the use of military force within the country. Under the proposal, any state official, except the President of Russia, would have been open to investigation. The law would also have given the legislature the authority to examine alleged cases of the violation of human rights during states of emergency or under martial law. The bill was seen off by the pro-presidential majority.

Politics and the law

The rule of law is the basis of democratic politics. In the Russian Federation there is a fully articulated structure for delivering justice and settling disputes, and there is a legal profession formed in academic institutions of great accumulated expertise. Many of the state's leaders have had a legal training, including, notably, Putin himself (see Box 2.2, p. 28), Dmitri Medvedev, the head of his Administration, and Dmitri Kozak, who has held a series of high-profile posts. None the less, there are numerous examples given in this book of ways in which the courts have been used to deliver politically convenient judgements. It is the courts that are finally responsible for finding guilt when the law-enforcement agencies present them with alleged wrong-doers, so that they have been brought to play a central role in suppressing opposition to the authorities – in addition, of course, to dispensing justice without political bias in the mass of everyday cases that they deal with. In cases concerning the media or the environment and research involving foreign partners, the justice delivered has very often had a political purpose.

On many known occasions the support of the law has quite simply been withheld from citizens charged by the Procuracy, a prominent case being that of Platon Lebedev, the chairman of the board of Yukos's financial arm, Menatep, who in July 2003 was denied legal counsel while he was being interrogated.[8] The excuse (that there was no free room in Lefortovo prison for the interrogations) itself reproduces the stratagems that used to be a characteristic of communist rule. Not even the Supreme Court is immune from them. In a celebrated example from 25 September 2003 it upheld on appeal a ruling by the Chechen Supreme Court that the registration of Malik Saidullaev, one of the candidates in the upcoming presidential election in Chechnya, was invalid. The Chechen court had ruled that more than half the signatures supplied by Saidullaev in support of his candidacy were unacceptable because the signatories had either not indicated their date of birth or had failed to give Chechnya as part of their home address.[9] This could be held to be a worthy example of attention to detail, were it not for the fact that other candidates for the Chechen presidential election were being forced out from the contest at the same time.

It is not always Putin and the central administration that benefit from this political use of the law. Very often it is a regional governor arranging affairs in his own bailiwick and using the courts to bolster his position when it is contested. After the hostage-taking at the Dubrovka theatre in October 2002, a Moscow district court rejected claims for compensation from the city authorities for damages suffered during the incident, on the prompting of the mayor, Yuri Luzhkov. The decision was upheld by the Moscow municipal court on the grounds that the terrorists themselves were responsible for any damages. The decision then became a precedent for rejecting some 20 further lawsuits.[10]

At other times the beneficiary is a social group whose aims are supportive of the central authorities. On 11 August 2003, a Moscow district court refused to support the Procurator-General's Office when it laid charges of hooliganism against two Russian Orthodox believers who, with a number of accomplices, had vandalised an anti-clerical exhibition organised by the Andrei Sakharov Museum in Moscow in January.[11]

There are, however, other causes for the failure of the rule of law to be applied and for the wheels of the judicial system to turn unfairly. One of the major problems is that Russia, at this particular juncture, is so violent a society. Rather than develop a framework of protection through use of the courts, people have preferred to settle disputes by resorting to violence, including contract killings at an all too frequent extreme. By the same token, it is difficult to find people willing to act as witnesses in trials. According to the Ministry of Internal Affairs, of those who come forward to act as witnesses in criminal trials in Russia, about a quarter are later led to change their testimony as a result of threats made against them or their families.[12] At the end of March 2003, Putin put before the Duma legislation that would increase the protection offered to witnesses and their families. It would include guards, new places of residence, new identities and even plastic surgery.

Assessment

The political culture of a society is expressed in the language of that culture – in fact, language and culture cannot be prised apart. This means that key terms are difficult to translate. One, essential for this chapter, is the Russian *gosudarstvennost* (literally 'stateness'), the sense of which is a belief that the integrity and the authority of the state are pre-eminent values. The idea of the primacy of the state, however, is part of a more general Continental European tradition, characteristic particularly of those societies where the state and its bureaucracy have a long history, as in both Russia and France, for example. France provides an important point of comparison, because the French revolution developed this notion of the primacy of the state from the 'I am the state' of Louis XIV to a republic of citizens and to the idea of the sovereignty of the people, which provided the basis for a democratic state capable, after two centuries, of adapting to a globally interconnected world. In Russia, however, the Marxist doctrine of the Bolsheviks that the self-rule of the victorious proletariat would make the state itself redundant fell away very shortly after the revolution. The primacy of the state reasserted itself with a vengeance under Stalin, but in a form that emphasised the state's integrity while foreclosing on the development of citizen self-rule.

There is a strong continuity from Soviet times in the way Russian political leaders think of the state. The Soviet planning mechanism was coterminous with the state and was designed to resist influences from beyond it. Today still, a Russian sense of self-sufficiency, arising from the country's size and its detachment from the mainstream of Western industrial development, has contributed to the high value placed on the integrity of the state. Even after the collapse of the Soviet Union Russians see the state not as an impediment to social progress but as the main driving force for change.

Such ideas have important implications for Russian politics today. First, they make it easy for Putin to use the security forces and the law-enforcement agencies in pursuit of his goals. Their function being to protect the state, they see the rule of law in terms of the rule of law enforcement – that is, of policing. This personalises the rule of law, making a nonsense of a principle that relies for its meaning on being depersonalised. It is a continuation of the patrimonialism of the Soviet period and is therefore anachronistic. Indeed, it prolongs the life of a factor that was instrumental in causing the collapse of the Soviet order.

Second, economic activity that escapes the control of the state, and above all such of it as introduces the foreigner into the Russian economic patrimony, is seen as suspect. In this way of thinking it made sense to lock up Mikhail Khodorkovsky (see Chapter 11).

Third, the nation state everywhere else in the advanced industrial world is seeing its traditional monopolies eroded, through international treaties, the internationalisation of finance, the expansion of multinational companies and the movement of substantial populations around the globe. The Soviet Union, having in any case the characteristics more of an empire than a nation state, resisted these pressures, and in the end paid for the choice with its existence. It is doubtful, however, how long the new Russian Federation can sustain its traditional view of the state.

Finally, there are a number of reasons concerned with the transition from communism for Putin's favouring a 'dictatorship of law'. The circumstances of the transition engendered lawlessness as new economic practices were allowed without adequate regulation and they have led people to settle accounts with each other by violence rather than resorting to legal channels, with which they are not familiar and which they are not inclined to trust.[13] Also, Russia has had to develop whole new areas of law connected with the onset of capitalism – business and financial law, external trade, buying and selling land – and compliance with unfamiliar regulation was difficult to achieve.

Further reading

An English translation of the 1993 constitution can be found at:
www.constitution.ru/en/10003000-01.htm
A bibliography on Russian law can be found at:
www.llrx.com/features/russian.htm#codes

W. E. Butler, *Russian Law* (New York: Oxford University Press, 1999). This is a comprehensive textbook in five substantial parts. Parts I and II deal with the legal setting and the legal system. Part V includes tables of legislative acts and of treaties.

K. Hendley, 'Legal development in post-Soviet Russia', *Post-Soviet Affairs*, 13:3 (1997), 231–56.

K. Hendley, 'Rewriting the rules of the game in Russia: the neglected issue of the demand for law', *East European Constitutional Review*, 8:4 (1999), 89–96.

S. Holmes, *et al.*, 'Reforming Russia's courts', *East European Constitutional Review*, 11:1/2, 90–130.

V. Pastukhov, 'Law under administrative pressure in post-Soviet Russia', *East European Constitutional Review*, 11:3 (2002), 66–74.

R. Sharlet, 'Putin and the politics of law in Russia', *Post-Soviet Affairs*, 17 (2001), 195–234.

P. H. Solomon and T. S. Foglesong, *Courts and Transition in Russia: The Challenge of Judicial Reform* (Boulder, CO: Westview Press, 2000).

Notes

1 H. J. Berman, *Justice in the USSR: An Interpretation of Soviet Law* (Cambridge, MA: Harvard University Press, revised edn, 1963).

2 G. Gill, 'Ideology, organisation and the patrimonial regime', *The Journal of Communist Studies*, 5:3 (1989), 285–302.

3 *Vremya-MN*, 22 July 2003; *Russian Political Weekly*, 23 July 2003.

4 'The important thing is that...', *Izvestiya*, 15 May 2003.

5 *Sunday Times*, 9 November 2003.

6 'The former head of the Petersburg electoral commission is being sued', *Kommersant-Daily*, 7 June 2003.

7 *Argumenty i fakty*, 2003, no. 31

8 'Apatit has gone forever', *Kommersant-Daily*, 7 July 2003.

9 *RFE/RL Newsline*, 12 September 2003.

10 *RFE/RL Newsline*, 30 April 2003, citing NTV and TVS.

11 www.strana.ru, 11 August 2003.

12 *RFE/RL Newsline*, 30 April 2003.

13 K. Hendley, 'Rewriting the rules of the game in Russia: the neglected issue of the demand for law', *East European Constitutional Review*, 8:4 (1999), 89–95.

Part III

Parliamentary representation

7

The Federal Assembly

Background

When Mikhail Gorbachev introduced his reforms from 1985, participation in politics in Russia acquired a new meaning. Until then, elections and the work of the soviets had been a matter of the involvement of the masses in which the masses were not called upon to make the decisions that determined their lives. Now participation was beginning to bring citizens voice and choice – through freedom of opinion and the press, through a free electoral process and through the ability of interests to take organisational form.

This was a novel situation. For a decade at the beginning of the twentieth century in tsarist Russia political parties had been enabled to form and their candidates had been elected to a newly created parliament, the Duma, albeit on a restricted franchise. Despite stern censorship, public opinion at the time enjoyed freedom of expression among an extremely restricted political class. The political power monopoly of the Soviet years stifled these first shoots of representative democracy for little short of 70 years. By the time the communist regime fell, too many generations had passed for so brief an experience to leave a mark or to give rise to any nostalgia. At the same time, the Soviet regime had transformed society in industrial and social terms. Russian citizens could now expect to enjoy political practices appropriate to a highly urbanised, technology-based society, culturally the equal of the leading industrial nations.

The Soviet Union's central legislative body – the Supreme Soviet – was filled through elections that did not involve choice (see Chapter 8), since the Communist Party nominated the sole candidate on the ballot papers. Twice a year Ivan Ivanovich left his workbench and took a paid trip to Moscow for a session lasting two or three days. He cannot have understood much about the intricacies of the budget, but his vote for the government's measures made them legitimate. It was therefore a revolutionary step when Gorbachev persuaded the Party to replace the Supreme Soviet at state level with a Congress of People's Deputies elected on a largely free basis in 1989. In the Russian Republic itself, a Congress of People's Deputies was elected in the following year on substantially the same basis. It was this Congress that Yeltsin confronted when he launched his radical economic reforms and which he sent packing in September 1993, as described in Chapter 1. The parliamentary structure that interests us here is the one established in the new Russian Federation by the constitution passed in the aftermath of that confrontation.

From that point, the new Federal Assembly had to learn to work in a context of open and competitive politics. This was the arena in which democratic politics were to be learned. On the other hand, there was one sense in which it was not entirely a novel institution. It retained the central constitutional function of giving legislation the stamp of approval as law. From this point of view, a distinction must be observed between the Assembly and the political parties that came into being to fill its lower house, the State Duma. With one exception – the Communist Party and some minor parties stemming from it, with which all other major parties refused to have relations – the political parties were new and had to learn to play a novel role. The importance of making this distinction is that, as long as the political parties were weak, there was always the possibility of tradition reasserting itself, with a powerful executive pulling the Assembly back into its previous and familiar role as simply a validating mechanism for decisions made elsewhere.

The Federal Assembly

The legislature of the Russian Federation today comprises two houses, together forming the Federal Assembly – a lower chamber, the State Duma, and an upper chamber, the Federation Council. They sit separately and their members are chosen according to different principles, which reflect differences in their functions. The two houses share a few important prerogatives. Together they ratify the President's nominees for the posts of director of the State Bank and the head of the Audit Chamber, and each of them ratifies the appointment of half that Chamber's members. In October 2004, in the wake of the Beslan crisis (see Box 2.1, p. 25), Putin proposed that a new Public Chamber be created, to which bills should be submitted before being presented to the Assembly.

The State Duma

The Duma (Figure 7.1) is elected for a four-year term and is made up of 450 deputies. They are elected through proportional representation on the basis of party lists (this is the result of ongoing change in the manner of the Duma's recruitment – see Chapter 8).

To stand for election to the Duma, a candidate must be at least 21 years old. A member of any other representative body in the state structure, and anyone holding a post in a body of federal or local government, can stand for

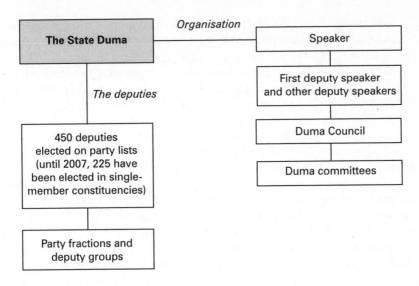

Figure 7.1 *The State Duma: deputies and organisational structure.*

election to the Duma but cannot hold both positions simultaneously. When an official working in the Ulyanovsk oblast legislature neglected to leave his post on election to that legislature in May 2003, the oblast procurator intervened to remind him of this rule.[1] It is a common practice for parties to place some well known figures near the top of their federal list to attract voters, who then resign their seats after the election.

When a newly elected Duma convenes, it elects a speaker and a number of deputies (eight were appointed for the Duma elected in December 2003). Duma deputies are required by the constitution to have no other paid employment, except for work as a teacher or in scientific or other creative activity. The grandeur of the cars in which many of them arrive at the Duma building suggests that this requirement is honoured more in the breach than the observance. They can stand in regional elections but must relinquish one of their mandates if elected. Members of the Duma are immune from prosecution while they are serving, which has made Duma membership attractive to the criminal fringe.

What does the State Duma do?

Legislative role

First, the Duma legislates. It discusses draft laws that have either originated in the Duma or been introduced from other sources (the President, the government, the regional legislatures or the high courts – i.e. the Constitutional

Court, Supreme Court and High Court of Arbitration) and it votes freely on them, using an electronic system. Bills must be passed by the Duma before they complete the legislative cycle by being sent to the Federation Council and then to the President for signing. In principle, draft laws involving funding from the budget may be submitted to the Duma for debate only when the government's opinion is known, though this rule is not always observed.

Holding the executive to account

Second, the constitution provides for the accountability of the executive to parliament, but hedges it about. Thus the appointment of the Prime Minister by the President is subject to parliamentary approval, but through a procedure that gives the President the advantage over the Duma (it is for the President to propose a name for ratification by the Duma – see Chapter 3). Similarly, the Duma can call the government to account by passing a vote of confidence (this is the standard term for what is usually, in fact, a vote of no confidence), but at the risk of it bringing about a dissolution of the house. For a vote of confidence to succeed, a simple majority of the total membership of the Duma is required. If it is passed, the President is entitled either to dismiss the government or to reject the Duma's decision, but if the Duma passes a second vote of no confidence within three months, the President either dismisses the government or dissolves the Duma. The government can itself call for a vote of confidence. If this fails, the President has to decide within seven days whether to dismiss the government or dissolve the Duma.

No vote of confidence has so far succeeded in the Russian Federation since the adoption of the 1993 constitution, though the system has been tested, as in March 2000, when an attempt by the Communist Party of the Russian Federation to dislodge the government failed. In late April 2003 the Communist Party and the Yabloko party tried to drum up support for a vote of confidence against the government of Mikhail Kasyanov, at a moment when the Duma was responding to a suggestion by President Vladimir Putin that Russia should move to a system of cabinet formation by Duma majority. The vote of confidence failed; the government showed its disdain for the process by not even sending one its members to the Duma to defend its position.

The fact that Putin has assured himself of a Duma majority in his favour since the beginning of the third Duma, in 1999, clouds the issue of accountability, and casts the emphasis on to the means by which he achieved this outcome. Chapters 8 and 12, on elections and the media, will show how the question of accountability cannot be reduced simply to the relative constitutional powers of the executive and the Duma, since the presidency has had a strong influence on which individuals and which parties are to be represented in the Duma. As with so many aspects of the political system in Russia today, reality departs from both the provisions of the constitution and the democratic promise of the transition from communism, but it is none the less better than the reality of Soviet days.

Table 7.1 *The public's confidence in national institutions, 2001 (percentage of survey respondents)*

Institution	Level of confidence			
	Full	Some	Not much	None
The churches	19	28	26	16
The armed forces	14	36	29	13
State television	13	44	31	8
Radio	12	41	26	7
The press	7	40	34	8
Independent television	7	31	28	12
Government	7	24	46	19
Parliament	2	14	47	28
Political parties	2	9	42	37

Source: S. White, 'Ten years on, what do Russians think?', *The Journal of Communist Studies and Transition Politics*, 18:1 (2002), 42.

Debating and airing issues

Third, the Duma debates and airs issues. It is in this role that the Duma departs most markedly from the Soviet past. Though the broadcasting of Duma debates on television is selective, they are fully reported in the press. Certain deputies, however, have taken advantage of the exposure to the media provided by Duma debates to promote themselves as individuals, which contributes to the very low ratings that parliament is given in public opinion surveys (see Table 7.1).

Representation

A fourth role of the Duma – its representative role – serves partly the same function as the debating role. It is a feature of liberal-democratic politics that political parties not only represent political cleavages in society but to an extent give them form by reducing the many views and interests in society to a manageable few. But the formation of a party system with clearly defined programmes and constituencies of support is taking time in Russia, and two dominant factors are holding it up, indeed, stalling it completely – on the one hand, the near universal appeal to a single national patriotic interest and, on the other, the ability of the President to make support for him and his policies the determining factor in the loyalties of deputies. The same factors go a long way to explaining why the deputies have not formed any clear and consistent pattern of regional and sectional representation, on the pattern of the US Congress.

Sectional representation, however, has at least gained a foothold, through the development of lobbying as the predominant way in which deputies have interpreted their role. Lobbying is, of course, a form of representation, but it places the emphasis on individual deals and influence, rather than on the articulation of broad group interests. *Nezavisimaya gazeta* publishes frequent tables ranking public figures in terms of their lobbying prowess. In October 2003 *Vedomosti* pointed out the number of executives from the consumer-goods industry who were standing in the December elections of that year, some for single-member constituencies and others on party lists. They included the owner or general directors of the supermarket chains Sedmoi Kontinent, Perekrestka, Tri Kita, Grand and Yevroseti. *Vedomosti* claimed that some 44 per cent of all direct investment in 2002 went into goods and services, and the sector now sought ways of asserting its interests.[2] *Moskovskie novosti* identified a number of links between individual deputies and interests in society, though it did not offer actual evidence of permanent lobbying relationships. According to the paper, the oil and gas companies, a number of holding companies in other extractive industries, the insurance business and, as noted, retail trade all have contacts on relevant committees and often with committee chairs. It mentioned also cases of deputies being 'delegated' to the Duma.

At the same time, the success of United Russia in the 2003 Duma elections (49 per cent of the seats and sufficient allies to ensure a majority) had the effect of sharply narrowing the possible targets for lobbyists, since all decisions about legislation from that point on passed through a single office on the sixth floor of the Duma building, that of Yuri Volkov, head of United Russia's group of deputies – and a reserve officer in the Federal Security Service.[3]

The extent to which Duma deputies take their duties seriously as representatives of their individual constituents varies. Not even election from a single-member constituency guaranteed it, since these deputies had no required connection with the locality and were often established national figures selected for their prestige.

Political leadership

Within important limitations, the Duma plays a fifth role, as a source of political leadership and advancement, partly as a result of the publicity that it offers. Insufficient time has passed since its birth in 1993 for this role to be tested, but two contrasting cases illustrate the present reality. While Gennadi Zyuganov, as leader of the Communist Party, owes his prominence to his emergence over time at the head of that organisation, the Duma was the forum in which he created the public image that he used – admittedly without success – to challenge Vladimir Putin for the presidency in 2000. Rather different is the case of the flamboyant Vladimir Zhirinovsky, who owes his prominence in Russian politics entirely to the Duma. At first his extravagant statements and performances on the floor of the Duma made him appear less than serious as a politician, but in fact he saw how exposure in the Duma and media coverage of his antics could fuel the consolidation of the political party that he created on this basis – the Liberal Democratic Party of Russia. Between these two extremes, many other Duma politicians are constantly in the public eye and consequently in a position to attract a following and build up a political position. The fact that the members of the federal government, including the Prime Minister, are not drawn from the Duma means that there is no direct career path from election to the Duma to government office, but Duma deputies have stood for election as regional governors (until that procedure was abrogated in 2004) and indeed for the presidency. Apart from these executive destinations, the Duma itself, through its committees and its lobbying possibilities, offers value to the ambitious.

Powers of appointment

Finally, as noted, the Duma has certain powers of appointment. Jointly with the Federation Council, and on the President's nomination, it appoints the director of the State Bank and the head of the Audit Chamber, together with half its members.

How the Duma conducts its business

When a new Duma convenes, it elects a speaker and a number of deputy speakers. It also elects the Council of the Duma, which has the task of organising the legislative timetable.

The newly elected deputies form parliamentary 'fractions'. Any party that has won 7 per cent or more of the party list votes (5 per cent until 2007) can form a fraction on its own, which deputies from that party elected in single-member constituencies normally join. Deputies of other parties, and independent deputies, may form a 'deputy group' if they can assemble at least 55 members (only 35 were needed in the third Duma, of 1999–2003). Finance for staff and other administrative expenses is assigned to the fractions and groups (henceforth simply 'groups'), with the result that almost all deputies are attached to one or other of them. A great deal of the Duma's business is transacted by the parliamentary groups, and it falls to the Duma's Council to arbitrate in the many disputes that arise among them. Leadership of a group is an important political post. Two central figures of the third Duma were leaders of groups – Nikolai Kharitonov, leader of the Agro-Industrial group, and Gennadi Raikov, leader of the People's Deputy group.

Under legislation approved by the Duma in March 2004, each deputy is allowed a staff of five assistants and 40 'public assistants'. The bill also deprived deputies' assistants of immunity from arrest (they were suspected of undertaking nefarious tasks on behalf of the deputies who employed them) and of their right to free travel on public transport.

Duma committees

One of the chief administrative tasks of the deputy groups is to distribute membership of the Duma's standing committees and their chairs. There were 28 committees during most of the third Duma and this became 29 in the fourth Duma. The Budget Committee is naturally of particular importance.

The allocation of committee chairs is a key political event at the start of any newly elected Duma. The distribution in principle follows the comparative strengths of the parties represented in the house. However, as the parliamentary forces supporting Putin consolidated their position in the third Duma, their manoeuvring came to centre on the chairs of the Duma committees. The Communist Party had won a significant victory in the 1999 elections and on that basis was allocated the chairs of nine committees. On 3 April 2002 the Duma voted to replace all but two of them with members of the pro-Kremlin parties and groups. At the same time, the parties supporting the President took control of the Council of the Duma – its organisational apparatus. Further details are given in Chapter 9.

With its sweeping victory in the elections of 2003, the United Russia party was able to make an even cleaner sweep of committee chairs, taking all 29 of them and leaving the other parties with eight deputy and first-deputy chairs between them.

Behaviour of deputies

The Duma has an Ethics Committee, charged with overseeing the behaviour of deputies. Zhirinovsky has frequently been at the centre of cases of misbehaviour, his use of colourful language in reference to the US President George W. Bush being brought before the Ethics Committee in early February 2003. Galina Strelchenko, the committee's chair during the third Duma, had to intervene more than once in the case of the Communist deputy Vasili Shandybin, who, in the same month, like Zhirinovsky on other occasions, engaged in fisticuffs with another deputy (the victim in this case, Alexander Fedulov, had contrasted Zyuganov's conduct unfavourably with Zhirinovsky's). Three months later Shandybin shouted out at the close of the President's address to parliament on 16 May 2003, 'There will be only thieves, bandits, and bribe takers in the next Duma!', for which misdemeanour his right to speak in the Duma was revoked for one month.[4]

Proxy voting and its misuse

The Duma's rules permit proxy voting, but some deputies have charged that the practice is out of control. It arises largely from the rule that, to be successful, a motion has to secure the vote of 50 per cent plus one (or more) of the whole house, not just of those present and voting. Absenteeism is in any case a major problem for the Duma. In September 2002, in a vote on amendments to the federal law on referendums, four members of the majority centrist deputy groups each voted on behalf of some 30 colleagues. This led a number of Communist deputies to challenge the amendments in the Constitutional Court, expressly citing the widespread practice of proxy voting as a violation of proper procedure, which they held should invalidate the amendments. It is not only the Duma that is plagued by absenteeism. In April 2003 the Federation Council submitted to the Duma an amendment to the law on the status of State

Duma deputies and Federation Council members that would forbid members of both chambers to vote on behalf of their colleagues.[5] The proposal was seen as unlikely to have a future, given the vested interests of the very people who would be required to vote on the issue. Indeed, so lax has behaviour become in this regard that proxy voting has come to be permitted in committee meetings as well as in full meetings of the Duma.

The dangers of being a Duma deputy

When Sergei Yushenkov, the leader of one wing of the split Liberal Russia Party, was assassinated on 17 April 2003, he was the ninth Duma deputy to be killed since 1994. The case acquired a high political prominence, but remained overshadowed by the shooting in 1998 of Galina Starovoitova, one of the original leaders of the democratic movement in the perestroika period and a prominent advocate of human rights.

The Federation Council

Each of the Federation's 88 subjects sends two representatives to the Assembly's second chamber – the Federation Council – which is therefore composed of 176 'senators', as they have come to be called. The way in which they are selected has changed twice. Until 1995 they were directly elected, but under a law adopted in that year the heads of the executive and legislative branches in each region automatically became members of the Federation Council. One of Putin's earliest measures in 2000 was to change the system again with a view to reducing the power of the regions. Today, one of the representatives is elected by the region's legislature and the second is selected by its executive. This results, in formal terms, in a mixture of nomination and indirect election at regional level, but there is a clear tendency for Federation Council members to be parachuted into that role through the patronage exercised by the President and his Administration.

The regions were given a right to recall their executive's nominee (on grounds of failing to attend Council meetings, for example). In January 2003 the State Duma considered amendments to the law on forming the Federation Council that would protect senators from being recalled during their first year of service. The bill included a provision that a two-thirds vote in the Federation Council would be required to approve a proposal from a regional legislature to recall a senator.

The Federation Council elects a speaker (Sergei Mironov held this post in Putin's first presidency and into the second) and a number of deputy speakers. Something can be gleaned about the Council and its workings from Mironov's abrupt dismissal of the deputy speaker, Andrei Vikharev, in June 2003 and the fact that his proposed replacement, Valentina Petrenko, was twice rejected.

Mironov had powers to dismiss, but an appointment required the approval of the Council. Mironov attributed the rejection to his failure to acknowledge pressures that had built up for appointments to follow the rotation principle. There has been a growing tendency to make appointments to positions such as the deputy speaker according to gender.[6]

The Federation Council's committee structure resembles that of the Duma, but in the Council's case there is an emphasis on regional affairs. A 'profile committee' prepares business and vets important legislation before it is presented to the house.

What does the Federation Council do?

- The Federation Council shares the Duma's legislating role but its composition obviously gives it a particular interest in legislation affecting the regions. As a second chamber it serves to refine bills that have passed through the Duma.
- It ratifies appointments to a number of high offices. Presidential nominations to the posts of justice of the Supreme Court, the Constitutional Court and the High Court of Arbitration, and to that of federal Procurator-General require ratification by the Federation Council. Jointly with the Duma it ratifies the President's nominees for the posts of director of the State Bank and the head of the Audit Chamber, and it ratifies half the Chamber's members.
- A presidential decree to introduce martial law or a state of emergency also requires the confirmation of the Council, as do proposals to change the borders between subjects of the Federation.

The Federation Council meets at least monthly. During the spring session of 2003 it held 11 plenary meetings, at which 121 federal laws were examined, 10 of which were rejected. As noted above, absenteeism is even more frequent than it is in the Duma. This is both a cause and an effect of the low esteem in which the Federation Council is held. It has also created problems. For example, journalists seeking information and copy tend to turn to the Council's standing staff if deputies are not available, which puts pressure on the staff and can lead to leaks. Staff have had to be put on their guard officially against this. Absenteeism, with rather similar consequences, led to a celebrated scandal in the Council's affairs when it was discovered that two senators who were recorded as having voted for amendments to the law on communications in June 2003 were in fact out of the country at the time. The staff of the Council were apparently admitting administrative assistants of Council deputies into the chamber during the vote.[7]

Putin has clearly seen the Federation Council as a bulwark of support for himself against the Duma. This was well illustrated in a meeting that Putin held on 25 April 2003 with Mironov, his four deputies and the heads of all of the Council's committees, together with their deputies. At the meeting

Putin was critical of the State Duma to the extent of suggesting that the Federation Council should exercise a particularly keen watching brief on the work of the Duma and its deputies during the legislative elections due in the following December. Putin's aim, no doubt, was to enlist the support of an ally in countering the populism to which the Duma can tend. It is also one illustration of the extraordinary lengths to which Putin went in order to ensure that United Russia, the party with which he was associated, would triumph in the elections. Nothing should be left to chance.

In general, the Federation Council has shown itself to be ineffective in the Russian political system. Not being directly elected, its membership has been open to manipulation in the way it is recruited. The Council has come, in fact, to reflect the dominance of the centre over the regions.

The legislative process

After an initial vetting by the Public Chamber (see below), all legislation starts in the Duma. It can be initiated by a number of sources: the President, either house of the Assembly, their individual deputies, the federal government, the legislature of any of the Federation's subjects, the Supreme Court, the Constitutional Court and the High Court of Arbitration. In the Duma a bill has a first reading before going to a committee. There follow a second and a third reading.

Once a bill has been given a favourable vote in the Duma it is considered by the Federation Council. If the Federation Council rejects the bill it can go before a conciliation commission, which attempts to resolve differences, or the Duma can override the rejection. For this a majority of two-thirds is required. When the bill has passed both houses it goes to the President for signing.

If the President signs the bill it becomes law. If he rejects it, it goes back to the Duma for reconsideration. The President's rejection can be overridden, but for this a two-thirds vote in each house of the Assembly is required, unless the President's amendments are accepted, in which case a simple majority suffices.

The Public Chamber

The function of the Public Chamber, when its creation was proposed by Putin in October 2004, was to oversee the work of the legislature while at the same time admitting representatives of civil society directly into the legislative process. The proposal was part of Putin's response to the Beslan crisis of September that year, and was inevitably seen by commentators as a softening measure to compensate for the streamlining of the executive through the central nomination of regional governors and the likely abandoning of the single-mandate system in elections to the Duma. At the time of writing it was still not clear how the members of the new Chamber would be recruited. What was clear was that a freely elected Duma was not viewed as an appropriate or sufficient way of ensuring the representation of civil society.

The Assembly's relations with the executive

Constitutionally, the relationship between the Assembly and the executive is based on the European tradition making the latter responsible to the former. This is not upheld, however, in the way political life is actually led.

The fact that there is a dual executive means that the Duma has to hold two bodies accountable to it, which makes for ambiguity, and this in turn can weaken accountability. True, the government has so far been merely an extension of the President's power, but the constitutional mechanisms for accountability at the Duma's disposal (impeachment of the President and the vote of confidence in the case of the government) separate the two functions. Again, a dual executive is in itself no bar to the proper functioning of democratic processes. France has a dual executive, divided as in Russia between the presidency and the government. In France, however, though government ministers do not sit in the Assembly, they are identified with the Assembly's political parties. Representation passes from the people through the electoral process to the parties and thus to a government formed from whichever party can command a majority in the Assembly. In the Russian Federation, in contrast, the government is detached from the Duma *and* from the structure of representation at any level. Government ministers come to the Duma from outside to explain their policies and actions. No party in the Duma can control the government, nor does the government govern according to a programme generated directly by a party or parties in the Duma.

Second, the constitution prevents the same person from holding both a government position and a seat in the Federal Assembly at the same time. At the present stage of the system's development this has the effect of strengthening the President yet further in relation to the Assembly, because it prevents Assembly politicians from increasing their political profile. At present the Assembly lacks prestige and it would increase its standing if its members had the visibility of a government post. This may be only a temporary matter. The separation of powers in the United States does not diminish the prestige of Congress or of its members, while in France politicians move more readily between posts in government and in the Assembly than has yet been the case in Russia.

Finally, the counterpart of the weakness of the Duma is the strength of the presidency. The presidency becomes overpowering if the incumbent uses the media, the electoral commissions and, if deemed necessary, the law-enforcement agencies to provide himself with a subservient Duma.

However the success was achieved, the party supporting Putin won a massive majority in the 2003 elections, and Putin continues to be given an approval rating of 60–70 per cent in opinion polls. Moreover, many people in Russia associate democracy with the disasters and the plunder of the nation's wealth of the Yeltsin period. Since, in comparison with the economic gulf into which the Russian electorate fell in the 1990s, that electorate has nowhere to go but up, it may be some time before executive power in Russia has to face a real challenge from within the Duma.

Meanwhile, it is revealing that, after the 2003 elections, Putin offered jobs in the government to former deputies of defeated parties, such as Yabloko – and that they accepted.

Assessment

The Federal Assembly is essential to the ability of citizens to influence the state and to protect themselves from it. This chapter, however, has shown that the existence of an assembly is in itself no guarantee of accountability. All depends on how it is filled. If it is filled by the state's nominees, direct or indirect, it can still serve a legislative function, but it cannot claim to be a means of ensuring accountability to the people.

The political role of the Supreme Soviet in the communist days was to rubber-stamp measures taken elsewhere and validate them as law. Today's Duma, unlike all but one of the parties represented in it, must be seen as part of the Soviet legacy. There are people in positions of power in the Russian Federation today for whom the supreme representative body once played a strictly formal role, one that was none the less functional and, above all, did not threaten the coherence of the ruling party's policies. As long as the movement for change initiated by Gorbachev maintained its forward momentum, this image was eclipsed by the expectation of an assembly that would guarantee accountability of the government. Once that momentum was first halted by Yeltsin's curtailing of the powers of the Duma in 1993, and then reversed under Putin, the image of a rubber-stamp parliament was likely to revive in the minds of an authoritarian leadership. The extravagant behaviour of some prominent Duma deputies, moreover, could only lower the esteem in which the Assembly was held.

Others, however, could cast their minds back to the historic day in May 1989 when the new Congress of People's Deputies, with certain reservations freely elected, met and engaged in an open discussion. Before their television sets people watched and listened, amazed, as speaker after speaker contributed to a tumult of complaints, expectations, criticisms of the past and hopes for the future. The Congress, with an inner Supreme Soviet elected from it, went on to pass the laws that established the basic democratic freedoms and ensured that the mass of new issues stemming from the policies of glasnost and perestroika were publicly debated. Blocs formed around these issues within the Congress. However, the atmosphere in the Congress of People's Deputies throughout the

Gorbachev period was that of a constituent assembly discussing a future that was being made. It was a long way from a parliament assembling the spokes-people of formed bodies of interest and opinion in society, differentiated by a history of interaction and by programmes shaped by that interaction.

The interlude between the end of the Soviet Union and the election of a State Duma in the new Russian Federation in 1993 was occupied by the con-flict between the Supreme Soviet and Yeltsin, which put the development of a constructive parliamentary life on hold. The new Duma's political role that emerged must be seen against the assertion of the presidential power by Putin from 2000, and the steps he took to ensure, first, that the Federation Council would not develop an independent representative role and, second, that the electoral process would produce a State Duma dominated by his supporters. These developments fly in the face of his stated aim, backed by the 2001 Law on Political Parties, to make the Duma a site for competitive politics and other statements advocating direct accountability of the government (though not, in these statements, the President) to parliament.

The Duma retains what it had in Soviet days – the prerogative of placing the stamp of law on legislative proposals. It debates those proposals, and indi-vidual deputies may make them, but the vote will be determined by a majority crafted by the executive, and only bills presented from within that majority have a chance of succeeding. Issues are now aired in public in the Duma, but reporting on the debates falls under central control of television, and the circulation of newspapers is very small. In general, the Russian Duma is one of the weakest legislatures in Europe, and is held in deservedly low esteem by the population. Change is represented to a certain extent by the opportunities for individual lobbying that Duma membership offers. The beneficiaries of that lobbying are largely the deputies themselves, amplified to some extent by the benefit that their own advancement can bring in its train to a certain sector, or a certain region. Apart from that qualification, however, the Duma is today what the Assembly of the French Fourth Republic was charged with being – a house without windows.

Further reading

P. Chaisty, 'Legislative politics in Russia', in A. Brown (ed.), *Contemporary Russian Politics: A Reader* (Oxford: Oxford University Press, 2001).

J. Hahn (ed.), *Democratization in Russia: The Development of Legislative Institutions* (London, M. E. Sharpe, 1996).

T. F. Remington, *The Russian Parliament: Institutional Evolution in a Transitional Regime, 1989–1999* (Newhaven, CT: Yale University Press, 2001).

J. Shevchenko and G. Golosov, 'Legislative activism of Duma deputies, 1996–1999', *Europe–Asia Studies*, 53:2 (2001), 239–62.

S. Smith and T. F. Remington, *The Politics of Institutional Choice: The Formation of the Russian State Duma* (Princeton, NJ: Princeton University Press, 2001).

Notes

1 *RFE/RL Newsline*, 2 June 2003.
2 'The consumer lobby might sharply increase in the new State Duma', *Vedomosti*, no. 181, 6 October 2003.
3 *Moskovskie novosti*, no. 11, March 2004.
4 *RFE/RL Newsline*, 10 February 2003.
5 www.gazeta.ru, 30 April 2003.
6 ITAR-TASS news agency, 12 June 2003; *Izvestiya*, 10 June 2003.
7 *Vremya-MN*, 1 July 2003; *RFE/RL Newsline*, 19 and 26 June 2003.

8

Elections

Background

During the communist period, elections were held for the soviets at each administrative level of the Soviet Union. However, until 1987 they did not involve choice, as a single name was put forward by the 'Communist Party and non-Party bloc' and the Party was in a position to prevent any rival candidates from being presented. Why, then, did the Party run elections at all? The answer is that elections served as referendums confirming the Party's authority and celebrating its achievements. On election day the country gave itself a pat on the back for progress made since the last elections and the Party-controlled press played its part by displaying that progress. Headlines such as 'I vote so that my motherland may prosper', accompanied by before-and-after photographs showing how some major construction project had emerged from the forest or tundra, emphasised the national interest and a national solidarity. In such a context, to divide the nation by an appeal to one particular section of society could be made to appear antisocial. Not to vote at all laid one open to the same charge and turnout was always close to universal.

One aspect of open and free elections, however, is that they provide information about preferences among individuals and between policy options. It followed from Mikhail Gorbachev's concern to free the circulation of information through glasnost that an element of choice should be introduced into the electoral process. Multiple candidacies were allowed in a restricted number of electoral districts in 1987. In elections to the new Congress of People's Deputies in 1989 a radical step was taken by making all seats competitive, though competition for a third of them was restricted to the various 'social organisations'. This assured the Party of a reserved bloc of seats in the 2,250-member Congress, since not only was it a social organisation but it controlled the others as well.

Since 1993 there have been no restrictions on the franchise (apart from those arising from a lower age limit, certified mental incapacity and incarceration), and the freedoms of speech and assembly that have been instituted mean that in principle elections are free and open, and the ballot is secret. In any electoral system, the rules of competition can to some degree be stretched, distorted or at times ignored, but this chapter describes the particular manipulations to which elections in Russia have been subjected. It records also a particular feature of the Soviet electoral system that was carried over into the practice of the new Federation. This is the 'against all' vote. When competitive elections were first introduced in 1989, it was possible for electors to vote 'against all' candidates. The aim, when the procedure was originally introduced, was to increase voter participation. This has been carried over into today's electoral system in Russia, with results that will be presented below.

The organisation of elections

The Central Electoral Commission

Overall charge of running elections in the Russian Federation is given to the Central Electoral Commission (CEC). Its head is chosen by the President, subject to ratification by the Federation Council. Alexander Veshnyakov held the post from the beginning of Vladimir Putin's first presidency and into his second, having been reappointed on 26 March 2003. The President, the Federation Council and the State Duma each choose five members for the Commission, the State Duma's selection being made according to the relative strength of the party groups. In the third State Duma (1999–2003) Unity, Yabloko, the Communist Party of the Russian Federation (KPRF) and Fatherland–All Russia (see Chapter 9 on the political parties) each contributed one member each and the last was provided by the People's Deputy party group. United Russia's success in the 2003 Duma elections enabled it to predominate in the State Duma's allocation of Commission seats (see below).

The CEC has the power to issue regulations that have the force of law – on, for example, the vetting of candidates. This has been of considerable political significance, since the composition of the Commission and the work that it does are themselves in the control of people who might not be disinterested in the results of elections, given that the President nominates five members, and that five further members are chosen by a State Duma, which is itself dominated by the parties supporting the President.

The CEC heads a structure of electoral commissions that extends down into the regions, and which has been organised into a single vertical framework. The chair of the electoral commission of a subject of the Federation must have a higher legal education or an academic degree in law.

Registration and the role of the Ministry of Justice

The Ministry of Justice has played an important role in the formation of the Russian party system, because political parties have to register with it in order to participate in elections. In fulfilling this role it uses as its reference the 2002 Law on Elections of Deputies to the State Duma of the Federal Assembly of the Russian Federation, and the 2001 Law on Political Parties. Since these pieces of legislation are recent, and since it is difficult to get every detail right when applying for registration, the Ministry of Justice can affect the fortunes of political parties by the degree of tolerance or rigour that it brings to individual applications. Nor do the possible difficulties stop there, because the taxation authorities, also, can prevent parties from participating in elections if they have not presented their latest financial accounts.

The electoral system and its effects

Voting

The electoral system used in elections to the first four State Dumas was similar to the one used in Germany since the Second World War (the 'additional member system'). It found particular favour among states that had emerged from communist rule and were reconstructing their representative institutions. Its advantage is that it balances proportional representation for the political parties with a direct link between a parliamentary deputy and a local electorate. Under the Russian system, the 450 State Duma seats were filled in two different ways, and voters correspondingly had two votes. For half the seats, registered political parties presented a list of candidates. Voters used one of their votes to vote for a party list. The proportion of votes in the whole electorate given to a party (say, 10 per cent) entitled the party to that proportion of the 225 seats assigned to the party lists, in this case 22. So the top 22 candidates on the national party list got seats.

The other half of the 450 seats was filled by simple majority vote in 225 constituencies. Candidates could stand for particular parties or as independents, so that they might be well known local figures or perhaps less well known figures whom voters might favour partly because of their party ties. In the earliest days of the new Russian Federation, when the KPRF was the only federal party with any real existence in the regions, 'single-member constituencies' returned a great many independent State Duma members, who formed alliances once they assembled in Moscow, but the independent element has since diminished.

It has been one of Putin's aims to create a party system of a few consolidated parties, to give stability to the infant representative structure. It was no doubt with this in mind that, in September 2004, very soon after the hostage-taking crisis in Beslan (see Box 2.1, p. 25), he proposed that all Duma seats be filled by party lists, eliminating the single-member element. This had, in fact, been under discussion for some time. Having secured the domination of the Duma by United Russia, the Kremlin could, through the placing of names on the party list, effectively nominate a large section of the Duma's membership.

Meanwhile, increasing control over the other parties in the system is well on the way to delivering a State Duma that is unlikely to generate meaningful opposition to the President's policies and decisions.

The percentage threshold

To prevent the proliferation of small parties in the State Duma, with consequent difficulties in forming stable coalitions, a party has to win a certain percentage of the party-list vote to be allotted party-list seats. Until and including the 2003 State Duma elections, the figure was 5 per cent, but the 2002 election law stipulated that it would be increased to 7 per cent in 2007. Seats won by a party's candidates in single-member constituencies did not count for this purpose, though they meant that the party's total size in the State Duma would usually be more than its allocation on the party-list vote.

Other technical issues

- In a single-member constituency the seat was awarded to the candidate who gained a simple plurality of the votes cast.
- Under the election law, when a deputy elected on a party list gives up his or her seat before the term expires, the seat passes to the next person on the party list.
- The election campaign must last no longer than one month.
- A pattern has been established whereby elections to the State Duma precede

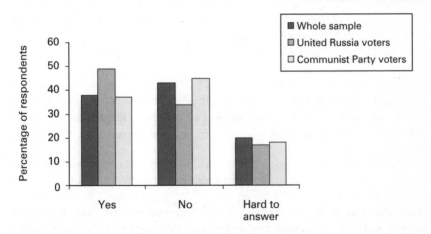

Figure 8.1 *Opinion poll responses to the question 'Do election results reflect popular opinion?' (percentage of respondents). Source: Public Opinion Foundation, 3 July 2003.*

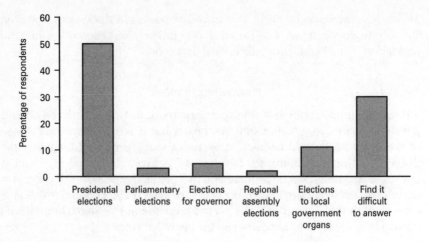

Figure 8.2 *Opinion poll responses on the relative perceived importance of elections at different levels (percentage of respondents). Source: Public Opinion Foundation, 3 July 2003.*

presidential elections, but it is the latter that are the focus of attention, since the presidency so far outweighs the Assembly in political importance. Until 2003 elections to the Duma were held on the second Sunday of the month in which the stipulated date for the expiry of the sitting Duma fell. This was changed for the 2003 elections to the first Sunday, on the grounds that the second followed shortly on the heels of the Constitution Day holiday, on 12 December (leading one wag to comment that United Russia's view of itself as the party of the majority might work against it, since on that day the majority would be happily drinking).

Public perceptions

The public's perceptions of whether the election results accurately reflect popular opinion and of the importance of elections at different state levels are illustrated in Figures 8.1 and 8.2.

Electoral legislation

When Putin assumed the presidency, elections to the State Duma were regulated by a law of 1998, itself revising an electoral law of 1995. In June 2002 he introduced into the State Duma a further revised electoral law, the aim of which was to promote the consolidation of the party system through the creation of a few fully viable parties. The law of 2002 on Elections of Deputies to the State Duma of the Russian Federation based many of its clauses on a Law on Political Parties of 2001 (see Chapter 9), whose provisions included a requirement that a party must have branches in at least half the Federation's regions in order to qualify to present a federal electoral list. More generally, the law set out the procedures for the proposal and registration of candidates through party lists or (at that time) in single-member constituencies, as well as for voting and for the counting of votes. The law also covered the financing of candidatures. Parties and electoral blocs are now allowed to spend up to R250 million on their campaigns (at the time of writing $1 was worth around R30). Candidates for single-member seats were required to lodge a deposit of R2 million. Winning candidates are rewarded with R1 of public money per vote. State finance is thus awarded after and not before the election.

Taken together, these measures were intended to yield a system of a few parties, organised Federation-wide and publicly funded. In another provision the law confirmed existing practice. The 1995 electoral law had required electoral associations and blocs to divide their lists into a federal and a regional section, the former not to exceed 12 candidates. The aim of this requirement, which came to be known as the '12 apostles rule', was to ensure regional representation. However, it was held that it had gone too far in that direction and was impeding the formation of major party formations at central level, and the number was consequently increased to 18 in the 1998 law. The effect of this was that the Zhirinovsky Bloc in the third Duma contained only members from its federal list (Zhirinovsky Bloc was the name under which the Liberal Democratic Party of Russia fought the 1999 Duma elections – see Chapter 9). In the 2002 law the number of 18 was retained (the majority in the State Duma's Institutions and Systems Committee voted to go back to 12; other versions favoured 15 and even 21).

The 2002 Law on Elections to the State Duma made reference not only to the earlier law on political parties, but also to a major 'framework' law, also of 2002, to cover the full range of electoral issues. This Law on the Basic Guarantees of Electoral Rights and the Rights of Citizens of the Russian Federation to Participate in a Referendum set the broad parameters to which the electoral process and electoral legislation were to conform. The law, together with a number of later amendments, had made the following provisions:

- Only political parties and their regional branches are recognised as 'electoral associations' (the official term for an organisation fully registered for participation in an election) in elections at federal and regional level, but at local level this recognition is extended to other 'public associations' (these being defined as organisations and movements).
- 'Electoral blocs' can be formed as alliances of one or several political parties, with or without participation from one or two All-Russian public associations whose charters provide for participation in elections but an electoral bloc may not contain more than three member units.

- At least half of all seats in regional assemblies must be filled on the party-list system.
- No fewer than half the members of electoral commissions in the regions must be appointed on the basis of proposals from political parties that have party groups in the State Duma or regional assembly.
- Public servants, including people holding high administrative posts, must be released from their official duties during the period of their participation in elections.

At the same time, parties were to be penalised for acting irresponsibly. Parties and electoral blocs that had not paid media outlets for airtime they had used in the 1999 election campaign were disqualified from free airtime in the 2003 elections. Veshnyakov, the head of the CEC, had gone further in 2002, claiming that 25 electoral blocs that had offended in this way should be required to reimburse the national and regional broadcast companies and periodicals for the free campaign advertising that they had enjoyed. The rule has been that parties and individuals obtaining under 2 per cent in the list and single-seat votes respectively have had to pay for airtime. This will apply only to party lists when the single-seat candidatures are abolished.

The vote 'against all' candidates

It was seen above that there is provision in the electoral rules of the Russian Federation at all levels for a vote 'against all candidates'. Designed originally to promote voter turnout, this provision has played a significant role in elections since 1993 and has survived the various redraftings of the electoral rules. In presidential elections its actual effect has been limited. In both the 1996 and 2000 presidential elections, campaigns were organised to muster an 'against all' vote. The figures for this 'against all' vote in presidential elections are given in Table 8.1. In the 2000 election the vote 'against all' came sixth in a field that it shared with 11 flesh-and-blood candidates.

In elections to the State Duma, the number voting 'against all' candidates have in many cases been much higher. Here a distinction has to be made between the vote for single-member seats and that for party lists (which, it will be recalled, each filled 225 of the 450 State Duma seats). In the first category

Table 8.1 *The 'against all' candidates vote in presidential elections (percentages)*

	First round	Second round
1996	1.54	4.83
2000	1.88	No run-off
2004	3.45	No run-off

Table 8.2 *The 'against all' candidates vote in State Duma elections (percentages)*

	Vote for single-member seats (mean)	Vote for party lists
1995	9.9	2.8
1999	11.5	3.3
2003	12.9	4.7

in the 1999 elections, 'against all' won a plurality in no fewer than eight constituencies, so requiring a further election to be held, and in many other cases 'against all' out-voted many of the flesh-and-blood candidates. In the 2003 State Duma elections, single-member constituencies in St Petersburg city, and in Ulyanovsk and Sverdlovsk oblasts, were 'won' by the 'against all' vote. The overall 'against all' vote for the State Duma appears in Table 8.2.

However, there is a wide variation in the 'against all' vote at regional level. In elections held in Rostov oblast in March 2003, several voting districts returned a vote 'against all' ranging from 22 to 28 per cent. The highest 'against all' vote was in small cities and in some neighbourhoods in the town of Rostov-on-Don itself. In the Komi Republic in the same month, difficulties were experienced in getting city councils elected because of the high 'against all' vote, which made it necessary to call fresh elections. Only nine of the 25 seats on the council of Syktyvkar, the republic's capital, were filled on the first round, and 12 out of 25 in the case of Vorkuta. The figure for the 'against all' vote in the republic as a whole was as high as 20 per cent in six of 30 electoral constituencies.[1]

The election for governor of St Petersburg in September 2003 was discussed in Chapter 4 to illustrate of the kind of people who stand for such posts. In the election almost 11 per cent of voters cast their vote against the whole list of candidates.

The tendency for voters to record a high 'against all' vote naturally forces the political parties to react accordingly. In a fully formed party system an 'against all' option would be trimmed by party competition, discontented voters giving their support to opposition parties in protest against the perceived failures of a party in office. In the March 2003 regional elections in Rostov-on-Don, United Russia apparently took account of the 'against all' threat by supporting independents instead of putting up its own candidates. *Kommersant-Daily* claimed that of four members of the party's regional branch who participated in the election, only one publicly declared his affiliation.[2]

Given Putin's clear intention to dominate the electoral system, together with the outcome of elections, it is highly unlikely that the vote 'against all' will survive for long. It gives a greater hostage to fortune than is to be encountered in the electoral systems of Western liberal-democratic countries. In Putin's Russia – one of the guiding principles of which is that nothing must be left to chance – the vote 'against all' appears more and more to be out of phase with the evolution of an increasingly authoritarian political system.

Table 8.3 *Turnout at federal-level elections (percentage of electorate)*

Date	Election	Turnout
1989	Congress of People's Deputies	86
1993	State Duma plus referendum	55
1995	State Duma	65
1996	Presidency	68
1999	State Duma	62
2000	Presidency	69
2003	State Duma	56
2004	Presidency	64

Participation in elections

Table 8.3 gives the figures for turnout in elections to both the presidency and the State Duma. The 1989 figure is exceptional – that was the first occasion when a free election was held. The consistently high figures for presidential elections reflect the respect in which the presidency is held, but it is worth noting that the vote (for the federal President) is highest of all in those ethnic republics with the most authoritarian leaders. Figure 8.3 records people's responses when asked how often they participate in elections.

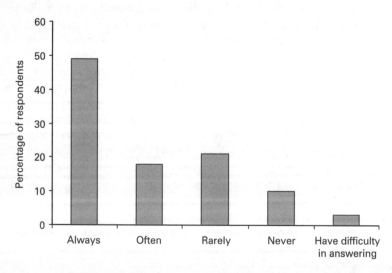

Figure 8.3 *Opinion poll responses to the question 'How often do you participate in elections?' (percentage of respondents). Source: Public Opinion Foundation, 3 July 2003.*

The problems of Russian elections

The problems impeding the formation of a competitive party system in the Russian Federation and the development of the parties themselves have also affected electoral behaviour, as has the strong directing role that Putin has played in attempting to put in place an electoral system that incorporates democratic norms while preserving the 'power vertical'. The result is that the realisation of those democratic norms has been hindered by factors coming from two directions. First, Putin's intervention in the process has led to over-steering, with the electoral commissions at every level tending to play a determining role in both the running and the outcome of elections. Second, the initial adoption of open and free elections, without a culture of mutually accepted constraints that a fully formed party system generates, allowed all manner of malpractices to arise. Given that the controls from above are themselves open to abuse – through bureaucratic intervention but also through outright corruption – Putin's professed aim of developing democratic norms is a long way from realisation. No open political system can escape a degree of ingenious manipulation in elections. It can, indeed, be held to be a mark of competition in the system. Democracy requires, however, that elections be not only open but also fair, and it is in ensuring fairness that the Russian electoral process has had severe problems.

The list of those problems is long and it starts in the Kremlin itself, with control over the election committees at all their various levels. We have seen that through his control of the State Duma majority, Putin has been able to determine the membership of the CEC. This could change at central level with a different composition of the State Duma, but for the time being the electoral commissions form a structure that has a very strong influence on the outcomes of elections. They in turn are dependent on officials – the CEC on officials in the Kremlin, the republican and regional ones on the governors, and the local ones on local officials.

The CEC itself at times will recommend names for the chairs of local electoral committees and effectively appoint to the position. *Vedomosti* carried a report on such a case in Volgograd oblast in August 2003.[3] The CEC had recommended for the oblast electoral committee the head of the local Unity election bloc. Volgograd town and oblast lie in the so-called 'Red Belt', where the KPRF is strong, and an election for mayor was shortly to be held there, followed after a three-month interval by the State Duma elections. To nominate a candidate so closely connected to a political party – and to the party supporting the President – was provocative. In this case the oblast procurator intervened, but that control is not always forthcoming.

Regional electoral commissions can arrange for a favoured candidate to face little competition and, conversely, they can refuse to register candidates from a party that they do not favour. Or television journalists can find themselves dismissed if they are working for a local figure who has a rival with close links to the Kremlin.

A photograph reproduced by *Nezavisimaya gazeta* in April 2003 showed a resolution of the general council of the United Russia party on 'The participation of UR [United Russia] in the formation of the electoral commissions of the subjects of the Russian Federation'.[4] The State Duma parties do have a right to nominate to the electoral commissions, but the fact that the resolution stated that United Russia should send in its nominations to the local commission before the process of electing the commissions had even begun, and that the party's general council should, moreover, send them also to the CEC (point 13 of the resolution), marked an unwillingness to leave things to chance.

Political and administrative interference in areas beyond the composition and activity of the electoral commissions comprises a second category of practices that can impede the fairness of the electoral process. Organisation for Security and Cooperation in Europe monitors, having witnessed the State Duma 1999 elections, recorded cases of this kind that it had encountered. The list included failure to allow opposition parties and candidates to hold public meetings; dismissal from employment; the mounting of extraordinary tax inspections; the selective imposition of administrative fines; and embarking on criminal prosecutions that were later found to be groundless.

Going beyond the administrative into the political realm was the restructuring in the autumn of 2003 of the board of directors of the All-Russian Public Opinion Research Centre (VTsIOM), the most highly regarded of Russia's survey organisations. The restructured board was to contain new categories of membership, including representatives from the Administration of the President's Affairs. Once again, with elections impending, nothing that it was in the Kremlin's power to control was to be left to chance and the VTsIOM, not having been privatised, was legitimate prey.

The most blatant case of political interference with electoral freedom, however, was not at all irregular but took the form of a proposed law. In February 2003 Putin presented to the State Duma a bill on the media that would effectively have prevented candidates from engaging in electoral campaigning. This is treated in Chapter 12, where it will be seen that in the end the more restrictive proposals in the bill (but only they) were dropped.

Overt moves of this kind not surprisingly give rise to suspicions that parallel moves are afoot elsewhere in the political system. Thus, when the Primorye krai administration (around Vladivostok) announced that it was going to cut down on the number of US films and programmes shown on television in the region (to challenge American dominance in the provision of programmes, but in particular because of coverage of the war in Iraq), this was widely interpreted as an initiative by the governor, Sergei Darkin, to increase his control over the regional media as the 2003 State Duma elections approached. Putin himself has not been averse to a little personal intervention; for example, he allowed his face to appear together with that of Valentina Matvienko on an election poster when the latter was standing for the governorship of St Petersburg in September 2003, alongside the slogan 'Together we can do anything!' This led two other candidates to demand (unsuccessfully) that Matvienko's candidacy be annulled. Rather more surprisingly, Matvienko was able to find protection in a rule that allows the head of state's image to be used, with his permission, for campaign purposes.

It is important to note, however, that steps have been taken to ensure objectivity in the counting of votes. In the past, it was at this stage of the electoral process that manipulation to obtain the right result was most obtrusive. *Nezavisimaya gazeta* listed the common past irregularities:

- *The merry-go-round*. Officials would persuade the voter to put an already filled-in slip into the box and take a blank one, which the official would fill in and give to the next voter.
- *Stuffing*. Officials would stuff a packet of filled-in slips into the box.
- *Beyond the observation zone*. Advance voting and postal votes offered chances of manipulating individual votes beyond the eyes of witnesses.
- *The duty guard*. Duty guards worked for one of the candidates and, in collusion with the electoral commission, would get hold of the ballot papers of alcoholics, Jehovah's Witnesses, young drug addicts and so on. If they could obtain the ballot papers of other members of the family, so much the better.
- *Good counting*. Counters would spoil papers where the tick was for an undesired candidate, or put them under the table, in bunches so as to minimise the risk of being seen.[5]

In the 2003 State Duma elections, the votes were counted by electronic means. The GAS Vybory (state automated system elections) method should rid the electoral process of these malpractices, though it remains to be seen whether this technology is not itself open to manipulation. Before the reorganisation of the security forces in March 2003 (see Chapter 5), votes were counted by the Federal Agency of Government Communication and Information (FAPSI), one of the successor organisations of the dismantled Committee of State Security (KGB). When the FAPSI was in turn dismantled in March 2003, the bulk of its functions were transferred back to the Federal Security Service (the successor to the KGB).

However, spoiling activity is not restricted to the polling booth. Particularly prominent is what is called 'black PR' – the blackening of a rival candidate's reputation and the distribution of disinformation about his or her policies. There are also the cases where a bogus candidate is proposed with a name very like an official candidate in order to diminish the latter's vote. In a rather different case with similar aims, a group of political consultants in Yekaterinburg decided to nominate 'Garri Ivanovich Potter' as a candidate in the September 2003 elections for governor in Sverdlovsk oblast, where Yekaterinburg lies ('Garri', of course, being a transliteration of 'Harry').

Box 8.1 considers the process of the presidential election of 2004.

Box 8.1 The 2004 presidential election

Observers from the Organisation for Security and Cooperation in Europe reported that the presidential election of 2004, which was won by Vladimir Putin, was well administered but lacked elements of a genuine democratic contest. It is likely, following freely conducted opinion polls, that popular support for Putin at the close of 2003 was sufficient in itself to account for his sweeping victory in the election, but the steps taken to ensure that result are pointers to many of the political factors shaping political life in Russia as described in this book.

- The fact that those steps were taken itself illustrated the survival, on the part of Russia's power elite, of the Soviet tendency to political overkill, to leaving nothing to chance.
- Putin himself did not campaign, either as an individual or as the representative of a political party, because he did not need to. His control of television was by that time complete. His campaign managers, in the United Russia party and in his own Administration (Vladislav Surkov is attributed with the role of supervising elections on behalf of the presidency), could ensure the ubiquity of his image at the expense of other candidates. An enormous poster, the length of a whole block, in central Moscow opposite the State Duma portrayed Putin as the people's President, without any recommendation to vote for him. No other candidate could display his or her image in this way.
- Public meetings scheduled by the candidate with the greatest chance of defeating Putin, Sergei Glazev, had to be cancelled, or held out of doors, because of untimely administrative impediments (power failures or reports of a bomb threat). His permitted television slots were curtailed (on one such occasion the CEC accepted that he had been disadvantaged, but disadvantaged he remained). Another candidate, Irina Khakamada, also suffered from difficulties in holding meetings for the same reasons. A warrant for the arrest of a major Yukos shareholder, Leonid Nevslin, was issued less than two weeks after he had offered to help plan her campaign. One of her television

---

The regional dimension

The important questions that arise about the electoral process in the regions concern, first, the extent of freedom that the regions have to vary electoral practice, and second, the degree to which powerful regional leaders or the Kremlin itself can determine the outcome of elections in the regions.

For the first, regional elections have to be held in such a way that they conform to the federal constitution, but a ruling by the Constitutional Court on 18 July 2003 that it alone is competent to decide whether local legislation

broadcasts was cut off when a well known actress asked her a question critical of Putin.

- In places across the Federation, local pressures were applied to ensure turn-out – in itself a means of promoting democratic participation, but not in such unequal circumstances. There were carrots (free tickets to popular events, offers of free transport, reductions in housing rents) and sticks (people without a valid certificate of having registered as a voter were turned away from public services).
- The sudden five-day disappearance of one of the candidates, Ivan Rybkin, to Kyiv in Ukraine at the height of the election campaign, and his subsequent withdrawal from the contest, raised questions so complex that it can be used only as an example of the very many strange coincidences that affected Putin's competitors in the election.
- On the other hand, Putin's majority was substantial enough to outweigh manipulation of the actual voting procedure (the results of the election are given in Table 2.3, p. 27). The vote 'against all' was significant, and high in certain locations, but not sufficient to invalidate the popular choice. Turnout was high (highest in regions with authoritarian leaders – 89.3 per cent in Bashkortostan, over 94 per cent in the Kabardino-Balkar Republic).

These features of the 2004 presidential election cannot be seen in detachment from the overall return of central control into the hands of an authoritarian power in the Kremlin during Putin's first presidency. Equally, however, they bespeak the acquiescence of Russian voters in this authoritarian return, shaken by the deprivations of the Yeltsin years and the despoliation of society's riches by a handful of financial speculators, all in the name of an alien-sounding 'democracy' (to which, in website discussions, they opposed 'people's self-government').

Even before the election, on 17 January 2004, *Ekho Moskvy* announced the creation of Free Choice 2008, a group formed to ensure that the next presidential election would be more fairly run. It contained a number of former and actual State Duma representatives and personalities from the cultural field.

complies with federal laws had the effect of allowing the regions to escape uniformity and to adopt practices of their own in the detail of the electoral process. An example is the decision of the assembly of St Petersburg, taken already in the preceding June, to reduce the turnout required for an election to be valid from 50 per cent to 20 per cent. It had also increased the maximum permitted size of a candidate's election fund by five times.

For the second, in early 2003 Putin instructed his President's Envoys to the seven federal districts to ensure that federal laws were being observed in the regions, with a particular emphasis on the introduction of the mixed electoral system (that is, the standard two-vote system). Apparently there was still a good way to go to achieve this. Georgi Poltavchenko, the President's Envoy to the Central Federal District, admitted that only three out of the 18 regions in his district – Belgorod, Tver and Vladimir oblasts – had aligned their electoral laws with federal norms.[6]

Of far greater significance was the decision taken at the end of 2004 to make republican presidents and regional governors subject to nomination by the President (with ratification by the regional legislature) and not to election. Not only did this inevitably weaken further the already weak republican and regional legislatures, but it foreclosed on the development of meaningful political participation in the localities – that is, given the severe restrictions on democratic procedures at the centre of the system, the sphere where change could conceivably come about organically through the impatience of local opinion leaders. Almost immediately calls were made in the Duma for the change to be extended to the appointment of mayors.

The way in which the vote 'against all' is amplified in certain regions, and particularly the more outlying, has been recorded above. In the remoter corners of the Federation there is also clearly a lack of understanding of what

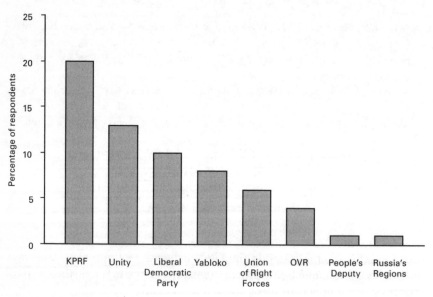

Figure 8.4 *Visibility of political parties. Opinion poll results for the question 'Which of the parties and party groups in the State Duma participate actively in the life of your region?' (percentages of respondents, who could name more than one). KPRF, Communist Party of the Russian Federation; OVR, Fatherland–All Russia. Source: Adapted from New Russian Barometer X. Nationwide Survey, 17 June – 3 July 2001 (Centre for the Study of Public Policy, University of Strathclyde).*

competitive elections are expected to achieve. The idea still lingers that elections are top-down affairs, organised by the authorities in support of themselves. The website www.regions.ru related the case of a letter being sent by the villagers of Bubnyi, Smolensk oblast, to the chairman of the oblast electoral commission informing him that they did not intend to vote in the upcoming State Duma elections because the local authorities had not yet built the road to their village that they had repeatedly requested.[7]

Figure 8.4 shows the extent to which people see the federal political parties as being active in their region. In one respect – the high score for the KPRF – the findings might have been expected. In another respect they are at first glance surprising. People's Deputy makes a populist appeal at federal level, but clearly that is not how it is perceived in the localities. Again, OVR is a coalition of two formations – Fatherland and All Russia – formed to promote the interests of the regions. Within the coalition the leaders of the two formations have spoken chiefly for the interests of their own regions (Yuri Luzkkov for Moscow and Mintimer Shaimiev for Tatarstan). They were, however, as individuals drawn by the magnet of central power to join the forces supporting the President. They kept their local visibility (and power bases), but the figures presented here show that OVR's visibility across the Federation has been low.

Referendums

The constitution of 1993 states that one of the powers of the President is to schedule referendums, and the holding of referendums was included in the provision of the 2002 Law on the Basic Guarantees of Electoral Rights. The constitution itself was submitted to referendum in 1993. Two million signatures are required in support of a demand for a referendum to be held.

Amendments to the 2002 law have stipulated that no referendum can be held during the final year of a term of office of the State Duma or the President. In May 2003, however, as the debate on the buying and selling of land built up to its climax, the KPRF challenged the legality of the previous year's amendments, with a view to calling a referendum on the land issue. In the highly charged political atmosphere surrounding this divisive question, the matter was sent to the Constitutional Court, but the KPRF's cause failed.

The referendum was used to good political effect by Putin in March 2003, in an attempt to damp down the tension in Chechnya by submitting to referendum a new republican constitution, together with draft laws on elections to the Chechen presidency and parliament. The Kremlin devoted a quite extraordinary effort towards acquiring a positive result and in the event, on 23 March 2003, 85 per cent of the Chechen electorate were reported to have voted on the proposals, while over 90 per cent of voters were reported to have approved the new constitution. However, the exercise did little to lessen the tension in Chechnya. On 9 May 2004 Akhmed Kadyrov, the new president, voted in on the provisions of the referendum, was the victim of a bomb explosion in the Dynamo stadium in Grozny.

On 19 May 2004 Putin submitted to the State Duma a draft constitutional law on the holding of referendums. It would make the terms under which a referendum could be demanded more difficult to fulfil. The resulting law refined the need for two million signatures in support of a demand for a referendum, by stipulating that the demand must come from at least 100 people in at least half the Federation's subjects.

Assessment

Chapter 7 showed that the existence of an assembly is in itself no guarantee of accountability, everything depending on how it is filled. The present chapter has dealt with the extent to which the organs of the state intervene in the process whereby the Federal Assembly is recruited. After the departure from the norms of Soviet rule under Gorbachev and the disorder of the Yeltsin years, Putin's call to order has revived features of Soviet practice in the electoral field. A system for competitive elections is in place, but the extent of interference in its functioning advantages one competitor over others, sharply reducing the effect that competition has on choice between candidates and parties.

A parliament accountable to the electorate, a freely operating electoral system, freely circulating information and opinion, even if these are never complete and flawless, are society's lifeline against the state and the requirements that the state chooses to make of its citizens. To these, given recent experience, should be added the market. These mechanisms guarantee voice and choice in politics and in the economy. Without them, citizens become subjects.

Putin's choice to interfere so strongly in the electoral process reflects both the dynamics of the transition from communism and inherited beliefs and practices. First, in times of political change, free elections can increase the nervousness and unpredictability characteristic of transitions from authoritarian rule. When communist Yugoslavia held a first tentative free election, the result in some cases was that anti-system nationalist candidates were given large majorities. A Russian President who sees his role in terms of countering a threat to the viability of the state might be tempted to take measures to guard against destructive developments from unexpected quarters.

Second, electoral competition in Russia goes against beliefs and patterns of political behaviour inherited from the past. The Soviet Communist Party inculcated a collectivist view of political organisation (including at the societal level), according to which the interest of the organism as a whole transcends individual and group interests. The term that the Communist Party used in its doctrine to encapsulate social and political relationships built on this view was 'democratic centralism'. The obverse of democratic centralism, its deadliest opponent, was 'fractional activity'. In this way of seeing things, an election, whatever other purpose it serves, should not involve choice, since parties are divisive. Later chapters will show how this thinking still produces a form of collectivist nationalism that is not outwards directed, but sees the deliberate and open expression of conflicting interests as destructive of society.

Taken together, these two aspects of the state's interference in the electoral process recall one of the basic tenets of the holders of state power in the Soviet Union – that nothing must be left to chance.

Further reading

R. Rose and N. Munro, *Elections Without Order: Russia's Challenge to Vladimir Putin* (Cambridge: Cambridge University Press, 2002).

R. G. Moser, *Unexpected Outcomes: Electoral Systems, Political Parties and Representation in Russia* (Pittsburgh, PA: University of Pittsburgh Press, 2001).

H. Oversloot, J. van Holsteyn and G. P. van der Berg, 'Against all: exploring the vote "against all" in the Russian Federation's electoral system', *The Journal of Communist Studies and Transition Politics*, 18:4 (2002), 31–50.

D. Hutcheson, 'Disengaged or disenchanted? The vote "against all" in post-communist Russia', in E. A. Korosteleva (ed.), *The Quality of Democracy in Post-Communist Russia* (London: Frank Cass, 2004).

S. White, R. Rose and I. McAllister, *How Russia Votes* (Chatham, NJ: Chatham House Publishers, 1997).

M. Wyman, S. White and S. Oates (eds), *Elections and Voters in Post-Communist Russia* (Cheltenham: Edward Elgar, 1998).

Websites on Russian elections

www.rferl.org/specials/russianelection
www.russiavotes.org
www.cikrf.ru (look for 'English' button)
www.cikrf.ru/m_menu_i.htm (Central Election Commission)

Notes

1 *RFE/RL Newsline*, 1 April 2003 and 4 March 2003, citing ITAR/TASS news agency.
2 *Kommersant-Daily*, 31 March 2003.
3 *Vedomosti*, 6 August 2003.
4 *Nezavisimaya gazeta*, 17 April 2003.
5 *Nezavisimaya gazeta*, 27 June 2002.
6 *Kommersant-Daily*, 13 May 2003.
7 www.regions.ru, 9 October 2003.

9

Political parties

Background

Political parties are the heart of political life in democratic politics, where they combine a representative function with a main aim of winning and exercising governmental power. They shape political debate by reducing many contending voices to a manageable few. Within the parliament they give political issues a full airing. Important also has been their role in civilising competition between elites. In established parliamentary systems they have normally been shaped over time and they have set great store by forming a loyal electorate.

Political parties in Russia today cannot be said to conform to this model. With a single very important exception – the Communist Party of the Russian Federation (KPRF) – all the parties represented in the Russian State Duma have come into being since 1990. Until shortly before that, the communist monopoly of power had ruled out autonomous organisation of any kind, and today's KPRF is a rather surprising transformation into competitive politics of the party that imposed and ran that monopoly. It is not surprising that in its early stages the party system has been unstable – a 'floating system' as Richard Rose put it, on the analogy of floating voters.[1] There has been no clear acceptance of what constitutes a political party in a competitive system. There have been (with that one exception) no existing structures to generate a leadership cohort and no tradition of internal debates and inter-party strife to provide clear ideologies and programmes. The parties were mostly created by individuals or groups of individuals seeking a political means for the promotion of their views, interests or, usually, themselves. Other reasons for the lack of substance of political parties have been the weakness of the State Duma in which they operate, the fact that the government is independent of the political parties and the expansion of presidential power.

Establishing a party system

The party system of the Russian Federation has passed through three phases since 1993. With hindsight it is possible to see how the final phase, reached in

2003, was prefigured in the earlier two phases. At the time, however, it seemed that other futures were possible. Those 10 years saw the steady consolidation of a dominant party around a President powerful enough to ensure the domination of that party and the failure of all others. They saw also, as part of that process, the gradual, and in the circumstances probably inevitable, marginalisation of the one party that could challenge it in terms of electoral strength – the KPRF.

- The first phase, 1993–99, is that of the creation of new political parties alongside the already numerically strong KPRF. The key event in the evolution of the party system in this phase came right at its end, with the formation of Unity around the incoming President, Vladimir Putin.
- The second phase covers almost the whole period between the Duma elections of 1999 and 2003. In this period Unity was consolidated, becoming United Russia, as it was joined by particularly influential leaders of other parties, who saw their interests and those of their formations best served by supporting the presidential party of power. In this period United Russia systematically weakened the other political parties by all means at its disposal, the KPRF being the principal target.
- The third phase took shape in the campaign for the 2003 Duma elections, and the results of the elections gave it its final outlines. The election campaign showed the lengths to which the President and his party (without his actually needing to be a member of it) were prepared and able to go in order to eliminate political opposition and to ensure the continuing domination of United Russia into the foreseeable future.

During the second of these phases, Putin presented legislation with the purported aim of giving political parties a secure corporate basis and of generating a stable party system containing a few, large parties. Given his destruction of the existing infant party system, this design is best seen as a further example of Putin's fondness for creating orderly schemes of governance that are in fact eclipsed by more real sources of power that lie outside these schemes.

In what follows, the party system as it had formed by the end of the first phase is presented. That is followed by an account of Putin's measures intended to shape the party system. Then the second and third phases are described. The small extent to which differentiated party programmes and clear party constituencies of support have been able to be established is then examined, before the overall assessment is given.

The first phase: the party system in 1999

Forty-three parties presented party lists in the 1999 elections. Of these, only six won the 5 per cent of the party-list vote required at the time for a proportional share of the 225 seats allocated to party lists, though eight further

Table 9.1 *Elections to the State Duma, 1999*

	Party list		Single-member constituencies	
	Vote (%)	Seats	Vote (%)	Seats
KPRF	24.3	67	13.7	46
Unity	23.3	64	2.2	9
OVR	13.3	37	8.8	31
SPS	8.5	24	3.1	5
Zhirinovsky Bloc	6.0	17	1.4	0
Yabloko	5.9	16	5.0	4
Other parties	13.4	0	10.8	16
Independents	–	–	43.2	105
Against all	3.3		11.8	
Turnout	61.7			

parties secured representation through single-member seats (Table 9.1). The parties in the Duma elected in 1999 elections fall into five categories:

- the 'party of power', Unity, which will be treated separately as a case on its own below (see p. 151);
- parties unequivocally committed to economic reform;
- parties stemming from the defunct Soviet Communist Party;
- national-patriotic parties;
- parties representing regional interests.

The parties of economic reform

The first category comprises the parties unequivocally committed to maintaining the forward movement of the economic reforms. The party in this category that had been longest in existence was Yabloko ('apple' in Russian but the title was also an acronym derived from the names of the party's three original founders), led by Grigori Yavlinsky, a young economist who had played a prominent part in the debates over economic reform in the Gorbachev period. It was present in both previous Dumas, and has consistently defended a policy balancing market liberalism with the maintenance of a social safety-net. Its vote has been strongest among the intelligentsia in the larger cities. Despite the relatively long time that it had been in existence, its share of the party-list vote in 1999 was only 5.9 per cent.

Close to Yabloko in policy preferences, though less concerned with social welfare, was a new arrival on the political-party scene – the Union of Right Forces (SPS). A number of groups had formed to promote the reform process during the second Duma. One was the creation of Boris Nemtsov. Nemtsov had had a remarkable career already by this time. After heading the administration of the economically important Nizhni Novgorod oblast he served twice as deputy Prime Minister during the presidency of Boris Yeltsin. Other groups promoting the market reforms were led by Irina Khakamada, Sergei Kirienko and Yegor Gaidar. In the period leading to the 1999 State Duma elections they and Nemtsov saw that their fortunes in the contest depended on their presenting a united front. The lead in bringing the various possible components together in the SPS was taken not by any of these four but by Anatoli Chubais, who, like Gaidar, had been prominent in directing the reforms in the early 1990s, but it was Nemtsov who emerged as the party's authoritative spokesman in the 1999 election. The SPS obtained 8.5 per cent of the party-list vote.

The combined score of 14.4 per cent of the party-list vote for the liberal parties augured well for the formation of a right wing in Russian party politics – provided that they could consolidate this support through organisation in the localities and could prove capable of forming an electoral coalition. In this respect their lack of a deep organisation and the corresponding domination of individuals in their leaderships augured a good deal less well.

The Communists and fellow heirs of the Communist Party of the Soviet Union

A second group of parties that contested the 1999 elections stemmed directly or indirectly from the Communist Party of the Soviet Union (CPSU) or from splits in its successor party, the KPRF. In 1999, fear of a return to communism still existed, despite the fact that the KPRF had accepted the reforms in general and had embraced the democratic changes that had destroyed the power monopoly of its Soviet predecessor. Indeed, other parties were more outspoken in their call for a reincorporation of the former Soviet territories. However, while the KPRF no longer called for a return of the Soviet Union, it carried a dual heritage from Soviet times: on the one hand, it retained the nationalism which had always sat awkwardly in the CPSU's professedly internationalist ideology; on the other, partly because of its links with organised labour, it consistently spoke out against reform measures that pressed hard on poorer households. This did not prevent it from accepting financial aid from business sources.

With 24.3 per cent of the party-list vote (and 25.6 per cent of the seats when single-member seats had been factored in), the KPRF was numerically the winner in the 1999 elections. It had recovered from the trough into which it had fallen when the Soviet Union fell and it was benefiting from its inherited organisational base in the localities, which no other party came near to rivalling. The party put the number of its local 'cells' (it retains the Leninist term) at 17,636, and the strength of its local implantation was reflected in the number of deputies elected in 1999 from single-member constituencies (46 out of a possible 225).

The KPRF maintained (and still maintains) an umbrella organisation that enrols well known figures from all walks of life to act as sponsors for the party without actually being members of it – the People's Patriotic Union of Russia (NPSR). This reflects the KPRF's inherited tradition of claiming to speak for the nation as a whole rather than any particular constituency within it. At the same time, there is always a risk that the NPSR's leader will be a powerful source of opposition to the KPRF's own leader.

Two other parties stemmed from the CPSU – Women of Russia and the Agrarian Party. Both had won single-member seats in the 1995 Duma elections, but neither cleared the threshold of 5 per cent for representation through its party list. This brought a benefit to the KPRF, since these two parties had until then drawn votes away from it. Women of Russia was not present at all in the third State Duma (1999–2003) but the Agrarian Party secured enough single-member seats to form the Agro-Industrial deputy group, under the leadership of Nikolai Kharitonov, who went on to stand against Putin in the presidential election of 2004 but as the KPRF's candidate.

The national-patriotic parties

Hurt pride at the loss of superpower status and of a substantial portion of the Soviet Union's territory, together with resentment at a perceived defeat at the hands of the West, had led to a wave of nationalism that affected almost all the Russian political parties to a greater or lesser extent. The Liberal Democratic Party of Russia (LDPR), led by Vladimir Zhirinovsky, had sat in the first two Dumas, which were alternately entertained and dismayed by the antics of the party's leader. The party was forced to contest the 1999 elections under the convenience title of the 'Zhirinovsky Bloc', as the LDPR had been accused of fielding candidates who were under criminal investigation or who had withheld details of their finances. The party's main appeal was for the restitution of the borders of the defunct Soviet Union (it has branches in many of the Soviet Union's former republics) but, as the creation of one man, the LDPR stood for the preoccupations of its creator at any given time. Its success has owed much to Zhirinovsky's ebullient personality and to his astute use of the media in projecting it. A persistent rumour has held that the security forces played a role in the formation of the LDPR.

Less strident in its nationalist appeal than the LDPR and rather less opportunistic in its strategy was the People's Party of Gennadi Raikov. As with the Agrarian Party, the People's Party failed to win representation through the party-list vote, but formed a deputy group – People's Deputy. Raikov was far from unique among party leaders in having a past in the Soviet *nomenklatura*, but was a good deal less reticent than others in parading either it or populist views redolent of his former party home.

The regional interest

A fourth category was constituted by parties defending regional interests. One of these, All Russia, formed by the dynamic president of the Tatar Republic, Mintimer Shaimiev, merged with Fatherland, a party created by another powerful regional leader, Moscow mayor Yuri Luzhkov, to form Fatherland–All Russia (OVR). Once the party had been formed, however, it gave its support to the centralising policies of the President, to yield an important feature of Russian politics under Putin – strong regional leaders defending a local power base but within a centralised power structure.

The regional interest was articulated less ambiguously by a deputy group entitled Russia's Regions, which brought together independent deputies who had won single-member seats in the regions. But it, too, was to throw in its lot with the coalition that supported the centralising President during the third State Duma.

The party of power: Unity

During his presidency, Yeltsin had stood as the leader of the movement for reform, and had made himself personally responsible for the shift from a planned to a market economy. He was accepted as the champion of change by the early movement leading the reform, Democratic Russia, and then by the political party Russia's Choice, which stood in the 1993 election under Yegor Gaidar, who was steering the process of economic change. Already by the 1995 election, Our Home is Russia, the party associated with Yeltsin and led by his Prime Minister, Viktor Chernomyrdin, had become a focal point for groups and individuals whose interests lay beyond a mere concern for furthering the economic reform. With the end of the Yeltsin presidency, and with the arrival at the centre of political life of an authoritative figure intent on asserting the centralising power of the Kremlin, the balance tipped, and the party associated with the President became essentially a party of power for its own sake (Box 9.1). It donned the mantle of leader of the reform process, but Putin's determination to stabilise Russia, coupled with the attraction to the party of conservative political leaders (notably regional governors concerned to secure their power base by courting the President) meant that its actual commitment to change diminished. The creation of the political party Unity on the eve of the 1999 elections to the State Duma to provide an organisational base for Putin in his bid for the presidency in March 2000 was the catalyst of this change (see Box 9.1).

Unity's full name was the Inter-regional Movement 'Unity' (Medved). 'Medved' is an acronym for the main part of the party's title; it is also the Russian word for a bear – an important Russian folk symbol, awesome yet familiar. Putin himself was not a member of any political party; nor, indeed, did he associate himself directly with Unity when it was formed under the leadership of the popular Minister for Emergency Situations, Sergei Shoigu – Putin contented himself with saying that he approved of its aims. Unity won 23.3 per cent of the party-list vote in the 1999 State Duma elections. Our Home is Russia failed to obtain 5 per cent of the party-list vote (it achieved a mere 1.2 per cent). What had happened was that one political party whose reason for

---

Box 9.1 'Party of power'

In formally competitive political systems where the representation of sectional interests is either permanently or temporarily weakened, a party sometimes forms as a rally in support of a leader or government already in power. In such circumstances the party presents itself as the defender of the national over sectional interests, as the RPR (Rassemblement pour la République) did, for example, in Gaullist France. It also tends to act as a magnet for those seeking influence or position, who might see their fortunes better served by courting the party of power than by entering into conflict with it. In Russia, from the birth of the Russian Federation, the development of a party of power can be seen taking place, from Russia's Choice to Our Home is Russia, to Unity and then to United Russia. The following is an illustration of how a party of power sees its position. It is taken from the time when Unity and Fatherland–All Russia were coming together to form United Russia.

In early 2003, workers in the Tula armaments factory were all given a form to fill in if they wished to be supporters of the United Russia party. It contained a section that ran:

Declaration: I support the aims of the programme of the All-Russia party 'Unity and Fatherland – United Russia', I am ready to take part in the socially important measures and programmes that the Party sponsors. While remaining outside all political parties I wish to be counted as a supporter of the Party 'United Russia'.

The organisation of supporters of United Russia in the region was headed by Sergei Kharitonov, who was the chief federal inspector for Tula in the administration of the President's Envoy for the Central Federal District (*Nezavisimaya gazeta*, 12 March 2003).

---

existence was to support the President had passed the baton to another such party, hastily created for the transfer. Once Putin had been elected President, Unity became the focal point of power and patronage in the State Duma.

This left Yabloko and the SPS fulfilling the roles of joint conscience of the reform and of free-market opposition to the President and his government, as Putin's ability, or even willingness, to promote reform during his first presidency perceptibly slackened.

Legislating for a party system

Putin's approach to party politics was characteristic of his general style. It combined a formal acceptance of democratic procedures with an authoritarian determination to fix their guidelines and to ensure that those guidelines were followed. But the existing electoral practice was itself less than democratic. The threshold of 5 per cent (to be 7 per cent in the 2007 elections), taken together with the great number of parties presenting lists, meant that all the many votes for unsuccessful party lists were wasted. In 1995 as much as 49.5 per cent of the vote went to the 39 parties that failed to reach the threshold. This fell to 18.9 per cent in 1999, which was still a substantial proportion of the electorate. Putin's answer was to have legislation passed that would enable political parties to establish accountable leaderships and stable Federation-wide constituencies, so as to promote their role as a link between people and authorities in a democratic society. The result was the Law on Political Parties, which was promulgated in July 2001. Its aim was to produce a party system of from two to four parties.

The Law on Political Parties

The law stipulated that in order to register as such, a political party should have no fewer than 10,000 members and should have regional branches, each with not less than 100 members, in more than half the subjects of the Russian Federation (in an important development, the former number was raised to 50,000 in a bill presented to the Duma in October 2004). An important article (9.3) banned the creation of parties on a professional, racial, national or religious basis.

The main objectives of a political party were given as (article 3.4):

- shaping public opinion;
- political instruction and the education of citizens;
- the expression of opinions of citizens on all issues of public life;
- making the general public and the bodies of state power aware of these opinions;
- the nomination of candidates in elections to legislative (representative) bodies of state power and representative bodies of local self-government, and participation in elections to these bodies and in their work.

It is to be noted that there was no mention among these aims of contending for and exercising executive governmental power.

The law covered also party organisation and finance. In order to be registered, a party had to have held a constituent congress at which a resolution had been passed establishing the party, the party statutes had to have been duly adopted and a programme approved, and the leading and supervisory–auditing bodies elected. A limit was put on the donations that a party, including its regional branches, could receive. Parties were to be funded also by the state from a total sum that related the minimum monthly wage to the number of voters on the voters' lists at the latest elections to the State Duma or the presidency. That sum was to be allocated proportionally to parties that either had

---

Box 9.2 How are the political parties financed?

Political parties in the Russian Federation draw their finance from three very different sources. The first is the state, which funds parties according to a formula that relates the minimum monthly wage to each qualifying party's vote in State Duma and presidential elections. To qualify for such support a party must either have polled not less than 3 per cent of the party-list vote, or else have at least 12 of its candidates elected in single-mandate districts.

The second source of finance is subscriptions. These serve a further purpose in creating a bond of loyalty between the subscriber and the organisation, the subscription being a marker of commitment. Subscriptions vary among the parties. Yabloko requires none (which is presumably connected with its weak implantation in the localities). United Russia and the KPRF each require 1 per cent of wages as a subscription (in the former case only if the wage exceeds a certain level). The SPS has a relatively high subscription of R300 a year (R20 for students), which is substantially higher than the 1 per cent of wages required by the KPRF and United Russia.

The third source is business. Here figures are hard to come by. According to *Argumenty i fakty* (no. 12, March 2003) the money flowing for the 2003 elections from business into the coffers of United Russia as the party of power had reached $1.2 billion. Other parties could hardly compete, but it is claimed that practically all the major oligarchs, with the exception of Oleg Deripaska and Roman Abramovich, contributed to the SPS's 2003 electoral fund. Yabloko has had the misfortune of being financed originally by Vladimir Gusinsky, whom Putin drove into exile on assuming the presidency, and more lately by the Yukos oil company, another target of Putin's displeasure. Even the KPRF derives financial support from business, primarily from Yukos (until autumn 2003) and Vladimir Potanin's Interros empire. Mystery surrounds the financing of the LDPR, but its Duma deputies have proved themselves adept at using their lobbying power to build up the party's funds.

---

polled not less than 3 per cent of the party-list vote, or else had at least 12 of their candidates elected in single-mandate districts (see also Box 9.2).

The second phase: change in the party system during the third Duma, 1999–2003

The party system during this period evolved particularly markedly in three broad areas, corresponding in part to the categories of party presented above:

- the parties supporting the President and his government;

- relations among the market-oriented liberals;
- tensions and divisions in and around the KPRF.

Parties supporting the President and his government

The most significant development in the party system during the third Duma was the coming together of Fatherland–All Russia with Unity to form United Russia. On 8 and 9 February 2002 all three formations (Fatherland and All Russia had maintained separate structures within their alliance) held congresses in Moscow at which they agreed to dissolve their respective political organisations and to create the new party. Its stated aims were highly significant in that they were not sectional but general – the promotion of 'patriotism and democracy, freedom and justice, and a strong state'. United Russia held its first all-Russia party congress on 25 April 2002, with about 1,000 attending.

Box 9.3 The organisation of United Russia

The party's highest leading body is its congress, which meets once every two years. The congress elects a central political council, a central council of audit and a general council. These provide the formal organisational hierarchy of the party. The congress also elects a supreme council of the party.

The central council of audit has charge of the party's finances and acts as the party's organisational watchdog.

The central political council has a membership of 100 chosen from the congress by show of hands.

In the intervals between the meetings of the central political council, the party's business is conducted by the general council, which is given in the statutes as 'the party's highest political organ'. It has 15 members, drawn from the central political council. It meets at least once a month. It has a presidium, comprising its head (the secretary of the general council) and his or her deputies. The general council elects a central executive committee.

The fact that the statutes state that the general council is the party's highest political organ makes the role of the supreme council difficult to place in formal terms, but it is clearly what its name suggests. It has an inner body, the bureau, which comprises the chair of the supreme council, his or her deputies, and the presidium of the general council. The statutes state that the supreme council is 'chosen from the leading social and political figures of the Russian Federation'. The statutes do not state whether these personalities must be members of the party. It would be hard to find a better example of how the party views it role in Russian politics.

Source: www.edinros.ru/section.html?rid=47#y, taken at 9 June 2004.

United Russia made immediate strides in organising itself as a mass party. On 29 March 2003, at the party's second congress, Boris Gryzlov announced a membership of 400,000 (this had reportedly doubled by 2004). The party was well implanted regionally but it was at the party's apex that its growing strength was evident. When seven new members for the party's central political council were elected, no fewer than six of them were regional governors. By April 2003 the total number of governors on the party's central political council was 12. They included such political heavyweights as Luzhkov (Moscow), Eduard Rossel (Sverdlovsk oblast), Egor Stroev (Orel), and the Tatarstan president Mintimer Shaimiev.[2] The central political council contains spokespeople of each of the party's component organisations and constitutes the party's main directing body (see Box 9.3).

Two further formations in the State Duma were already aligned with United Russia, both of them deputy groups: People's Deputy and Russia's Regions. Together with these two groups United Russia now formed a presidential coalition that dominated the State Duma. At the heart of the People's Deputy group was Raikov's People's Party. This party at times played an independent role within the presidential majority, reflecting its links with a faction within the Administration of the President's Affairs. Its occasional waywardness, however, was never enough to harm the coalition.

Having secured a solid party machine in his support, Putin took a number of steps to ensure its election. He had already assured himself of favourable coverage from the television channels, which were now entirely in his control. In Chapter 12 it will be seen how he introduced legislation that would have effectively abolished campaigning for a political party, though he was led to backtrack on that initiative. Other steps conformed to his style of indirect operation and appeared as fortunate coincidences. It was announced in May 2003 that all workers in the public sector – which includes teachers and doctors – would be given a 33 per cent rise in pay from October. At a meeting that Putin held on 16 July 2003 with the chairman of the Pension Fund, Mikhail Zurabov, it was decided that pensions would be increased by 8 per cent instead of by the 7.4 per cent originally planned, Interfax reported.[3] An increase in state spending of R68.9 billion decided by the government in October did no harm to United Russia's electoral chances.[4]

Putin, meanwhile, maintained his detached position. He had said in his address to the Federal Assembly on 16 May that he did not plan to join any political party, and that 'United Russia is not a presidential party, but only a pro-presidential party' (but see Box 9.4).[5] This did not prevent him saying on 20 September that United Russia was 'undoubtedly the leader' of the Russian political scene.[6]

With a dominating position in the State Duma, control of the media, last-minute redistributive government actions and public forums and displays, United Russia was well placed for the December elections. When its party list for the State Duma elections was presented, the party's leader, Boris Gryzlov,

---

Box 9.4 'Together with the President!'

In Soviet times a common theme on posters before elections to the Supreme Soviet was 'I vote so that my country may prosper!' The same appeal to a national constituency, avoiding sectional or programmatic appeals, was characteristic of United Russia's campaign in the 2003 elections. Its political broadcasts regularly ended with the words 'Together with the President!' and had the following voice-over:

> Everyone has his own Russia. The one he sees, the one nearby. For one person it's a factory, for another a [farmer's] field. We all have our own little Russia, and only if you put them all together is the picture unified, and we can see how great and rich Russia is. It has everything for building a decent life for each person. Together with the President, choose United Russia!

Voice-over cited by Laura Belin, *RFE/RL Endnote*, 8 December 2003.

---

was in first place, followed by Minister of Emergency Situations, Shoigu, the Moscow mayor, Luzhkov, and the Tatarstan president, Shaimiev.

The market-oriented liberals

Throughout the life of the third Duma, relations between Yabloko and the SPS were affected by the same hostile rivalry as had prevented them from uniting for the 1999 elections. As the 2003 elections approached, the dangers that this posed became clear, but they were not adequately appreciated, partly because opinion polls showed that each of the parties stood a chance of winning over 5 per cent of the party-list vote. Thus proposals for a merger made by the SPS were written off as opportunism by Yavlinsky. With 64 regional organisations when it was registered and a total membership of 15,000 (according to the Ministry of Justice; 82 and 20,000, respectively, according to the party itself) the SPS prided itself on the quality of its organisation, and made use of public relations professionals in its leading councils. Yabloko could claim to have been longer in existence. A major cause of its inability to compromise was the personal rivalry between Yavlinsky and Chubais, who had been placed in a leading position on the SPS's party list as an attraction to voters.

By September 2003 the two parties had accepted the urgency of at least an electoral alliance, if a merger was impossible. The SPS had won 8.5 per cent of the party-list vote in 1999. The sum of that and Yabloko's 5.9 per cent, together with the multiplier effect of a more substantial profile in the party-political scene, would have given the joint formation a significant presence and perhaps secured its future. A suggestion put forward by Yabloko that the SPS should coordinate candidatures with it in 50 of Russia's 225 single-mandate districts was reciprocated, and the SPS agreed not to put up candidates in single-mandate districts that had been selected by Yabloko as particularly promising for it.[7] But even this failed, with spokespeople from each side blaming the other for the breakdown in negotiations. Speaking on RTR television on 14 September, the SPS's campaign organiser, Alfred Kokh, and his Yabloko counterpart, Sergei Ivanenko, each said that his party was willing to coordinate candidatures, but claimed to be awaiting a response from the other. By this time tensions had arisen within Yabloko over Yavlinsky's leadership and a 'Yabloko without Yavlinsky' movement had made its appearance – to be written off by the party leadership as 'black public relations' ('black PR' is a current expression in Russian political discourse; 'PR' has in fact been adopted in Russian as *'piyar'*).[8]

Tensions in and around the KPRF

The KPRF lived a life of perpetual tension in both the second and the third Dumas. In both the 1995 and 1999 elections its performance had been strong. It had accepted the rules of democratic party politics and had shed a good many of its doctrinal Marxist positions, but it had been unable to divest itself of another aspect of its ideology – its mission as the single authentic voice of the social interest. It was unwilling to move to the social-democratic programmatic position that the spectrum of possible party positions offered it and instead continued to make patriotism its basic appeal. But the issue created stresses, which were compounded by strong personal rivalries and, increasingly, by discontent with the leader, Gennadi Zyuganov. Looming splits continually threw up contenders for the leadership position but resulted in the discomfiture of the challenger rather than a division in the party.

An informal split in the KPRF within the State Duma, however, was engineered by the presidential majority in April 2002. As noted in Chapter 7, the allocation of chairs of Duma committees follows the comparative strengths of the parties at the start of a newly elected house, but during the third Duma a redistribution of committee chairs came about as part of the party of power's move to secure its position. Having won a significant victory in the 1999 elections, the KPRF had originally been allocated the chairs of nine committees. But on 3 April 2002 the State Duma voted to replace seven of the nine occupants of these chairs, all but one of them by members of the pro-Kremlin parties and groups. At the same time, the parties supporting the President took control of the council of the State Duma, its organisational apparatus.

The pro-Kremlin parties also moved to oust the speaker, Gennadi Seleznev, who was from the KPRF, but the President intervened to support him and the move was abandoned. In his role as speaker, Seleznev had been accommodating to the President and this overt support now put him under pressure from his party, which called for both his resignation and those of the two committee chairmen who had been spared the purge. They refused, and were expelled from the party and the KPRF Duma fraction. The Kremlin had succeeded in sowing discord in its chief rival (which was at the time showing a lead in polls of 30 per cent against 27 per cent for the pro-presidential United Russia). Needless to say, the change in allegiance of the State Duma's speaker from his party to a power outside the State Duma could not but weaken the parliamentary process as a whole.

At this stage of its fortunes the KPRF had some 500,000 members, but they were ageing, with pensioners accounting for a third of its vote in 1999. While it avoided a formal split in the years between the 1999 and 2003 Duma elections, the pressure that it was coming under from United Russia and the Kremlin weighed heavily on its internal life.

A further shock to the KPRF, coming as the third Duma was in its final months, was the creation of a new party with aims and ideas very similar to its own and appealing to the same constituency. According to the rumours with which political life in Russia abounds, this initiative was encouraged by the Kremlin. It took the form of a proposal to found the Motherland–People's Patriotic Movement, which constituted a further informal split in the party, in that it aimed to draw away a part of the KPRF's membership. It was made by Sergei Glazev, who had for some time been talked of as a possible replacement for Zyuganov at the head of the KPRF, and Dmitri Rogozin, chair of the State Duma's international relations committee and a member of the People's Deputy group in the State Duma. The linking of these two names suggested already that the new initiative was going to make a broad appeal.

Though not actually a member of the KPRF, Glazev had joined its parliamentary fraction, and was co-chair of the People's Patriotic Union of Russia. During the summer he held discussions with the leaders of a range of movements and small parties, including the philosopher Alexander Dugin, leader of the markedly anti-Western Eurasia Party. In August he made his move, announcing the creation of a 'left-patriotic' bloc and inviting the KPRF to join it. Glazev claimed that there was a constituency of people who wanted to vote for a left-patriotic party but were not prepared to vote communist. This defection from the KPRF parliamentary fraction, added to that of Seleznev, further weakened the KPRF. Motherland included a number of small parties with low expectations of Duma representation. Apart from the two leaders, the bloc's electoral list included two bankers, a popular Air Force general and one of the plotters in the attempted coup of 21 August 1991. It was a strange mixture, representing a move away from the formation of a party system with differentiated programmatic appeals. The broad range of its sponsors made it inevitable that Glazev's emphasis on combining the demands of social justice with those of economic growth would be eclipsed by the universalising populist appeals that Russian political parties seem rarely able to avoid.

Other blocs and alliances

By the time of the 2003 Duma elections (see Table 9.2) a number of other parties and blocs had achieved political prominence or, in the case of the first of
those listed here, retained it.

- The Agrarian Party maintained its existence during the fourth Duma, partly
  due to its role at the core of the Agro-Industrial deputy group. It remained
  allied to the KPRF and tended to vote with it, though debates arose between
  the two, and among the Agrarians, over the form that privatisation of the
  land should take (see Chapter 13). The party received 3.6 per cent of the
  party-list vote in the 2003 Duma elections.
- Pensioners have been among the social groups most adversely affected by
  the economic reforms in Russia. During the third Duma the Russian Party
  of Pensioners and Social Justice was formed to articulate that interest; it
  gained 3.09 per cent of the party-list vote in the 2003 elections.
- A rather different reflection of social and economic change was the emergence of New Course – Motoring Russia. Arising over issues such as the
  proposed obligatory motor insurance in 2003, this new political party
  obtained 0.84 per cent of the party-list vote.
- An important strand of thinking and action developed, from the early years
  of the transition from communism, around the idea that Russia was not
  European, but straddled Asia and Europe. An example of such thinking was
  that closer ties with Muslim Iran could help Russia from being drawn too
  far down the road to Western liberalism. 'Eurasianism' finally took party-
  political form as the 2003 Duma elections approached, in the form of the
  Great Russia – Eurasian Union bloc, constructed round Alexander Dugin's
  Eurasia Party (it received 0.28 per cent of the party-list vote).
- Two small parties created by the speakers of the State Duma and the Federal
  Council, Seleznev and Sergei Mironov, respectively, developed during the
  third Duma and came together to form a bloc for the 2003 elections: the
  Party of Russia's Rebirth – Russian Party of Life (it received 1.88 per cent of
  the party-list vote).

The intervention of Khodorkovsky

A major stone was thrown into the pool of Russian politics when it became
clear that Mikhail Khodorkovsky, the head of the giant oil company Yukos,
was making financial contributions to a number of political parties opposed to
the government, including Yabloko and, to general surprise, the KPRF. Other
reasons also were given for the arrest of Khodorkovsky on 25 October 2003, as
will be seen in Chapter 12, but the arrest in any case signalled that the Kremlin
intended to impose the terms of an informal agreement that Putin had made
with certain oligarchs in 2000 that their title to the wealth accumulated in

the privatisation process would be respected as long as they refrained from aspiring to a role in Russia's political life.

The third phase: United Russia's final domination of the party system

The impact of the 2003 elections

The results of the 2003 State Duma elections are shown in Table 9.2. The new State Duma had only four party fractions and no deputy groups. The percentage shares of the seats are shown in Figure 9.1.

The overall effect of the elections was to block the development of a party system with clearly differentiated programmes based on sectional appeals and to encourage the perpetuation of multiple appeals to a populist nationalism. It also crowned the efforts of United Russia to dominate the electoral field and present itself as the one true representative of the national interest. With all major parties making substantially the same non-sectional appeal, with United

Table 9.2 *Elections to the State Duma, 2003*

	Party lists		Single-member constituencies	
	Vote (%)	Seats	Vote (%)	Seats
United Russia	37.6	120	23.5	102
KPRF	12.6	40	10.9	12
LDPR	11.5	36	3.1	0
Motherland	9.0	29	2.9	8
Yabloko	4.3		2.6	4
SPS	4.0		2.9	3
Agrarian Party	3.6		1.8	2
Russian Party of Pensioners and Social Justice	3.1		0.6	0
Party of Russia's Rebirth – Russian Party of Life	1.9		2.6	3
People's Party	1.2		4.5	17
Development of Entrepreneurship	0.4		0.4	1
Great Russia – Eurasian Union Bloc	0.3		0.8	1
New Course – Motoring Russia	0.8		0.4	1
Other parties	5.1			0
Independents	–			68
Against all	4.7			
Turnout	55.7			

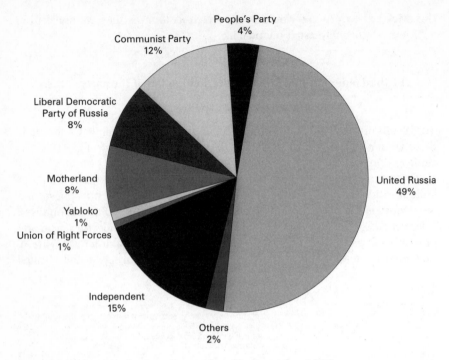

People's Party
4%

Communist Party
12%

Liberal Democratic
Party of Russia
8%

Motherland
8%

Yabloko
1%
Union of Right Forces
1%

United Russia
49%

Independent
15%

Others
2%

Figure 9.1 *Seats in the State Duma elected in December 2003.*

Russia having established itself as the privileged voice of that appeal, and with those parties that made a sectional appeal having effectively been erased from the party political competition, Russia had once again acquired a single party dominating the political system, with all the supports necessary for consolidating that domination in the future. This was not yet a return to the Soviet single-party state, but the way in which United Russia presented itself, together with the steps that it had taken to ensure its success (in particular, the exclusion of other parties from airtime on television and from public advertising, coupled with extravagant promotion of its own views and images), certainly spelled a partial return to the Soviet tradition. The important factor here is the trend, which was away from full representation of competing electoral forces and back to their suppression.

The sharp drop in the vote for the KPRF, which was an objective of the presidential majority, duly transpired. Deprived of airtime on television the KPRF was unable to attract a vote much above the core of supporters whom it was still able to mobilise in the localities. Also, it suffered from the emergence of Motherland, which was now campaigning on the KPRF's political territory. Glazev's belief that there was a substantial number of communist voters prepared to vote for that party's values but not prepared to vote for Zyuganov

Table 9.3 *Approval ranking of leading Russian politicians (at January 2004)*

Rank	Name	Post
1	Vladimir Putin	President
2	Sergei Shoigu	Minister of Emergency Situations
3	Vladimir Zhirinovsky	Leader of the LDPR
4	Yuri Luzhkov	Mayor of Moscow
5	Sergei Glazev	Leader of Motherland

Source: Interfax, interview with pollster Yuri Levada, 19 January 2004.

had borne fruit. Zyuganov's defeats in the presidential elections of 1996 and 2000 also told against him to some extent. The pressure that the party was now under increased the tensions within it. In particular, the ever-present potential rivalry between the leaderships of the KPRF and its front organisation, the NPSR, rose in salience, with the KPRF's presidium instructing all party members working on the executive political committee of the NPSR to cease their cooperation with that body, in a bid to clip the wings of its leader, Gennadi Semigin. A split was to develop within the party during 2004, as a section of it, led by the governor of Ivanovo oblast, Vladimir Tikhonov, held a separate congress. The Justice Ministry, however, declared the splinter group illegitimate, on the grounds that the documents submitted for registration were faulty.

Tensions that were latent in the Motherland–People's Patriotic Movement sharpened after the elections, which greatly reduced the political value of its electoral success. Glazev himself was voted out as the leader of the party's fraction in the Duma. One of the party's components, Dmitri Rogozin's Russia's Regions deputy group, registered as a political party under the single-word title of Motherland. Glazev thereupon attempted to rename the weakened electoral bloc 'For a Worthy Life', but the Justice Ministry refused to register it. The main effect of Motherland's sally onto the party-political scene had been to contribute to the weakening of the KPRF, until the 2003 elections still the main source of opposition to United Russia. After the elections there was no significant opposition at all.

The success of the LDPR was the result partly of support built up over the years and partly of very energetic campaigning by the party leader himself across the length and breadth of the Federation, according to reports distributing in places R100 notes to prospective voters.[9] The LDPR's electoral appeal supported rather than conflicted with the positions and policies of United Russia, while its role as a political sideshow destructive of the Duma's standing was confirmed.

Meanwhile, the virtual exclusion of both Yabloko and the SPS from the State Duma (without party-list representation they were not entitled to state funding) spelled the departure from the forefront of the political scene of the only parties whose appeal was not based on a broadly defined patriotism.

Programmes and issues

Given the virtual obliteration from the political scene in Russia of party programmes with a sectional appeal, it makes little sense to seek lines of cleavage in the party system. There are, indeed, tensions between definable social groups in Russia, and there are intense struggles at times over policy, but the process of party formation had not succeeded in building those tensions and struggles into clear competitive programmes before the elections of 2003, when the chances of that happening at all were dealt what may turn out to be a death blow. The reasons for this failure are as follows:

- To repeat a major theme of this book, the Soviet system was hostile to the notion of sectional interests in society, and in its ideological statements the ruling party presented society as an organic whole, and saw the political self-assertion of its parts as a threat to the health of the organism. That way of thinking acted against the very idea of sectional competition. It has historical roots much deeper than the Soviet system and it still permeates Russian political behaviour.
- It has taken time for privatisation to yield an economic differentiation of society into competing interests. Workers are still dependent on both their firms and the trade unions for many of their daily needs. In these circumstances the notions of 'us' and 'them' that arise take many cross-cutting forms and the political parties have not channelled those notions into clear political constituencies.
- When competitive political parties formed in the post-Soviet vacuum, they were in almost all cases the creation of individuals seeking a following rather than the organised expression of a particular group interest. These top-down formations, often entitled 'sofa parties' because of their small size, engendered a form of party competition in which personal self-assertion was not moderated by the structured life of a large organisation.

The result has been that the cleavages that certainly exist in Russian society do not receive clear representation in the party system. They can, none the less, be presented and the limited extent of their presence on the party-political scene assessed.

The limited development of a cleavage structure

In the early years of the transition from communism, the predominant political division was between those favouring the move to market liberalism and those striving to salvage the defeated system in some form or other. This reform–communism cleavage had lost a good deal of its salience by the 1996 presidential election, and it waned further by the time of Putin's accession to the presidency in 2000.

As calls for a restoration of communism lost their force, the reform–communism issue stratified out into three sources of tension that had been contained within it:

- Views differed on the extent to which Russia should accommodate the interests of Western powers with which it was becoming increasingly involved. In this case the entrenched anti-Westernism of the KPRF and other parties conflicted with the links that the reformers entertained with Western economists and economic interests. This can be termed the nationalism–cosmopolitanism axis of political competition.
- The reforms, which included the privatisation process, produced a tension between those favouring ownership and distribution of resources by the state and those favouring ownership and distribution by the market – that is, a state–market axis. Related to this was a tension over the particular issue of whether agricultural land should be available for sale and purchase, which rose sharply up the political agenda when the land code and the land law were debated in the State Duma in 2002.
- Independent of the reform–communism cleavage was a centre–periphery axis of political competition between the federal centre and the regions.

The term 'political' rather than 'party' competition is used here for the important reason noted above – that these divisions of interest and opinion are not neatly reflected in party positions, and there are often tensions *within* parties over the issues.

Nationalism–cosmopolitanism axis

The results of the 2003 elections confirmed a constant feature of Russian party politics – the vitality of patriotic appeals. With the failure of Yabloko and the SPS to pass the barrier for representation through the party-list vote, cosmopolitanism suffered a severe blow. This development was connected with the popular disapproval of the results of the privatisation process, which was running strong at the time, as a result of the Yukos affair. The patriotic emphasis was amplified by the surprisingly strong performance of Motherland–People's Patriotic Movement, whose name made clear where its priorities lay. Three of the four major Duma parties (the KPRF, Motherland and the LDPR), together with an increasing part of United Russia, placed patriotism high in their values. With the failure of Yabloko and the SPS to preserve their representation in the State Duma, the political forces espousing cosmopolitan values now lay outside the major Duma parties. They were the Kasyanov government, Putin himself (who has to present a cosmopolitan face in his role as spokesman for the nation) and the beleaguered, internationally linked oligarchs.

It is of the first importance to be clear on what this 'nationalism' represents. In only one case, that of the LDPR, is it aggressive in relation to other states. It is chiefly a defensive patriotism and seeks to prevent the dissipation of what is seen as the people's patrimony in a style of thinking inherited from Soviet days, and indeed before. A belief that both the internal market and international pressures might weaken the state is common to all four major parties of the fourth Duma. When, in June 2003, Glazev announced the formation of a Committee for the Protection of Russian Citizens' Rights to Mineral Resources, to prevent Russian mining companies from usurping national resources that rightfully belong to the entire country, he might have been speaking for any of the post-2003 Duma parties.[10] That is, parties have not gone for what divides people but for what unites them, which means that they all tend to stress the same themes.

State–market axis

The state–market axis is equally insubstantial as a current basis of party competition. All the major Duma parties have accepted the principle of owner-ship and distribution by the market, though all have reservations about the extent to which it should be pursued and about the conditions that should be imposed on it. In this case, too, the elections of 2003 removed from the State Duma those parties that were categorically in favour of market liberalism – the SPS and, with the qualification of its concern for a social safety-net, Yabloko. Their effective departure from the State Duma sharply reduced the salience of the axis as a whole.

Here again, the active political cleavage lay outside the State Duma, this time chiefly in factional differences within the Administration of the President's Affairs, where, as far as can be discerned, the issue has been very much alive.

Centre–periphery axis

The centre–periphery axis is a yet more remarkable example of the blurring of party competition through the dominance of a centralising presidency. It was the assertion of a true regional interest that led to the original forma-tion of each of Fatherland, All Russia and Unity in the period when Putin was preparing to curb the power that the regions had acquired under Yeltsin. This could have developed into a permanent and lively cleavage animated by regional interests. What happened, however, was that powerful regional leaders threw in their lot with the party of the centre, where power lay, to become an integral part of United Russia. The calculation was clearly that they could best achieve their goals within the party of power, rather than through party competition in parliament.

It is none the less possible, despite this damping down of party cleavages, to attach particular interests to particular parties to some degree. The links that the KPRF has with the trade unions mean that it defends a worker interest and opposes measures that threaten to impose social inequalities. When the State Duma voted on reform of the system of payment for housing and public utilities, which seemed likely to lead to price rises, the Communist party group opposed the bill – as did Yabloko, despite its basic support for distribution through the market. The Communists later organised protests also against the 2004 bill to replace benefits in kind with cash payments, which was widely seen as revoking an important feature of Soviet social policy. By the same token, by voting for the housing and public utilities reform, the parties supporting the presidency were taking a position clearly in favour of the market, in that sense positioning themselves on the centre-right of the political spectrum, in line with the government's position throughout Putin's first administration.

The tendency, however, has been away from the development of party competition through the political representation of sectional interests in the State Duma, and towards an effectively uncontested bloc of support for the President and his policies. At the same time, it is important to record that the voters themselves have acquiesced in this tendency.

Assessment

In principle, party competition in a differentiated party system should follow from a free electoral process through which multiple competing interests and demands are aggregated and so made easier to deal with. Yet one of the roles of political parties is precisely to bring about and promote this articulation and aggregation of interests and demands. It is a chicken-and-egg situation. To emerge from it successfully in circumstances of abrupt change, a party system would require time, stability and encouragement.

Putin has provided stability and the 'power vertical' has been presented as a means precisely of creating the conditions for the development of democratic politics. Encouragement was ostensibly offered by the Law on Political Parties and by various provisions of the 2002 electoral law. Yet the trend during Putin's first presidency was towards the atrophy of an emerging multi-party system. This in turn has had a negative effect on the development of the State Duma. The causes of the failure of a competitive party system to emerge must be sought on the one hand in Putin's actions in effectively destroying it, and on the other in the parties' own failure to secure their viability.

As to Putin's actions, there was, first, no reason why the President should willingly have accepted the restriction on his freedom of action imposed by opposition parties in a possibly recalcitrant State Duma, and his strategy towards the numerically strong KPRF in the 1999 Duma made clear his views on that matter. Second, one of his major aims was to prevent the oligarchs from using their economic power to make an entry into politics. Locking up Khodorkovsky, who was funding a number of political parties opposed to Putin, corresponded to this aim, as did reducing the number of parties susceptible to those siren voices. Third, as so often, the question 'Who is Putin?' arises. A role in emasculating the political parties must be allotted to the opaque factional rivalries within the Administration of the President's Affairs, in which are entrenched a number of people who would not be averse to responding to current demands in a traditional way. Political parties, yes – provided one particular party remains paramount. All are equal but one is more equal than the others.

In these adverse circumstances it is hardly worth examining the failure of the parties themselves to fashion a viable party system. There have been, none the less, failings independent of the pressures of the presidency. A prominent example is the failure of Yabloko and the SPS to unite, itself a reflection of the 'tadpole' nature of the new parties, whose leaders made party policy without reference to a slender membership, which had no party culture or identity fashioned in competition with other parties. The tendency of almost all parties to appeal to the whole people and – the obverse of this – a failure to exploit sectional interests reduced their capacity to mobilise a targeted support and obviously militated against programmatic differentiation.

Finally, there is the electorate itself to be considered. It was as new to this competitive game as were the parties themselves. Excited at first by the innovations of the Gorbachev period, completely disoriented by the events of the Yeltsin presidency and disillusioned by the privations of those years, the Russian people in the mass have a very low opinion of both political parties and the State Duma (see Table 7.1, p. 117). Moreover, they are as little inclined as the parties themselves to envision politics in sectional competitive terms. There has been little in Russian and Soviet history to mobilise them in that direction, while the pre-revolutionary social structure, and then Soviet doctrines emphasising the unity of the people around its Communist Party, have both militated against it.

Further reading

R. G. Moser, *Unexpected Outcomes: Electoral Systems, Political Parties and Representation in Russia* (Pittsburgh, PA: University of Pittsburgh Press, 2001).

R. Rose, 'How floating parties frustrate democratic accountability: a supply-side view of Russia's elections', *East European Constitutional Review*, 9:1/2 (2000), 53–9.

L. March, *The Communist Party in Post-Soviet Russia* (Manchester: Manchester University Press, 2002).

D. Slider, 'Russia's governors and party formation', in A. Brown (ed.), *Contemporary Russian Politics: A Reader* (Oxford: Oxford University Press, 2001).

S. Whitefield, 'Partisan and party divisions in post-communist Russia', in A. Brown (ed.), *Contemporary Russian Politics: A Reader* (Oxford: Oxford University Press, 2001).

D. Hutcheson, *Political Parties in the Russian Regions* (London: RoutledgeCurzon, 2003).

Notes

1 R. Rose, 'How floating parties frustrate democratic accountability: a supply-side view of Russia's elections', *East European Constitutional Review*, 9:1/2 (2000), 55.
2 *Argumenty i fakty*, no. 15, April 2003.
3 *RFE/RL Newsline*, 17 July 2003.
4 *Vedomosti*, 6 October 2003.
5 *RFE/RL Newsline*, 30 June 2003.
6 *Interfax*, 21 September 2003.
7 *Kommersant-Daily*, 8 September 2003.
8 *RFE/RL Newsline*, 16 September 2003.
9 www.gazeta.ru, 27 August 2003.
10 *RFE/RL Newsline*, 13 June 2003, citing RIA-Novosti news agency.

Part IV

Interests, social issues and the media

10

Groups in Russian politics

Background

It is an important part of pluralist democratic thinking that group interests should be free to find political expression and that government decisions should be affected in some demonstrable way by their input to the governmental process – that is, that political power and influence should flow upwards as well as downwards. Indeed, one version of the pluralist thesis has governments simply as brokers between competing interests.

In the Soviet Union, autonomous organisation for political ends was ruled out. On the other hand, there was a dense mass of organisation that was not autonomous and that the Communist Party had created to mobilise society in pursuit of the Party's developmental goals. Through these 'social organisations' – for example the Central Trade Union Council, and the Komsomol youth organisation – the Party could control strategic sections of society. It was a form of corporatism that enabled the Party to communicate with them without giving them an effective voice in the making of political decisions (corporatism, as used in this chapter, connotes the ability of government to coopt the leaderships of groups into its decision making, at the expense of the influence of the groups' grass roots). The rigour of this system of control has to be seen against the Party's developmental goals. The Soviet Women's Committee, for example, was formed partly to further the social position of women, though it also served to bring them into the labour force.

From Mikhail Gorbachev's reforms onwards, it has been accepted in Russia that citizens should be free to associate and to articulate their demands. This chapter examines the extent to which group interests have developed a capacity to lobby government and with what chances of success.

Categories of group formation

Groups active in the governmental process in Russia can usefully be presented in four categories:

- formally organised interest groups;
- social groups with a political salience;
- issue groups and non-governmental organisations (NGOs);
- informal groups.

Western discussion of groups in politics does not normally deal with the second and fourth of these, but in many ways it is these two categories, and particularly informal groups, that give Russian politics its flavour. A prominent feature of the communist Soviet Union was the prevalence of informal factions and clientelist relationships, most visible at the apex of power. We shall see that the formal introduction of the basic democratic freedoms has done little to rid Russia of its clientelism and factionalism. A theme running through the whole of this book is the distance in Russia between formal structures and actual behaviour in almost every area of political life. It is often the operation of informal networks that provides the clues as to what is actually going on.

What to look for

A first point of interest concerns the extent to which groups are able to form and engage in autonomous political activity in Russia today. Second, it must be asked what effect group action has on government decisions. Third, since this effect will vary, the factors that account for the variation become important. These questions must be posed against the background of a society in change, with all the implications of this – the nervousness arising from new political relationships, the influence of traditional pathways in political behaviour, and the pressures arising from the particular economic and international conjuncture. The overarching question that calls for an answer concerns the extent to which Russia has moved away from the incorporation of strategic groups into the state, which was characteristic of the Soviet system. It will be seen that Russia has indeed moved away from that extreme form of corporatism, but that it has left strong residues. It will be seen also that the vast number of groups that have formed in the past two decades is not matched by the extent of their political leverage.

Formally organised interest groups

Professional and consultative associations

Russia shares with the countries of Central and Eastern Europe a strong tradition of chambers that regulate the professions. In the Soviet Union, such organisations chiefly served purposes of control, but by the 1970s they were already exhibiting an independence of view, and glasnost gave them institutional freedom. In September 1994, for example, three already existing chambers of lawyers formed a new association to regulate their own affairs, though it was not until January 2003 that the First All-Russian Congress of Lawyers met and approved the Lawyers' Code of Professional Ethics. Similarly, a National Association of Television and Radio Broadcasters was created in 1995 and the new Media Union was set up in December 2000.

It has been easy for the state in the Russian Federation to accommodate regulatory bodies of this kind, which serve as a buckle linking government to defined areas of professional activity. The relationship is free of the nervousness that affects government's relations with NGOs and the independent trade unions. It is an area where a degree of pluralism can develop, but in a confined field and always subject to vertical pressures. Vladimir Putin's Russia, and indeed the preceding administration of Boris Yeltsin, have been able to accommodate mediating bodies of this kind, representative of professional groups.

Employer, business and financial groups

An organisation that came quickly to acquire authority among enterprise chiefs in the Gorbachev period was the Scientific-Industrial Union, led by Arkadi Volsky. On the demise of the Soviet Union it became the Russian Union of Industrialists and Entrepreneurs (RSPP). In partnership with other groups, Volsky's organisation entered the electoral field and contested the 1993 election as a political party opposed to the policy of economic 'shock therapy' launched in 1992. The initiative failed and the RSPP settled into its present role as an extra-parliamentary interest group, for example contributing a version of its own in the discussion in 2003 of an administrative-reform plan for the federal government. Other bodies promoting an industrial and business interest emerged, such as the Federation of Manufacturers of Russia, the League for Support of Defence Enterprises and the Association of Russian Managers.

Differing from Volsky's organisation in an important way has been Evgeni Primakov's Chamber of Commerce and Industry (TPP). Primakov also was a critic of Yeltsin's shock therapy and was appointed Prime Minister in August 1998 after those methods had led to an acute crisis in that year that had caused a sharp devaluation of the rouble (Chapters 1 and 11). While both he and Volsky were critical of the radical reforms, they differed in their views on the new political opportunities: Volsky favoured an external form of action, maintaining an independence from government, while Primakov preferred an internal approach, which showed a continuity with the Soviet past and its patrimonial, collectivist underpinnings. It was in keeping with his view of the TPP's role that in May 2004 Primakov suggested its powers be increased to encompass state regulation of entrepreneurial activity.[1] Another example of the internal approach is the National Association of Stock Market Participants (NAUFOR in its Russian acronym) – a case of an organised group forming in a sphere of activity novel to Russia. In fact, it has undertaken a central task of the reform programme on the government's behalf, working in a

175

tripartite arrangement involving, apart from itself, a commission set up by the government and the US Agency for International Development.

When the financial adventurers who had made colossal gains from the privatisation process of the 1990s sought protection and respectability, it was naturally to the RSPP that they turned rather than to the TPP, and by 2001 over 25 of them had joined that organisation. This may explain, at least to some extent, the timid reaction of the RSPP to the arrest of Khodorkovsky in the Yukos affair in the autumn of 2003. Though that response was divided, even at its most assertive it took the form of a defensive letter to the President in early July complaining that an atmosphere of fear was not conducive to business activity. However, a number of influential members disapproved of Khodorkovsky's entry into the political field. Volsky's own view, illustrating his idea of the RSPP's role, was that he had 'always been against businessmen having political ambitions'.[2] Later, on 29 January 2004, Vladimir Potanin, head of the Interros holding company, proposed to Volsky that the RSPP merge with two other business organisations, Support for Russia, an association of small and medium-sized businesses, and Business Russia, which enrolled medium-sized and large concerns, the aim no doubt being to dilute the RSPP's image as the oligarchs' union.[3]

Trade unions

The early Soviet trade unions lost their autonomy with the onset of Stalinism. Their role from that point on was to act as an arm of the state, in promoting production and distributing welfare benefits – in fact, they replaced the Ministry of Labour, which was abolished. Since it was through the trade unions that pensions as well as sickness and maternity benefits were paid, 98 per cent of employees outside agriculture were enrolled in them. The trade unions ran sanatoria, holiday homes and summer camps for the children. They did not bargain over wages at plant level – wages were centrally determined and the size of the workforce in a given workplace was given in the firm's plan. Employment, moreover, was guaranteed. It followed from this welfare role that, apart from military service, the trade union was the chief contact that most people had with the state.

In March 1990 a split in the Soviet All-Union Trades Union Council led to the creation of a Federation of Independent Trade Unions of Russia (FNPR), which inherited the structure, the enormous assets and almost the entire membership of its predecessor. It was therefore in a strong competitive position as new independent trade unions came into being, especially since it continued at first to act as a channel for the distribution of welfare benefits. It is not surprising, therefore, that its membership at the close of the century was still close to the 1990 figure of around 50 million.

Starting with a major strike of miners in the Kuzbas (Kuznetsk Basin) in 1989, and accelerating rapidly when the full impact of the policy of shock therapy came to be felt from 1992, there was a wave of protest that involved most notably miners but also health workers and, increasingly, teachers. Much of this protest action was led from within the major trade-union organisation. Such was the case with the strike action by the Union of Education and Science Workers, which closed schools in 86 out of the Federation's 89 regions (as there were then) during its high point between 1996 and 1998. But often it escaped the FNPR structures and led to the creation of new unions. Many of these new organisations mobilised workers in a single sector, as with the Independent Miners' Union and the Federation of Air-Traffic Controllers, both created in 1990 (see Table 10.1).[4] A strike by the air-traffic controllers in December 2002, which led to wage increases of almost 16 per cent, and of 28.5 per cent for specialists working at the busiest airports, illustrates the effectiveness that the independent unions can achieve.[5]

The major economic crisis of 1998 saw a peak in the activities of both the FNPR and the new unions, and provided reference points for future action, down to a tradition among miners of banging their helmets on the pavement at demonstrations, picked up in a protest action by the independent Union of Coalminers of Vorkuta in 2002. Since then the main features of post-Soviet trade-union organisation have settled into place. The FNPR has maintained its pre-eminence – vast in numerical terms, but dominant also in political influence. The independent unions have tended to form among groups where power is not commensurate with size, though larger umbrella independent organisations exist, including a Confederation of Labour.

Table 10.1 *Examples of large independent trade unions in Russia*

Name	Date founded	Place	Membership[a]
Union of Socialist Trade Unions (SOTSPROF)	1989	Moscow	20,000
Unity	1990	Leningrad	40,000
Independent Miners' Union	1990	Moscow	17,000
Association of Flight Personnel	1990	Moscow	10,000
Federation of Air-Traffic Controllers	1990	Moscow	60,000
Council of Kuzbas Workers' Committees	1989	Novokuznetsk	10,000
Union of Kuzbas Workers	1989	Kemerovo	7,000
Confederation of Labour	1990	Moscow	–[b]

[a] Estimated, 1995.
[b] Umbrella organisation.
Source: Derived from S. Davis, *Trade Unions in Russia and Ukraine, 1985–95* (Basingstoke: Palgrave, 2001). Membership numbers are from the All-Union Central Council of Trade Unions, which still existed at these dates. Claimed memberships were higher.

Many of the independent unions are local organisations and stand in sharp contrast to the major centralised unions, which have bureaucracies that can engage in corporatist discussions with government and employers. This differentiation means that the centralised unions tend to play a mediating role, defusing protest actions by a mixture of accommodation and negotiation. When the independent Chelyabinsk coalminers' union took its action to Moscow and mounted a picket near the government building in August 2002, its members were fobbed off by a ministry spokesman, who said that everything that concerned them would be decided on a local level. The unspoken argument was that if anything were to be decided centrally it would be with the FNPR's member trade unions.[6]

Workers are now able to make wage claims, but demands have also concerned increased involvement in a firm's management and at times go so far as to challenge government policy. The Vorkuta miners mentioned above were demanding higher pensions but also limits on imports of coal. A hunger strike of trade-union leaders in the massive Norilsk Nickel concern in early 2003 was over larger wages in compensation for a rigorous working environment and also more information about the company's finances.

The interventions of the FNPR, often accommodating and consensus seeking, must be distinguished from the spontaneous cases of direct action, which are in fact evidence of the FNPR's failure. Employees have made little progress in their ability to defend their interests against employers in the post-Soviet period. This comes about paradoxically not because they lack organisation, but because the well established structures that are there to protect them have retained attitudes inherited from the Soviet past. Moreover, the labour code adopted in 2001 institutionalised corporatist arrangements for tripartite discussions involving government, employers and the trade unions. According to its provisions, organisations below a certain size are not permitted to draw up collective agreements or to mount strike action. The effect has been to exclude the new independent trade unions as social partners of the government – and to drive their workers to take unofficial action. Employees may have gained possibilities of organising denied to them earlier, together with a certain tolerance of non-institutionalised action, but the trade unions show little sign of shedding a traditional, accommodating attitude to managerial and governmental authority.[7] Meanwhile, the FNPR is encountering difficulties in maintaining its earlier very high membership. Workers are less and less willing to pay dues to an organisation that is neither effective in bargaining nor any longer the sole source of social benefits.

Regional interest groups

The freedom of action that the regions acquired as a result of the collapse of the centralised Soviet regime and the ensuing weakness of the state led groups of adjacent regions with a common interest to form associations. Such were the Siberian Accord, the Greater Urals Association, Central Russia, Northwest, Great Volga and a group linking a number of agricultural regions in the 'black earth' area of Russia (and appropriately named 'Black Earth'). They do not serve as instruments of the state but play a mediating role between agencies of the state and the interests of individual regions. This has been most obviously the case with the Siberian Accord, which came spontaneously into being in 1990, when regional autonomy was at its highest. As early as 1993, however, it renounced its most extreme aims when the state began to reassert its power, and it survived into the Putin presidency, when it became common practice for it to meet together with the Council of the Siberian Federal District to discuss, for example, problems of illegal immigration from China and illicit deforestation. More radically, at a joint meeting in June 2003, the governors of Siberian regions complained about Moscow's control over natural resources (which was the centre of the Accord's demands when it was first formed).

The commission under Dmitri Kozak that produced new legislation on local self-government (see Chapter 4) elicited a collective response from within the regions – this time at municipal level – in the form of the Union of Representatives of Local Self-government Organs. This organisation, created in 2003, and bringing together representatives of 57 cities across Russia, came into being because the existing Congress of Municipal Organisations had adopted too passive a stance to the Kozak reforms. It therefore represents a spontaneous and independent initiative from below, and an organised political response to an important element of the reform programme.

Agricultural interests

There has been strong resistance to the privatisation of the land in post-Soviet Russia and the articulation of an agricultural interest has been chiefly in the hands of a lobby dominated by the former managers of the Soviet collective and state farms. This lobby is represented in the Duma by the Agro-Industrial group and the Agrarian Party itself. Outside the Duma there is an Association of Agro-Industrial Unions, which is quite prepared to criticise government policies, as with the delay in dealing with the overproduction of grain in 2002 – a bonanza that created just as many problems as the more usual underproduction. The Association charged the government with a lack of consultation and transparency, which it claimed had led to corruption. But despite these criticisms it is close to government. It has also been instrumental in retarding the development of pressure groups representing the interests of small-scale entrepreneurial farmers. These therefore resort to demonstrations, as in the aftermath of the 2002 overproduction, when farmers burned wheat in Kurgan town, and threatened to go to Moscow and burn it in Red Square. The demands on that occasion were for a cancellation of debts for agricultural enterprises, a limit on agricultural imports and a reduction in the costs of energy.

The representation of social groups

Ethnic groups

Ethnic groups and large-scale religious organisations have tended to fall outside the discussion on interest groups in Western liberal democracies. Moreover, the Russian Federation's constitution enrols the ethnic minorities in the state itself by giving them the status of subjects of the Federation. On the other hand, ethnic and administrative boundaries do not always coincide. Furthermore, the leaders of these constitutional units have shown themselves adept at manipulating the ethnic factor in political actions that go far beyond the constitutional workings of the state.

The influence of ethnic groups in the Russian Federation has overlapped with both regional and religious factors. The Tatars once again serve as a useful example. They are the largest of the settled ethnic minorities in the Federation and have a corresponding political weight. The 2002 census gives a figure of 5.56 million ethnic Tatars in the Russian Federation; by no means all of them live in Tatarstan – a substantial number, for example, inhabit the neighbouring republic of Bashkortostan. The president of Tatarstan, Mintimer Shaimiev, has played off against each other a number of organised groups within the republic of varying degrees of ethnic fundamentalism in pursuit of his political aims. These range from the moderate nationalist group Tatar Public Centre to the Chally Yoldyz *madrasah*, two of whose students were convicted of blowing up a gas pipeline in Kirov oblast near Tatarstan on 1 December 1999 (the group was later prohibited for promoting Wahhabism – the term usually used in Russia for Muslim fundamentalism).

It was seen in Chapter 9 that Shaimiev played a key role in the formation of the centralising United Russia party, but at the same time he defends both a regional and an ethnic interest. In fact, he uses a general Tatar 'we-feeling' to support the Tatarstan regional interest (which includes a sizeable Russian population) while, within United Russia, working to preserve the status of Tatars in the Russian Federation and to keep fundamentalism at bay.

Examples of organised representation of other ethnic groups are the Union of Armenians of Russia, which demonstrated in April 2003 against lack of protection from the law-enforcement agencies, and the All-Russia Azerbaijani Congress, one of several bodies that claim to represent the interests of the Azerbaijani diaspora in the Russian Federation. The troubles in Chechnya spawned a number of organised groups, such as the Chechen Anti-War Congress. The Association for Native Numerically Small Peoples serves as an umbrella organisation aimed at protecting the identities and interests of ethnic groups most threatened by processes of integration and, increasingly, by Russian nationalism.

Organised religion

Religion was not a causal factor in the fall of communism in Russia, but as the authority of the Soviet state weakened, religious loyalties came to have political salience. The two major confessional communities – Islam and Orthodoxy – were both involved. They are treated in this chapter as collective actors in the group process of politics in Russia; they are dealt with in broader terms in Chapter 13.

Islam

There are 14.5 million Muslims in the Russian Federation according to a preliminary report on the figures of the 2002 census, though the figure of 20 million, frequently mentioned, may be nearer the true mark. Islam as a spiritual force capable of attracting the loyalty of a significant section of the population is of the greatest salience in politics in Russia today, particularly in view of developments in global politics in the wake of the events in the United States of 11 September 2001. The fall of the Soviet regime brought Russia closer to the West in many ways, but by the same token it brought about strong nationalist reactions within Russia. These were noted in Chapter 9 in the case of political parties, but they have also been forcefully expressed by voices within both the Orthodox Church and the Muslim community. On this terrain there is a coincidence of sensibilities between certain currents within both Orthodoxy and Islam. As the leader of the Spiritual Directorate of Muslims of the Volga region put it, 'Only a strong Slavo-Turkic, Islamic Christian Russia can become a barrier to the Western expansion against the entire world'.[8]

There are spiritual directorates representing the Muslim interest in areas where Muslims have a strong presence – the Volga region, Asian Russia and the North Caucasus. But two larger entities, the Central Spiritual Directorate of Muslims of Russia and the European Countries of the Commonwealth of Independent States (CIS), with 49 member administrations, and the Spiritual Directorate of Muslims of European Russia, with 15, have a particular authority, though this is weakened at times by an intense rivalry between them. There is also an umbrella organisation, the Council of Muftis, in which an instance of these rivalries erupted in April 2003, after Telget Tadzhetdin, the supreme mufti of Russia and the European countries of the CIS, had pronounced a jihad against the United States in the wake of the attack on Iraq. The Council, which was led at the time by the head of the Spiritual Directorate of Muslims of European Russia, Ravil Gainutdin, condemned Tadzhetdin's 'emotional declaration', holding that it had done great damage to the authority of Russian Muslims.

Orthodoxy

The acceptance of the Orthodox Church into the mainstream of Russian politics has been one of the more notable features of the new order in Russia. The early revival of the Church in the Gorbachev period started as a movement for restoring the symbols of the Russian pre-Soviet past, but it empowered the Orthodox hierarchy, which went on to seek a greater political role. The resurgence of Orthodox influence has not included a re-establishment of the Orthodox Church, but the Church has frequently behaved as if this were the case – an attitude that has been encouraged by political figures making populist appeals at a time of political dislocation and uncertainty. This un-spoken but real fusion between state and church gives Orthodoxy's role as an interest group a particular corporatist character at the highest level of political interactions. The Church has not been backward, however, in taking advan-tage of the increased possibilities for collective action also at lower levels. For example, in February 2003 an Orthodox student brotherhood picketed the Ekaterinburg city administration in an attempt to force the closure of the city's first officially sanctioned gay club – the 'Clone'.[9]

The potential impact of the Orthodox Church on political issues was hinted at when its eighth council adopted a code of moral principles and rules for business, in February 2004. Reporting on this, *Vedomosti* cited the view of the former head of the National Strategy Council, Stanislav Belkovsky, that the Church was capable of acting as a mediator between business and govern-ment.[10]

The name of the Russian Orthodox Church raises a linguistic point with a relevance to many of the concerns of this book. The term 'Russian' in English fails to make a distinction of great importance in Russian, which uses the adjective *russkii* (feminine *russkaya*) for a man (woman) of ethnic Russian extraction, and *rossiiskii* (*rossiiskaya*) for a citizen of the Russian Federation. To confuse the two would be like confusing English with British, or Breton with French. The Russian Federation itself is the *Rossiiskaya Federatsiya*. The Russian Orthodox Church uses *russkii* in its name, thus identifying itself with the dominant ethnic group in the Federation, and by that fact emphasising that group's domination.

Issue groups and non-governmental organisations

Groups that have formed to promote particular issues are diverse in their organisation, the nature of the causes that they wish to further, the breadth of their support and their impact. But there are two factors that in particular affect the way they have come into being and the role that they play in the overall structure of group representation.

First, while the opening of the political system with the fall of communism has enabled these groups to form and to operate, the increasing intervention of the law-enforcement agencies during Putin's presidency has restricted their political possibilities and shaped their perception of their relationship to power, pressing them into a role of dissidence. In these circumstances, and with recollections of the Soviet Union still fresh in people's minds, issue groups themselves are naturally subject to feelings of impotence and to a perpetual suspicion of government. This affects the form in which they cast their appeals, which in turn seems to justify the authorities' view of them as spoilers. The position is still far from that in Soviet days, when the Party's monopolistic claim to speak for the social good meant that the dissenter was held to be either a traitor or dangerously misguided, but neither has the political system yet succeeded in acquiring forms of group action over contentious issues that are free of nervousness and over-reaction. The nervousness on the part of the authorities is not helped by the fact that the issue over which some groups mobilise is quite simply the failure of the authorities to measure up to their democratic claims.

The second factor is the influence that foreign actors have exerted on group formation and activity in post-Soviet Russia in certain areas, particularly the environment and human rights. In the case of international NGOs this has followed a number of patterns:

- International NGOs have opened branches in Russia, as was the case with Greenpeace and Worldwide Fund for Nature (WWF).
- Others have come to Russia simply as part of their international operations, such as Médecins sans frontières (one of the many international NGOs that were drawn into Russia by the wars in Chechnya) and the International Organisation for Migration, which has established links with the Russian Forum for Migration Organisations, itself an umbrella body within Russia created to encompass the interests of groups such as the legal network Migration and Rights.
- Sources of funding outside Russia have contributed to the work of groups within the country. For example, Citizens' Coalition was created in Yaroslavl oblast to promote transparency and openness about the budget resources of municipal organisations and has been supported by the British Westminster Foundation for Democracy.
- With Russia now open to the world, and its journalists part of a global information network, international NGOs can find themselves defending embattled Russian colleagues and in this way intervene in Russian politics from abroad. When, in 2001, the former military journalist Grigori Pasko, already under suspicion by the law-enforcement agencies, was denied a passport by a district court in Moscow, the authorities made much of the fact that he had been invited abroad by international NGOs, including Reporters Without Borders and Amnesty International. As another example, the Dublin-based Frontline Defenders has taken up the cause of protestors against the war in Chechnya.

All these cases stem from Russia's opening to the world and largely for that reason contribute to the jumpiness of the authorities about NGO activity.

Moreover, while the international NGOs do much to keep the object of their concerns in the eye of both government and population, their effect on the development of their Russian partners is not entirely beneficial. Being better endowed in terms both of finance and of expertise, they to some extent cut the ground from beneath local groups in the attempts those groups are making to gain a purchase of their own in the political system.

One of the less obvious influences from abroad has been simply the way in which the title of NGO is attached to issue groups of all kinds. This borrowing from a Western terminology is useful to groups that have a mission that can be construed as at all contesting the authorities, since in a sense it legitimises them – or, more significantly, delegitimises them in the eyes of authoritarian conservatives.

A prominent issue group formed within Russia with specifically Russian concerns was encountered in Chapter 5, on security – the Union of Committees of Soldiers' Mothers. One of the Union's main concerns was the high number of suicides caused by the brutality to which soldiers, particularly conscripts, were being subjected in initiation ceremonies, but also more generally. The authorities responded to the Union's actions in ways now familiar in Putin's presidency. In June 2003 the Ministry of Justice warned the group that its activities were religious and therefore did not correspond to its charter. This was because there happened to be religious posters and icons on the office walls.[11] When the Minister of Defence ventured to ask publicly 'Who keeps it going? Where does it get its money from?', the questions elicited a deluge of letters of protest from many of the organisation's regional committees to the Ministry of Defence and to the President himself.[12] In February 2004, the Union announced that it intended to form a political party.

Women have played a notable role in the formation and activity of issue groups, but also in less organised protest actions. A landmark occasion was the surge of anger on the part of the wives and mothers of the crew of the submarine *Kursk*, which exploded under water in August 2000. The women were incensed at the secrecy over the cause of the explosion, over the decision not to lift the submarine with their men in it – and over the absence of the President from the scene of the disaster.

Human rights and the environment

Relations between the authorities and human rights groups are particularly susceptible to nervousness. In 2001 the NGO Unified Europe won 18 local legal cases for violations of the rights of victims of political repression. In the following year it found itself the target of nationalists in the city and oblast of Orel, who painted fascist slogans on doors adjacent to its building. Not only did its complaints to the procurator's office meet with indifference but it found itself the subject of an inspection by that office.[13] In the actions and reactions of these three actors – the NGO, the nationalist group and the authorities – it is difficult to draw up a balance sheet between provocation, representation and responsible law enforcement.

Many of the most prominent activists in the human rights groups were major figures in the movements of dissent in the Soviet Union. The membership of groups such as Memorial, Common Action, For Human Rights, the Institute of Human Rights, Civil Assistance, and Ecology and Human Rights include leading veteran anti-Soviet activists such as Yelena Bonner, Sergei Kovalev and Lev Ponomarev. While these former dissidents are freer now to express their views, this does not prevent them from adopting a critical stance towards the limited democratisation that has taken place. At the very least they are anxious to mark progress achieved (Memorial, created in 1988, had a stele erected on Lubyanka Square in memory of the gulag). But almost inevitably they are concerned to push the process further than the authorities wish to go, and the authorities equally inevitably view them with much the same suspicion as their predecessors did.

The authorities have set up mechanisms for relations with issue groups. There is, for instance, a Human Rights Commission attached to the presidency, headed by Ella Pamfilova. This organised civic forums in November 2001 and October 2003, which assembled public officials and members of NGOs in Moscow. The Ministry of Justice also, however cavalier its attitude to issue groups, does have regional directorates to liaise with NGOs. The groups cannot be blamed for believing that these are merely examples of the time-honoured techniques of control that they know so well, but they nevertheless represent a change from the categorical ban on group autonomy of the Soviet years.

Effectiveness and targeting

The radical nature of the transition from the communist power monopoly to freedom of association has meant that simply the existence of autonomous groups is significant as a feature of politics in today's Russia. An assessment of the effectiveness of groups, however, has to range wider than simple existence, since so many organised groups involved in the governmental process already existed in the Soviet period. What is important is the extent to which they have shed their 'conveyor belt' character.

Any assessment of the effectiveness of organised groups in Russian politics must be based on the following considerations, which reveal its limitations:

- The government engages in discussion with business groups, the trade unions and professional chambers, but it does so from a position of strength. The FNPR is unwilling, and would probably be unable, to mobilise employee forces to contest or seriously influence government decisions. Such links as it has with parties in the Duma are worth little, in view of the emasculation of that body. The RSPP showed its feebleness in the Yukos affair, which also showed that the more aggressive business elements in Russia were to have no place in governmental discussions. Corporatism ('bureaucratic corporatism' is but one of the many names it has been given by Russian analysts) remains a feature of politics in Russia, but the fact that the bodies engaging in corporatist negotiations are organisationally autonomous distinguishes today's position to some extent from that in Soviet times.

- The possibilities for autonomous organisation have at least opened an arena in which groups can form. It is an arena that the central authorities accept with a better grace than they accept autonomous political parties. Corporatist links with interest groups leave the state as the key player, but they do at least constitute a paradigm that autonomous players can exploit (as with various regional organisations that have formed).

- While the Duma does not offer an arena for untrammelled party competition, it does offer lobbying opportunities for groups and not only individuals.

- Given the central controls on the media (see Chapter 12), the impact of issue groups is necessarily limited and acquires a flavour of dissidence, which is amplified in many cases by connections with foreign groups. Since television is centrally controlled and newspaper readerships are small, even the most determined of the groups working through public opinion, such as the Committees of Soldiers' Mothers, cannot hope for much publicity.

Informal groups

The discussion of group politics in Western political science has tended to privilege organised groups but there is also a substantial literature on informal group inputs into the political process, focusing on policy networks. Interestingly, such attempts as were made to discern signs of pluralism in the late years of the Soviet regime focused likewise on informal networks within the state and Party bureaucracies, which constituted, in the view of one major theorist, a form of 'bureaucratic pluralism'.[14] The use of the term 'pluralism' was contested, since such networks were not a part of a more general pattern of group interventions in politics in the Soviet Union, but the development of the phenomenon itself could not be gainsaid.

More widely accepted was another view of informal group influences on politics in the Soviet Union, this time with no suggestion that pluralism was involved. This view drew attention to the way in which clientelist networks were central to the process of elite recruitment in a political system that described itself in very formal terms but was in fact highly informal in its actual workings.

Both these features of Soviet politics have survived into today's political system. The first, indeed, is a necessary feature of all technology-based societies where specialised expertise and a complex state bureaucracy generate competing policy options, between which government must decide.

For example, the political analyst Mikhail Delyagin held that the resolution of a crisis in the banking system in mid-2004 was being complicated by competition between opposing influential groups.[15] Clientelism, on the other hand, can be embedded in a society's cultural folkways, and be both an impediment to the efficient functioning of an industrial society and an interference in a free competitive political process. In the Soviet Union it quite clearly acted as a substitute for election at the higher levels of politics. Today it is no longer a substitute for election. It remains, however, a prominent factor in recruitment to high administrative posts.

Clientelist networks

Patron–client relations in politics do not proclaim themselves and often have to be inferred from indirect evidence. The clearest examples of clientelist relations at work in the Russian Federation are to be found in appointments made by the Federation's first two Presidents. In Yeltsin's case it was the years that he spent as first Communist Party secretary in Sverdlovsk oblast that provided a pool of reliable contacts from which many of his key appointments were made. A further clientelist network centred on his family (his daughter, Tanya Dyachenko, had a particular influence on her father) and his immediate entourage, and the 'Family' remained a powerful faction almost to the end of Putin's first presidency. It included highly placed members of Putin's first administration, including the former Prime Minister, Mikhail Kasyanov, and a number of the 'oligarchs', whose sudden wealth dates from the Yeltsin privatisations, such as Roman Abramovich. The removal of a significant number of these figures in late 2003 and early 2004, together with an increasing pressure on the oligarchs, spelled a changing of the guard in the post-Soviet Russian elite.

In the case of Putin, it is to past colleagues from his years in the St Petersburg administration that he has turned for his closest collaborators (Box 10.1). He has relied also (as noted in Chapter 5) on an informal network of a less intimate kind in appointing to high positions throughout the political system members of the power structures – the Federal Security Service (FSB), of which he was the head immediately before being appointed Prime Minister in 1999, and the armed forces. There is a natural overlap between the two groups. There was public surprise when Putin nominated Mikhail Fradkov for the premiership in March 2004, but the website www.regions.ru published a report from three years previously which recorded that Fradkov was even then secretly in the frame for the job. At the time he was working as deputy to the secretary of the FSB in St Petersburg, directly under the future Minister of Defence, Sergei Ivanov.[16]

The extent to which these clientelist networks operate as clearly defined factional groups is extremely difficult to fathom. There is a hidden part of Russian political life that calls for the old techniques of Kremlinology – that is, the use of circumstantial evidence to discover who stands with whom on given

187

Box 10.1 The St Petersburg connection

The contacts that Putin made in his years in the St Petersburg administration and who were appointed to key political posts in his first presidency (throughout Putin's first presidency, unless noted), include:

- Dmitri Medvedev, head of the Administration of the President's Affairs from November 2003;
- Igor Sechin, deputy head of the Administration of the President's Affairs (Putin's assistant in the St Petersburg administration);
- Nikolai Patrushev, head of the FSB;
- Boris Gryzlov, Minister of Internal Affairs, later speaker of the fourth Duma;
- Sergei Ivanov, Minister of Defence (who started his career in the Leningrad Committee of State Security, KGB);
- Alexei Kudrin, Finance Minister;
- Sergei Stepashin, head of the Audit Chamber;
- Vladimir Rushailo, former secretary of the Security Council;
- Sergei Mironov, speaker of the Federation Council;
- Viktor Cherkesov, President's Envoy in the North-western Federal District, 2000–3 (earlier head of Leningrad FSB before joining Putin in the Moscow FSB);
- Georgi Poltavchenko, President's Envoy in the Central Federal District (with Putin in the Leningrad KGB);
- Ilya Klebanov, Minister of Industry and Science;
- Sergei Ignatiev, head of the State Bank from 2003.

---

policy issues. Yet factional conflict clearly takes place at the highest level on the most important issues, to the exclusion of the parliamentary representative institutions. The Yukos affair provides a striking example. In that case it was possible to discern at least some part of a factional struggle pitting part of the Administration of the President's Affairs against members of the Family. People from the St Petersburg group, however, were to be found on each side of the dispute. The fact that the two terms 'Family' and '*siloviki*' (the security services and, by extension, their supporters in high places) have been an essential part of the political discourse within Russia and among commentators outside reveals the importance of clientelist groups in Russian politics. On the other hand, it was clearly Putin's aim, having come to power with the aid of the Family, to reduce its influence. With the complete reshuffling of the government and his own administration as 2003 turned into 2004 this was achieved, with only a single member of the Family remaining in a ministerial job (Mikhail Zurabov, Minister of Health and Social Development).

Assessment

A group approach to politics in Russia reveals three categories of group formation and political intervention. There are: first, organised groups that have regular contact and cooperation with government; second, organised groups that do not have this contact and are often opposed to government policies; and third, informal groups bonded by personal links and by forms of mutual accommodation. Each of these categories has a particular relationship to the state. The third penetrates both state and society and is best seen as a central part of the cultural context in which political and economic life go on in Russia.

Some cases of the first category – FNPR was seen to be an example – still bear the marks of incorporation in the state in the communist period. Other cases of organised groups that existed in Soviet times, such as the various organisations representing the professions, show fewer signs of that legacy, and do not enrol large memberships that could easily conflict with the state. These more long-standing groups have now been joined by entirely new groups that organise over a wide range of interests. This entire first category constitutes a sphere of interest articulation that all advanced industrial states share, and differences within it concern the extent to which the state chooses, or can be forced, to accommodate these interests. In all cases, too, the state itself has an interest in dialogue with these groups. Establishing this, through the policy of glasnost, was one of Gorbachev's main contributions to Russia's political development.

In dealing with groups in this category the Russian government, from the President down, is engaged in a form of political interaction that, in its extent and its variety, is new to it, but which it must digest because of the costs of allowing relations to get out of hand. This is thus a key area, if an unsensational one, in which progress towards deeper and wider participation could develop, freed from the nervousness and unpredictability that impede progress in other areas, such as political parties. The record so far is mixed, and the overall domination of the state remains clear. This is at least one area where, under Putin, the development of political participation is not systematically frustrated.

The record is different in the case of the second category, which includes groups expressly concerned with the autonomous assertion of interests and opinions against the state. These are constantly victims of the manoeuvres of the law-enforcement agencies, and their effect on government decisions is negligible – though no smaller than that of many issue groups in Western liberal democracies. They can, as in the case of the Committees of Soldiers' Mothers, make an impact even if only indirectly. In their statements, attitudes and occasionally their membership, many of these organisations reproduce the dissident groups of Soviet times, but they espouse a significantly different cause. Their aim is no longer to supplant the system, but to make it work more accountably. The attitude of the state towards Russia's new NGOs reveals in an extreme measure the legacy of the past, particularly as concerns the foreigner, the figure who still gives rise to suspicions and to over-cautious reactions on the part of the ubiquitous security forces, and with whom many NGOs have financial but also less material links.

The legacy of the past is strong also in the case of the third category of groups, those constituted by personal linkages. Clientelism can be viewed as representing a traditional form of political relationships, which normally gives way to an impersonal and rational legality in the process of political development. Its essential characteristic is informality. The prevalence of clientelism is proportional to a weakness in the rule of law and the presence of informal patterns of political behaviour. In the Russian case it has historically been strong, making clientelism and corruption norms of the political system. Both remain strong in Putin's Russia.

These informal relationships continue, however, to render the study of groups in Russian politics difficult to conduct in the categories of interest groups as conventionally applied to the analysis of Western liberal democracies. A further impediment stems from the process of transition itself. Political parties have so far failed to establish clear constituencies and programmes. They are, moreover, not allowed a role in government formation. When these facts are taken together with the slow emergence and self-assertion of group interests in a society in flux and newly introduced to the modalities of political competition, it is not surprising that there has been confusion over the respective roles of parties and interest groups in a democratic polity. The Russian Union of Industrialists and Entrepreneurs, the Committees of Soldiers' Mothers, the car-owning lobby – all these have at one time or another opted for the political party as their mode of political engagement, and other cases could be cited. The articulation of interests in Russia has not yet acquired clear organisational contours. The conditions for its doing so are not propitious at present, but they do exist.

Further reading

A. B. Caiazza, *Mothers and Soldiers: Gender, Citizenship, and Civil Society in Contemporary Russia* (London: RoutledgeCurzon, 2002).

S. Clarke, *Management and Industry in Russia: Formal and Informal Relations in the Period of Transition* (Cheltenham: Edward Elgar, 1995).

S. Davis, *Trade Unions in Russia and Ukraine, 1985–1995* (Basingstoke: Palgrave, 2001).

G. Easter, *Reconstructing the State: Personal Networks and Elite Identity in Soviet Russia* (Cambridge: Cambridge University Press, 2000).

S. E. Mendelson and J. K. Glenn (eds), *The Power and Limits of NGOs: A Critical Look at Building Democracy in Eastern Europe and Eurasia* (New York: Columbia University Press, 2002).

L. I. Shelley, 'The changing position of women: trafficking, crime, and corruption', in

D. S. Lane (ed.), *The Legacy of State Socialism and the Future of Transformation* (Lanham, MD: Rowman and Littlefield, 2002).

F. Varese, *The Russian Mafia* (Oxford: Oxford University Press, 2001).

Notes

1 *Kommersant-Daily*, 11 May 2004.

2 'A statesman: Yevtushenkov sympathises with the authorities and not with Khodorkovsky', *Vedomosti*, 11 September 2003.

3 'Business should unite in one structure', *Izvestiya*, 30 January 2004. For more on this topic see S. Peregudov, 'The oligarchic model of Russian corporatism', in A. Brown (ed.), *Contemporary Russian Politics: A Reader* (Oxford: Oxford University Press, 2001).

4 S. Davis, *Trade Unions in Russia and Ukraine, 1985–1995* (Basingstoke: Palgrave, 2001).

5 *Kommersant-Daily*, 25 December 2002.

6 *RFE/RL Newsline*, 15 August 2002.

7 S. Crowley, 'Comprehending the weakness of Russia's unions', *Demokratizatsiya*, 10:2 (2002), 230–43.

8 D. Glinski, 'Russia and its Muslims: the politics of identity at the international–domestic frontier', *East European Constitutional Review*, 11:1/2 (2002), 73.

9 www.regions.ru, 18 February 2003.

10 *Vedomosti*, 5 February 2004.

11 *RFE/RL Newsline*, 25 July 2003.

12 *Nezavisimaya gazeta*, 13 January 2003.

13 *RFE/RL Newsline*, 8 August 2003, citing *Vremya novostei*.

14 J. F. Hough, 'Pluralism, corporatism and the Soviet Union', in S. G. Solomon (ed.), *Pluralism in the Soviet Union: Essays in Honour of H. Gordon Skilling* (Basingstoke: Macmillan, 1983).

15 *Moskovskie novosti*, no. 30, August 2004.

16 www.regions.ru, 5 March 2004.

11

The politics of economic reform

Background

Understanding the politics of economic reform in Russia from 1991 requires some familiarity with the Soviet system that was being replaced. The details given in Chapter 1 should be consulted before continuing. The account of the shift from a planned economy to the market that follows will emphasise the *politics* of the reform process. The interplay between political and economic actors is vital for judging the extent to which Russian society has made headway against a strong state tradition in the Russian Federation today.

The reform under Yeltsin

The first steps towards a market economy made with Mikhail Gorbachev's perestroika proposals were noted in Chapter 1. Those steps were hesitant and proceeded piecemeal, with scheme after scheme being put forward by the country's leading economists for ways of grasping the nettle of ending subsidies and freeing prices from bureaucratic state control. The uncertainty only increased existing problems, with inflation and the consequent need for stabilisation mounting. The definitive shift from a planned to a market economy was not made until the Soviet Union had collapsed. It comprised three elements: liberalisation, stabilisation and privatisation.

Liberalisation

Liberalisation was based on the reformers' conviction, formed in collaboration with Western advisers, that efficiency could be best achieved through competition in a market with prices freed to reflect supply and demand. It was held that an economy organised rigorously in this way would bring political change in its wake. In October 1991 Boris Yeltsin as President of the Russian Republic was given special powers by the Congress of People's Deputies to launch a programme of reform by decree. Nominating himself Prime Minister, he appointed Yegor Gaidar as first deputy Prime Minister in charge of reforming the economy. It was Gaidar and his team, working with Western advisers, who drafted the 'shock therapy' proposals that Yeltsin then put into effect in Russia in 1992.

To do away with the heavy subsidising of foodstuffs and other basic commodities, prices on almost all goods were freed on 2 January 1992. They rose 350 per cent in the first month. The effects were immediate and were particularly dramatic in the retail sector. As long as prices had been pegged artificially low, basic goods had been within reach of everyone's pockets. Consequently there was a perpetual run on them and queuing was a regular part of daily life. With prices freed, the shelves of shops began to fill and the queues disappeared.

Stabilisation

Stabilisation meant taking measures to control the budget deficit and inflation, above all by ending the credits to failing enterprises, which were a major fault in the Soviet economic system and were incompatible with the market reform. It had an international dimension because of the requirements of Russia's creditors, now that the country had re-entered the world economy. Indeed, one of the chief demands of the International Monetary Fund (IMF) in the discussions that it held with the Gaidar team in 1992 was that the budget deficit be kept strictly under control. This proved difficult to achieve, for two principal reasons.

First, it was intended that income into the treasury would be found by reducing tax privileges and by extending taxation to new areas, but difficulty in getting entrepreneurs to pay taxes was one of the greatest problems of the reform and was to remain so until Vladimir Putin came to power. It was one consequence among many of the weakening of the state at a moment when regulation was urgently required. In the Soviet Union, of course, there were no entrepreneurs and the state was the single paymaster. Now, an increasing part of the economy escaped the state's direct control.

The second problem was subsidies. It ran counter to the reform to continue giving subsidies to failing enterprises. On the other hand, the industrial economy would come to a standstill without them. In this sphere a tug-of-war developed between the Ministry of Finance (with the advice of the IMF), which was pressing for the reforms, and the State Bank, which was concerned to cushion their effects. In July 1992, Viktor Gerashchenko became head of the Bank and exercised a powerful influence in favour of state intervention, through credits from the State Bank to firms and to the government, earning himself the nickname 'Hercules'. This meant printing money, which in turn led to inflation. In 1995–96, however, there was a return to monetary discipline. Gerashchenko lost his job and inflation was contained.

The tug-of-war reached its apogee in 1998. The lack of liquidity in the economy did not favour the reformers' point of view. A great many transactions between enterprises were taking the form of barter and payments in kind, and the state itself was not able to generate sufficient revenue from taxation to cover its needs. It took to selling off assets, often at ludicrously low prices, to issuing short-term bonds (the so-called GKOs, government treasury bonds) and to borrowing from abroad. The beneficiaries of this situation were financiers who could exploit the state's weakness. The losers were the struggling industrial concerns and the state, which in the end succumbed to the pressures that it had itself created. On 13 August 1998 it defaulted on its debts and the rouble suffered a two-thirds devaluation. That date was to fix itself firmly in the public consciousness.

Privatisation

The third element of the reform programme was privatisation. This was taken to be an essential component of any thorough-going process of economic reform. It was seen as necessary in order, first, to produce capital; second, to eliminate 'soft' budget constraints and induce financial discipline in enterprises; and third, to produce effective corporate governance, through shareholders monitoring the efficiency of companies in their own interests.

Privatisation was effected in a number of different ways. First, the sale of shops and restaurants was put in the hands of the municipal authorities. Then, in 1992, a scheme was launched whereby vouchers with a face value of R10,000 each were distributed to all citizens of Russia. They could use these to buy shares in an enterprise, not necessarily their own; or they could sell them for cash; or they could place them in an investment fund. One of the ways of spending the vouchers was through a form of management–worker buyout. Managers and workers could buy 51 per cent of the shares in the enterprise at a low price, with the remaining 49 per cent going to auction, or being retained by the state for later sale. This method accounted for almost three-quarters of privatised enterprises. It was particularly popular with managers, since it offered them shares at a low price and an opportunity to purchase further shares from the workforce.

This, however, was only one example of the ways in which managers benefited from privatisation. Another very widespread way was insider, or *nomenklatura* privatisation, whereby directors of state enterprises hived off profitable parts of their firm and transferred them into a holding whose title they could appropriate, leaving just a shell of the unprofitable parts, which remained the property of the state. As a result, a number of enterprising people, often with no financial assets of their own at the start of the privatisation process, managed to acquire great wealth through manoeuvres of varying degrees of legitimacy and by launching often fraudulent financial schemes (see Box 11.1). The income to the state from these privatisations during Yeltsin's presidency was very small. The Audit Chamber estimated that the Russian government received just $9.7 billion for the privatisation of

---

Box 11.1 How to derive private wealth from a public company

When Rem Vyakhirev was replaced as head of Gazprom by Alexei Miller at the end of May 2001, it turned out that a whole series of subsidiaries of Gazprom (SibUr, Gazeksport, ZapSibGazprom, Itera, Rospan and others) had been created, and were leading to Gazprom's assets escaping its control.

How it was done:
First, a subsidiary was created, and given (from Gazprom) funds, some plant and some licences for digging. Or else an existing firm was bought. Next, the subsidiary was separated from Gazprom through diluting the shares of Gazprom in the firm by issuing new ones. Thus Gazprom's stake in ZapSibGazprom (Gazprom of Western Siberia) dropped from 51 to 34 per cent in August 2000. Friendly companies or shares belonging to the director, V. Nikiforov, took up the rest. Third, the assets of what had been a branch of Gazprom were transferred to a new company, which prevented Gazprom from recovering them. ZapSibGazprom set up SverneftGazprom and handed it the licence to exploit the Yuzhno-Russkii well.

Miller turned to the law, but it would take him time to recover the assets.

Source: Nezavisimaya gazeta, translated in *Courrier International*, 21–27 February 2002.

145,000 enterprises during that period – that is, approximately the amount that Russian tourists spent abroad in the single year of 2003.[1]

The greatest fortunes were made in banking and in natural resources (Box 11.2). In these sectors the newly rich were given a chance to multiply their initial wealth through a scheme in which the Yeltsin regime offered shares in the major industrial and extractive industries against loans to the exchequer. It was unlikely that the loans would ever be repaid, and indeed that possibility evaporated in the financial tribulations of the end of the Yeltsin presidency. The people in a position to profit from the opportunity offered by the 'loans for shares' scheme were bankers, such as Vladimir Potanin with Uneximbank and Mikhail Khodorkovsky with Menatep. In 1995 the first acquired 38 per cent of the equity of the nickel monopoly Norilsk Nickel and the latter 45 per cent of the oil major Yukos, both for derisory sums. Others acquired holdings at times in areas of political sensitivity, most notably the media. One of these, Boris Berezovsky, was indeed part of Yeltsin's team of advisers.

The economic and potential political power that these 'oligarchs' had acquired was one of the worst legacies of the Yeltsin presidency. It contrasted strongly with the near destitution that afflicted the general population in the 1990s and with the comfortable egalitarianism of the Soviet economy, which had been one of the chief targets of the reformers. After the rigour of Soviet

---

Box 11.2 Oligarchs

The *Forbes* magazine's list of the world's billionaires contained 11 Russians in the top 300 in its 2004 issue. The top three Russians, ranked 16th, 25th and 73rd respectively, were (with company, estimated worth and sector):

- Mikhail Khodorkovsky, Yukos, $15 billion, oil;
- Roman Abramovich, co-owner of Sibneft, $10.6 billion, oil and many other interests;
- Mikhail Fridman, Alfa-Group and Tyumen Oil Company, $5.6 billion, finance and oil.

Other billionaires listed in the top 300 were:

- Vagit Alekperov, LUKoil;
- Oleg Deripaska, Rusal/Basic Element, aluminium and finance;
- Vladimir Lisin, aluminium and other metals;
- Alexei Mordashov, Severstal, steel;
- Leonid Nevzlin, Yukos;
- Vladimir Potanin, Interros, including Norilsk Nickel, finance and nickel;
- Mikhail Prokhorov, Norilsk Nickel;
- Viktor Vekselberg, Tyumen Oil Company.

According to the magazine, no other city in the world rivals Moscow for its concentration of billionaires. The wealth of Russia's overall total of 36 billionaires equals one-quarter of the country's gross domestic product, or $110 billion, according to *RFE/RL Newsline* (13 May 2004, citing the *Moscow Times*). Forbes said that while individual billionaires were reluctant to disclose their wealth, the information, well testified, was always available from their rivals.

---

central command planning, the market seemed to offer economic freedom, which to an extent it did, but it was not sufficiently realised to what an extent a market requires regulation – in any economy. In neglecting to clad their liberalising policies in a framework of regulation, the Gaidar reformers contributed greatly to a weakening of the state already set in motion by the break-up of the Soviet Union and the uncertainties of the perestroika period. Moreover, the response of enterprises to the reform was not what the government and its Western advisers expected.

The breakdown of existing supply networks led enterprises to respond not by restructuring, but by stopping paying each other and by withholding delivery of goods. Three factors enabled people – and the state – to survive in this period of economic disruption. The first was that employees continued to benefit from a feature of the Soviet system – the way in which the workplace, including its trade-union organisation, provided many of their basic needs, for example in health or simply meals. The second was that the much-derided bureaucracy of the state had been little affected by the political and economic turmoil, and indeed played a key role in ensuring that the reform went ahead while reducing the strains that it was causing. The third was the informal networks of the 'second economy', inherited from the Soviet period and now revived and extended.

Putin's economic agenda

By the time Putin took office as President, the radical change in the economic system had, effectively, been completed, but the reform itself had generated problems that it fell to Putin to tackle. In addition he had his own agenda, aimed to a considerable extent at reining in the effects of the reform in certain areas. The problems that he addressed in his first term as President were as follows:

- He sought to curb the immense economic power that had accrued to the early beneficiaries of privatisation and to claw back as great an amount of illicit gains as possible. This was for Putin an immediate task, though it was not until towards the end of his first term that he challenged the oligarchs head on.
- In the area of finance, the banking sector required reorganisation and tax collection also called for urgent measures.
- Utilities, energy and housing provision all had to be restructured.
- Finally, the politically highly sensitive matter of land ownership had to be approached.

It was a huge programme that required a mass of legislation. Putin's first presidency opened with considerable dynamism, but the first tasks tackled were the easiest and, as time went on, the pace of reform slowed, almost to a stop as the Duma and presidential elections of December 2003 and March 2004, respectively, approached. Controversial matters still awaiting resolution were at that point shelved until after the elections had taken place.

The structure of the economy

Although this chapter is devoted to the political aspects of the economic reform, it is important to provide an outline of the structure of Russia's economy as the context within which change has been taking place.

First, the economy of the Russian Federation is heavily skewed towards production of raw materials. The figures for hydrocarbons vary but Russia's territory contains about 45 per cent of the world's natural gas, 23 per cent of its coal and 13 per cent of its oil. Oil accounts for some 50 per cent of

Table 11.1 *The Russian economy: percentage growth in gross domestic product and real incomes, and percentage inflation rates*

	2000	2001	2002	2003
Gross domestic product	8.3	5.0	4.3	8.5
Real incomes	9.0	8.5	16.6	14.5
Inflation	20.0	18.6	15.1	12.0

Sources: The Economist, Organisation for Economic Cooperation and Development, Ministry of Labour of the Russian Federation.

Russian exports and provides 25 per cent of income to the budget, which makes Russia's economic progress dependent at present on a high price for oil. The territory is also extremely rich in metals (notably nickel and aluminium), which account for 14 per cent of Russia's exports. There are also important deposits of gold and diamonds. These resources enabled the Federation to recover from the chaos of the Yeltsin years and the crisis of 1998 remarkably well (Table 11.1), but they are not infinite, and Russia's future progress lies in reducing its dependence on them and in developing other sectors.

Second, it had been rational in the Soviet planned economy to achieve economies of scale and best use of scarce resources by concentrating production in a few very large enterprises. The reform allowed these giant concerns to retain an effective monopoly, with all the disadvantages that monopoly brings, in terms of price setting and impediments to the creation of new business. But privatisation also meant that in a single deal a purchaser could acquire control of much of the production and distribution of a strategic good, if not all of it. Yeltsin's reforming team was prepared to take the risk of selling off strategic sections of the economy, but after the scandal of the 'loans for shares' affair Putin was naturally more cautious, with the result that at the end of his first presidency some of the major 'natural monopolies' remained in being and in the state's control (though not necessarily totally state owned; only 38 per cent of the shares of the gas monopoly Gazprom, for example, were owned by the state). Apart from the political question of ownership and control, it was not possible at a stroke to undertake a wholesale reconstruction of an economy designed around a few concentrated points of production, and these giant firms remain a feature of the Russian economy, and therefore of Russian labour relations and much else besides.

Third, the Soviet economy had been disproportionately geared towards defence and heavy industry. It was in fact a dual economy, with resources being concentrated on defence at the expense of the consumer sector. This was possible because of the Communist Party's control over a planned economy. The Party could pinpoint priority areas and direct resources to them. The country was provided with a highly developed technological base, but it was skewed towards military production. Civilianising the economy was therefore a major task of the reforms, though armaments still have an important place in the industrial economy. According to the Stockholm International Peace Research Institute's 2003 annual study, Russia surpassed the United States and became the world's leading weapons dealer in 2002, selling arms worth an estimated $5–6 billion to 52 countries.[2]

Fourth, agriculture is an area of particular weakness in the Soviet economy. The reasons are largely historical. The collectivisation of farms in 1928–29 allowed the Communist Party to control agricultural prices during the drive for economic construction, which in turn enabled it to privilege industry and the growth of towns. However, the resulting resentment created a permanent problem of individual motivation in the countryside, with consequent inefficiencies, while years of underinvestment in fertilisers and technology had resulted in very low productivity. Moreover, Communist Party leaders, whose technical competence was not generally great, had less compunction about launching campaigns in agriculture than about interfering in industrial matters. We shall see also that once farmers were technically freed from the collectives in the reforms, they faced all manner of impediments in setting up as individual producers.

Economic issues

Banking

When Putin took office in 2000, the banking system was in urgent need of reform. As noted, the State Bank had played an important moderating role during the Yeltsin period, but in those circumstances moderation meant reintroducing pre-reform measures, in particular giving credit to struggling enterprises and thus raising the old bogey of subsidies. Other major central banks called on to adapt to the new market conditions were the foreign-trade bank Vneshtorgbank, the agrarian Rosagranbank and the huge savings bank Sberbank, which until the reforms was the average Russian's only contact with a banking system serving a planned economy. With the reforms, new commercial banks sprang into being, with activities geared to speculation. The task of reforming this now heterogeneous sector was a formidable prospect, the more so as it was viewed as requiring a programme of privatisation. Reform was put off as the elections of December 2003 and March 2004 approached, but the *Strategy for Modernising the Banking System of Russia* was published in 2003, which proposed a reduction of the state's role in the banking system through the selling of some 150 banks (including Vneshtorgbank and Rosagranbank) and a rationalisation of the types of bank in the system. An important move was the appointment of Sergei Ignatiev to head the State Bank, who thus played a key role in effecting change.

There is also a lower-level story to be told, concerning the difficulties of setting up a system of personal banking. In the Soviet economy people had been paid in cash, though they could put money aside by placing it in the Sberbank. There was no facility for personal current bank accounts (it was impressive to see university professors lining up at the accountancy office window to get their monthly roubles). In the reformed economy the amount of money that people kept at home reached remarkable proportions, not least because, on at least two crisis occasions, in 1990 and 1998, people had lost most or all of their savings. Interfax reported in 2003 that the total amount of cash held by Russia's urban population at home was R243.7 billion ($13.5 billion at the time). It was estimated that the average Russian urban family held R6,980 ($223) at home, and a far greater number of dollars.[3] A law passed by the Duma in July 2004 increased confidence in the banking system for individual account holders by guaranteeing deposits at a uniform reimbursement rate.

Taxation

One of the first tasks of the reformed economy was to devise a taxation system to take account of private economic activity, which had not existed in the Soviet economy, except illicitly. It took a surprisingly long time for the reforming governments to do this and to set up a mechanism for collecting the taxes once a system had been devised. The reforms had released an appetite for speculation that went together with a reluctance to pay the state its due. The Federal Tax Police Service was created and photographs of its personnel in balaclavas dealing with the more flagrant cases of tax avoidance appeared in the press. As part of the reorganisation of the security services in March 2003, the functions of the Service were transferred to the Ministry of Internal Affairs, which was to form a new agency to combat economic and tax crimes. In October of that year Mikhail Kasyanov, the Prime Minister, could announce that success in tax collection had reached 96 per cent of the total assessed, against only 60 per cent in 1996. A failure to pay taxes was one of the main charges laid against Yukos in 2003.

Putin could claim considerable success in the field of taxation by the time his first presidency was nearing its end. In particular, his setting of a universal rate of income tax at 13 per cent had a pronounced stabilising effect.

Other implications of the market economy

The move from a planned to a market economy involved many other adjustments to the financial system:

- A stock market was created during Yeltsin's presidency, and in Putin's first presidency it developed remarkably, its capitalisation reaching over $165 billion by August 2003.
- A procedure to regulate bankruptcy had to be enacted and a bankruptcy law came into effect in December 2002 (some 105,000 bankruptcy cases

in the seven months from its enactment revealed the need that there had been for it).

- Private enterprise and personal responsibility brought a need for insurance, which was only slowly addressed. A bill requiring compulsory car insurance was introduced into the Duma in mid-2003 but the session ended before it could be completed. A requirement that flats be insured against natural disasters also came in 2003.
- Legislation on commercial secrets was required, to improve the climate for entrepreneurial activity and to put a stop to illegal leaks of valuable commercial information.

The problem of unpaid wages

The effects of moving to market relationships were naturally felt right across the economy, as not only enterprises but also public authorities had to pay for services rendered and could no longer rely on hand-outs from the state. At the same time, the monetarist policies that alternated with periods of relaxation of the money supply in the 1990s were creating a problem of liquidity in all quarters. In commercial contexts the problem was met, as noted, partly by payment in kind and partly by barter. For many workers the shortage of cash meant unpaid wages. This was a spur to the creation of independent trade unions in the mining industry, noted in Chapter 10, but it affected budget-funded workers in many fields, education most prominently. People survived by growing their own food in whatever plots in the countryside they had access to, while places of work normally provided meals and other essentials of life.

This was a problem to which Putin paid immediate attention, but it was not until late in his first presidency that real headway was made. *RIA-Novosti* reported as late as May 2003 that employees of the state across Russia were owed R1.3 billion (at the time $43 million), of which some R600 million was owed to teachers. The problem, however, was concentrated in certain regions, with wages being paid regularly in 70 out of the Federation's then 89 regions. The largest overhangs of unpaid wages were by then under a month (Kirov, Ulyanovsk and Amur oblasts being the worst affected).[4] In May 2004 wage arrears were still so frequent that enterprise directors in a number of regions were being prosecuted for failing to take effective action (which usually had the desired effect). In many cases, however, the problem of unpaid wages involved Russia's very many bankrupt enterprises and fly-by-night companies, where restitution was not likely to be forthcoming.

Communal services and housing

In the spheres of communal services – heating, lighting and water, for example – and housing the poor heritage of the Soviet system combined with new problems of the transition from a planned to a market economy to yield a crisis that came to a head in the winter months of 2001–2 and 2002–3.

The Soviet heritage was felt in the poor state of much of the energy infra-structure. The extensive building of large blocks of flats in the cities in Soviet times to house a rapidly urbanising population had been planned with com-munal services built in, with heating and hot water in the new blocks laid on for an entire district. But maintenance had been poor and, by the time of the reform, the system was plagued by rusting and bursting pipes. In March 2003 *Argumenty i fakty* pointed out that Russians 'used' 150 litres of hot water a day, against 30–50 litres in France and Germany, and 200 litres of cold water a day against 80 in Western Europe.[5] The Russian figures, based on what is produced and not on what is in fact used, show how much is lost through leaky and rusting pipes. In the winter of 2002–3, some 10,000 people in Novosibirsk were left without heat when a burst main left more than 100 apartment blocks without heating, at a time when the temperature was expected to dip to –7°C.[6] In 2003 the number of breakdowns in municipal utilities overall increased by 19 per cent over the previous year (2002–3 was the third in a series of very hard winters).

This was the context in which the transition from a planned to a market economy was launched. In Soviet times these services had been provided at a heavily subsidised price to the consumer, as was housing itself. One of the primary aims of the economic reform was to reduce or remove subsidies throughout the economy with a view to preparing firms for privatisation. This meant that the companies providing energy and communal services began to charge prices based on actual costs, with a resulting steep rise in domestic bills. Also, in Soviet times households underpaid for electricity while firms overpaid (so-called cross-subsidies). Regional energy commissions now began to set one price for all, which added to the pain that households were suffering. Debate arose over whether to make the population pay the full price before the infrastructure was put right or to put it right before imposing very high rates. Sergei Glazev, an economist close to the Communist Party, argued that it was unfair to put all the onus on users while the infrastructure was in such a bad state, and that the budget should first pay for the necessary repairs. This view did not prevail.

Energy

Problems stemming from the removal of subsidies were keenly felt also in the production and distribution of energy. At the heart of the reform programme in this area was a massive, state-owned conglomerate called United Energy Systems (EES, known familiarly as 'big energy'), which produced the power that other firms and local governments used and now had to pay for on market principles. The problems that had to be tackled were outlined in March 2003 by its chief, Anatoli Chubais. He pointed out that only some 20 per cent of payments (by regional distributors, for example) were being made in cash as opposed to barter and payments in kind, the structure and management of sales had collapsed, and wages were several months in arrears, leading to discontent and strikes. Chubais claimed that the company's performance was adequate, but that the energy that EES was producing was being wasted because of the inefficiencies of 'little energy' – the networks that delivered power and heating to the consumer. For example, EES said that it controlled only 30 per cent of the delivery equipment, the rest being maintained by municipal energy enterprises (Mosenergo in Moscow, and so on).[7]

Having now to charge for power at real prices, the local distributors began cutting off supplies to local authorities that could not pay. Suffering from both breakdowns and abruptly raised prices, people took to the streets. In early 2002, thousands of residents of Voronezh protested against the new arrangements, with municipal workers in Petropavlovsk-Kamchatsky going on strike for more than five weeks at the end of the year.

In early 2003, the government responded by lending EES R5 billion and transferring R10 billion to the regions for them to repair services to schools, hospitals and housing (though there were doubts about how much of this actually reached the municipalities). For his part, Chubais announced on 27 March 2003 that a number of large companies, including EES and Gazprom, had created a new company, Russian Communal Systems (RKS), to take responsibility for the whole range of communal services – water, power, heating and gas supplies, television and radio access, refuse collection and general maintenance – 'to establish order and move from the Soviet Mesozoic to normal business'.[8] The scheme's chief critics were the Communists and Yabloko, the two uniting in a view that, with the creation of a monopoly to manage housing and communal services, the EES would monopolise 'little' energy as well as 'big'. There was also apprehension that the scheme would lead to an extension of private ownership in a sector where state ownership predominated. A poll of 1,500 Russians conducted later in the year found that only 14 per cent of respondents approved of the government's intention to open the housing and communal-services sectors to private enterprise, with 41 per cent preferring an increase in state control in these sectors, and 73 per cent opposed to allowing foreign companies to run municipal services.[9]

Still in 2003, the State Duma passed a set of six bills reforming Russia's electricity sector. They provided for a consolidated national electricity power network, to be run by a public company. The federal government was to hold at least 52 per cent of the shares during a transition period, rising later to no less than 75 per cent. The bills were signed into law by the President on 31 March.

Housing

The drive to end subsidies had similar effects in the rented-housing sector, which accounts for the preponderant part of urban housing. On 9 April 2003 the State Duma passed a bill under which individuals could be evicted if they went six months without paying their rent. Yabloko and the Communist Party fractions voted against the bill on the grounds that the law was certain to lead to a rise in costs for vulnerable people. Concerns of a different kind were raised in the Federation Council (though it passed the bill), with some members voicing the house's usual complaint that the government was saddling local governments with additional responsibilities without giving them the revenue to pay for them. It was asked how this law corresponded to the proposed law on local self-government and what kind of tax base was being transferred to the regions. The President sagely signed the bill on 8 May, the eve of Victory Day, which is a public holiday in Russia. Putin showed his concern for the effects of these measures by confirming on 16 June that Vladimir Yakovlev had been appointed deputy Prime Minister with responsibility for reform of the housing and communal-services sectors (until he was made President's Envoy for the Southern Federal District in 2004).

Reduced social benefits

These measures in communal services and housing severely reduced the social benefits that the population had received in Soviet days. A further, and more acutely felt, reduction came in August 2004, when a law was passed that put onto a cash basis a number of social benefits that had to that point been freely provided – such as telephone installation and public transport for certain categories of people. The proposal raised a storm of protest from the public and also brought critical comments from a number of regional governors. It was a step of high symbolic value, since the increasing return to authoritarian Soviet norms in the political sphere was being accompanied, ironically, by the abandoning of progressive Soviet policies in social security.

Agriculture and the land

The farming sector has been one of the areas most resistant to change in the Federation's economy.[10] The reform programme implied that commercial relations should affect agriculture as much as industry, but for a number of reasons this has not been the case. First, with the collective farms broken up, the highly contentious issue of ownership arose and of whether land should be made available for purchase and sale, to whom and under what conditions.

Second, it was one thing to break up the collective farms of Soviet times but quite another to divest their managers of their influence. In *Argumenty i fakty* in 2003, a former worker on a collective farm recounted how, when the collective was wound up and its members became owners of their share of the land, the chairman placed the papers witnessing the registration of the individual distributions in his safe and ordered the workers to write a statement saying that they were giving their share to a new collective. The worker asked *Argumenty* whether he could now have his witnessed registration back and sell his portion. The editor's answer was that he very likely could, because the chairman had almost certainly not bothered to record the necessary measures or keep other documentation, the inference being that chairman was still confident that his power remained intact.[11] In these circumstances the collective and state farms remained effectively in being and under the thumb of powerful local figures.

Third, discussion of the whole question of the land was inflamed by collectivist notions about land tenure, the roots of which lie deep in Russian history and in the Russian consciousness. Those notions have strong political champions in an agricultural lobby within and outside the Duma (the so-called *pochvenniki* – 'people of the soil'), which mounted a formidable crusade against the buying and selling of agricultural land.

Taken together, these factors stifled the efforts of those who sought to take advantage of the new possibilities for private enterprise in agriculture. As late as mid-2003, the failure to institute real change in the countryside had left the managers of the state and collective farms with the means to engage in economic activity that could disrupt the employment structure in their area. There were cases in which farm managers intentionally brought their enterprises to bankruptcy so as to sell them off cheaply to companies specialising in deals of that kind, which created social disasters in rural areas where workers had no other possibilities of employment.

The land code

During the Yeltsin presidency a number of attempts were made to give effect to article 36.3 in the 1993 constitution, which had given citizens the right to own land as private property, but the Communists and the agricultural lobby in the Duma were able to halt any significant progress. The President consequently resorted to allowing the regions to enact their own land laws, with the result that, long before the land code was adopted in 2001, land was being bought and sold in a few areas. The change in party strengths in the 1999 Duma changed the position, as did the change in the way the Federation Council was selected, which had reduced its power.

In 2000, the framing of a new land code was embarked upon. The aims were:

- to extend a consolidated policy on market relations to this recalcitrant sector of the economy;
- to resolve contradictions in the existing legislation concerning the land;
- to create conditions favourable to the integration of Russia into the world economy.

The code, first, confirmed in their rights people who had already come into possession of land in one way or another. Second, it linked buildings with the land on which they stood – establishing this indivisibility was of great importance to investors. Third, it established the chargeable use of land – privatisation, in fact – but with agricultural land and (at that stage) sale to foreigners excepted. The land code came into effect in January 2003.

The land law

It was not until June 2002, however, that the question of ownership of arable land was finally tackled, when the State Duma passed a law establishing a market in agricultural land. As was to be expected, the Communist Party and Agro-Industrial group voted against the legislation, after unsuccessfully trying to limit the provisions of the law to allow only the leasing of land. Under the law, it is forbidden to buy agricultural land and then use it for another purpose. People without Russian citizenship have the right only to lease agricultural land, and then only for up to 49 years. The law came into effect in January 2003, at the same time as the land code.

The important question of how much land a single purchaser should be entitled to acquire was left to the regions to decide, but they were forbidden to set a limit of less than 35 per cent of the total amount of agricultural land in a given district that a single person or legal entity can own – that is, there was to be no ban on ranches. Some regions were more favourable to land sales than others. The governor of Krasnodar krai, Alexander Tkachev, announced that the new law would not be implemented on his territory. In some cases minimum plot sizes also were set. While a minimum of 100–200 hectares was being discussed in the Voronezh oblast assembly, some 100 farmers marched on the building demanding a minimum of five to six hectares (they did not get their way).

The economy and the state

The oil sector provides some invaluable perspectives on the interplay between the Administration of the President's Affairs and the oligarchs in the new Russia, and on the role that foreign capital and expertise can play in the Russian economy. It was also the field on which probably the most important battle of Putin's first presidency was waged. Unlike the gas and electricity monopolies, oil production passed to a great extent into private hands (though not the distribution pipelines, the main carrier, Transneft, remaining in public ownership). This in turn gave the people who run the industry the freedom to deal with foreign companies, which were not slow to reciprocate. The result was a triangular relationship between the Russian state, the oil oligarchs, and foreign oil majors.

These developments in a key sphere of the economy brought the policy makers of the Russian state face to face with the full implications of integration into the world economy and the threat to the prerogatives of the Russian state that it constituted. This reduction in the reach of the state and in its traditional monopolies had already long affected all the advanced industrial nations except the communist countries, whose whole political and economic systems were designed precisely to resist it. In the end they had almost all failed, and the question of how Russia would adapt to the changed circumstances was now posed by the possibility of foreigners acquiring a substantial stake in the state's patrimony.

The place of oil in this scenario of change was particularly important. The economic recovery under Putin's presidency had rested to a great extent on exports of hydrocarbons. It was not surprising that many of those in positions of power should wish to regain control of this vital sector, which the state had let slip in the privatisations of the 1990s.

On coming to power Putin had made an unofficial compact with the oligarchs, allowing them to keep their gains provided that they did not engage in politics. The arrest and imprisonment in July 2003 of Platon Lebedev, the chairman of the holding company that controlled 61 per cent of Yukos, Russia's largest oil company, announced the reopening of the affair. In June that year the head of a security section of Yukos had been arrested. It was already clear that Yukos itself, and its multi-billionaire head, Mikhail Khodorkovsky, would be the primary target of a campaign against the power of the oligarchs. Targeting the richest of the oligarchs was to serve as a warning to the others, who all thereupon sought forms of accommodation with the Kremlin (see Box 11.3).

Speculation arose at once regarding the full range of factors that had led to Khodorkovsky's arrest. A prominent explanation was that he had been financing opposition parties – the Union of Right Forces, Yabloko and even the Communist Party – and had openly expressed his intention of playing a role in Russia's politics. A second was that he was negotiating at that critical moment to sell a $25 billion stake in Yukos to the US company ExxonMobil. On the other hand, also during 2003, British Petroleum (BP) had joined the Russian Tyumen Oil Company (TNK) in the formation of a new company, which would be Russia's third largest oil concern. TNK is controlled by Alfa Group, whose head, Mikhail Fridman, is close to Putin, and the deal undoubtedly had the President's approval. International deals were clearly acceptable, provided that the state was in command of the transactions. A final reason was that Putin was anxious to recover as much as possible of the money that the state had lost through tax evasion and shady deals in the 1990s.

But all these explanations can be accommodated within a single conclusion – that those who wield the power of the state in Russia are still unwilling to cede the prerogatives that the state held in Soviet times. In the words of Kirill Rogov, 'Ownership is now a temporary right to conduct business and make a profit that is handed to a businessperson by the state and may be withdrawn or forcibly taken away at any moment'.[12] Putin's sustained high approval ratings during the crisis suggest that the population are in the main prepared

---

Box 11.3 The Yukos affair

At the end of May 2003 the Council for National Strategy, a think-tank close to the Kremlin, claimed to have detected an oligarchs' plot to transform Russia from a presidential republic into a parliamentary one, with Mikhail Khodorkovsky, the head of Yukos, Russia's largest oil company, as it chief ideologue. Questions over the claim's origin arose when it became clear that it had no substance.

On 2 July 2003 the Procurator-General's office called for the arrest of Platon Lebedev, chairman of Menatep, the financial arm of Yukos, on suspicion of embezzling nearly $300 million from the state during a 1994 privatisation deal. Reactions varied. Putin remained aloof: in cases of wrongdoing the law should take its course. The Prime Minister, Kasyanov, was opposed to reopening the privatisation issue, as were some of his ministerial colleagues. More surprisingly in hindsight, so were Putin's chief economic aide, Andrei Illarionov, and Sergei Mironov, chair of the Federation Council and one of Putin's firmest supporters. Many oligarchs sought protection by joining the Russian Union of Industrialists and Entrepreneurs (RSPP).

What was clearly a matter of controversy within the Kremlin itself had been resolved by 25 October 2003, when officers of the Federal Security Service arrested Khodorkovsky on his plane in Novosibirsk. The RSPP responded by sending Putin a letter complaining that business could not function in an atmosphere of fear. Opinion polls, however, had earlier shown that the great majority of Russians favoured a revision of the results of the privatisation process.

On 4 November Yukos announced that a US national, Simon Kukes, a petrochemical engineer who had led the Tyumen Oil Company (TNK) through a merger with British Petroleum (BP), was to replace Khodorkovsky as chief executive (the *Financial Times* noted on 3 November that, as a US citizen, Kukes would be less vulnerable to Russian prosecutors).

Between then and Khodorkovsky's trial in July 2004:

---

to acquiesce in this, indignant at the robbery of the Russian patrimony that the privatisation process had involved. Indeed, a survey by the ROMIR polling agency conducted on 6–14 July 2003 found that 77 per cent of Russians believed that the results of the country's privatisation process should be fully or partially revised.[13]

'Strategic enterprises' and strategic appointments

As events unfolded it became clear that, by design or through the logic of events, the Yukos affair was the opening stage of a recuperation of the state's control over the heights of the economy. An important development in that

- Yukos tried to salvage the benefit it had derived from a merger arranged in 2003 between itself and another major oil company, Sibneft. The merger had been called off at the start of February. In the original deal Yukos had received 92 per cent of Sibneft's stock in exchange for $3 billion and 26.01 per cent of its own shares, but the company did not get operational control over Sibneft. Following a ruling by the Moscow Arbitration Court on 1 March 2004, Yukos retained a blocking share of 35 per cent of Sibneft, but control of the company was maintained by the previous shareholders, headed by Roman Abramovich. It was expected that Sibneft would attempt to purchase Yukos's remaining 35 per cent stake in the company.
- In an apparently repentant essay entitled 'The Crisis of Liberalism in Russia', which appeared in *Vedomosti* on 29 March, Khodorkovsky bemoaned the 'capitulation of the liberals', and called the governments that presided over the 1998 financial crisis and its consequences 'irresponsible and incompetent'. Putin was no liberal or democrat, wrote Khodorkovsky, but be was none the less more liberal and democratic than 70 per cent of Russia's population.
- This did not prevent the Moscow Arbitration Court from freezing assets and shares of Yukos amounting to over R99 billion on 16 April 2004 – that is, about 10 per cent of the company's capital.

As the trial (twice suspended) opened in July it became clear that the $3.4 billion in back taxes and penalties required of Yukos by the Arbitration Court was likely to be used as a means of bankrupting the company so that it could be brought in one way or another under the state's control. In September Putin said that there were no plans to nationalise Yukos but if the company were to go bankrupt the state might buy it. Rumour had it that the Gazprom, Surgutneftegaz and Rosneft companies were interested in acquiring portions of it.

By October attention had come to focus on Yukos's biggest producing company, Yuganskneftegaz, and on 12 October the Ministry of Justice announced that Yuganskneftegaz was going on sale.

direction was a decree signed by Putin in August 2004 that established a list of more than 1,000 'strategic enterprises' over the ownership and management of which the state intended to maintain decisive control. The list included companies in oil and mineral extraction (such as Transneft and Alrosa) and in energy (Gazprom, EES) and extended to Russian Public Television.

At the same time, the most senior members of the Administration of the President's Affairs were being appointed to high positions in these companies. In July and August 2004, Igor Sechin and Vladislav Surkov were appointed respectively chairman of the board of Rosneft and a board member of the oil-carrier Transprodukt. Already by then, Dmitri Medvedev was chairman of Gazprom's board and Igor Shuvalov was on the board of Russian Railways.

Assessment

The decisive embracing of the market at the beginning of 1992 put an end to the system of central command planning and set the Russian economy on the path of a radical reform. The way in which the reform was embarked upon under Yeltsin's leadership, however, had a number of unfortunate results. A market requires regulation and yet many of the essential mechanisms for regulation had not been fully developed by the time a full-blown process of privatisation was undertaken. The most obvious case was taxation. For the state to gather the resources to meet its commitments in the novel circumstances, a new tax regime was required, the means of collecting taxes had to be put in place and – most difficult of all – some acceptance of a taxation culture had to be inculcated. These requisites had not been fully addressed before the economy was turned over to the market, nor could they have been, given the pace set for the reform process. If Russia had followed the example of the slower, more controlled reform offered by China, and paid less attention to models adopted in the smaller and more flexible economies of Central Europe, more favourable results might have been achieved in Russia.

In the event, a significant part of the country's wealth was allowed to escape any control by the state, with the active connivance of the reformers, who assigned a high priority to transferring property into private hands. This accentuated the inequalities that were an inevitable consequence of the reform and indeed – as a motor of efficiency – one of its aims. A related result was that the extraordinary wealth that a group of financial speculators appropriated for themselves became the most prominent symbol of the reform.

These unfortunate consequences of the way in which the reform was carried out affected the political development of the Russian Federation. The emergence of a business elite, which was a natural corollary of the reform, was distorted by the prominence within it of a comprador element.

Putin's move against Khodorkovsky was thus undoubtedly a major turning point in the evolution of post-communist Russia, involving far more than clipping the wings of a potential political rival. It forced, through fear, the entire new business elite into a position of subordination to an elite of which Putin had become the spokesman, its leading members being the officials who hold the key positions in the various organs of the state. The basis of their power is not economic, and economic power has been shown to be unable to prevail against them, but their dominance has profound economic repercussions. The Soviet Union had been a patrimonial system in the sense that the party-state had charge of society's patrimony of wealth and resources. Conceptualising the economy in these terms has carried over into the post-communist period and has implications for Russia's relations with the outside world. The statist elite is aware that Russia has been brought to join the world economy from a position of weakness, Russia's isolation having been one of the major reasons for the Soviet Union's collapse. This has left Russia's sense of vulnerability intact, even increased, and the statists' determination to prevent economic actors in Russia from transferring Russia's wealth out of the country is very reasonable in this logic. The irony is that an inherently unstable situation is being sustained by a state power prepared to preserve the status quo by firm political methods in a changing world to which Russia must adapt if it is to develop economically. This was the very problem that Gorbachev sought to solve when the reforms were launched in the first place.

So it comes about that apparently the great majority of the population, despite the attractions of McDonald's and Coca-Cola, see in the new order not the benefits accruing from a globalised economy but the spoliation of a patrimony that the state is ready to defend, as it has defended it in the past.

Further reading

M. Bradshaw, *A New Economic Geography of Russia* (London: RoutledgeCurzon, 2005).
T. Gustafson, *Capitalism Russian-Style* (Cambridge: Cambridge University Press, 1999).
H.-H. Schroeder, 'El'tsin and the oligarchs: the role of financial groups in Russian politics between 1993 and July 1998', *Europe–Asia Studies*, 51:6 (1999), 957–88.
B. Granville and P. Oppenheimer (eds), *Russia's Post-Communist Economy* (Oxford: Oxford University Press, 2001).
J. P. Hardt, *Russia's Uncertain Economic Future* (London: M. E. Sharpe, 2003).
S. Hedlund, 'Property without rights: dimensions of Russian privatisation', *Europe–Asia Studies*, 53:2 (2002), 213–38.
V. Volkov, *Violent Entrepreneurs: The Use of Force in the Making of Russian Capitalism* (Ithaca, NY: Cornell University Press, 2002).
L. Skyner, *Land Ownership in Russia* (London: RoutledgeCurzon, 2004).

Websites

The most useful websites are those of the major international economic agencies, such as:
www.imf.org (follow 'country info')
www.oecd.org (follow 'browse by country').

Notes

1 *Vedomosti*, 19 April 2004, citing the Audit Chamber.
2 *Moscow Times*, 2 March 2004.
3 Interfax, 8 April 2003.
4 *RFE/RL Newsline*, 15 May 2003, citing *RIA-Novosti*.
5 'Who will pay for the reform of the ZhKKh?', *Argumenty i fakty*, no. 11, March 2003.
6 *RosBalt*, 20 January 2003.
7 *Ibid.*; *Argumenty i fakty*, no. 9, February 2003.

8 *Kommersant-Daily*, 28 March 2003; *Vedomosti*, 31 March 2003.
9 'No private enterprise in the kommunalka', *Vedomosti*, 15 August 2003.
10 See L. Skyner, *Land Ownership in Russia* (London: RoutledgeCurzon, 2004).
11 *Argumenty i fakty*, no. 7, February 2003.
12 *RFE/RL Newsline*, 3 November 2003, citing www.gazeta.ru.
13 Reported in *Vedomosti*, 18 July 2003.

12

Information and the media

Background

In Soviet days, the ruling Communist Party had virtually complete control of television and the printed word. It was exercised not primarily through censorship but through the way in which the Party's power monopoly functioned. First, the absence of a market meant that it was not open to unauthorised people to buy the machinery and materials to print literature. Second, room for editorial freedom was reduced to a minimum through the Party's control over appointments. Adventurous editors would not last long in their jobs. Third, autonomous organisation for political ends was ruled out, which prevented the expression of public opinion outside the intimacy of the family, the student hostel or the bar. Not only was the expression of public opinion severely curtailed, but the Party insistently put out its own messages in the void it had created. Those messages stressed that Party policy was the sole expression of the social interest, and this was justified by the Party's claim that its ideas and policies were scientifically based.

This heritage of the Stalinist years lived on in its essentials right up until the fall of the communist regime, by which time its inhibiting effects were increasingly evident. But in fact from the time of Stalin's death, in 1953, developments took place which extended the area of what could be published. By the 1960s topics as contentious as the future development of the ethnic minorities of the Soviet Union were being openly debated in theoretical journals. While there could still be no expression of public opinion, at least scientific opinion was being liberated. General education itself was opening up rival channels of information. Foreign languages were widely taught and students could acquire a radio and be in touch with the world. Finally, access to an increasing mass of reproduction machinery made it possible for dissident works to be produced illicitly and circulated.

However, the power monopoly protected itself by its own mechanisms and could not be attacked successfully from below. When real change came it was from above, in the form of Mikhail Gorbachev's policy of glasnost, first enunciated in 1986. A law on freedom of the press was passed in 1990 and one on

Table 12.1 *Print-media output in Russia, 1980–2001 (total print runs in millions)*

	1980	1990	1995	2000	2001
Books/pamphlets	1,393	1,553	475	471	542
Newspapers/magazines	2,488	5,010	299	607	984
For comparison: theatre audiences (millions)	71.0	55.6	31.6	30.8	31.0

Source: Goskomstat.

freedom of association in the same year, which together removed the political restrictions on press freedom and created a framework in which autonomous organisation for political ends could be established. There followed an explosion of publishing activity, as a mass of independent pamphlets and newspapers appeared, printed often on the presses of the major, now also independent, newspapers. The new general interest weekly *Argumenty i fakty* was listed in the *Guinness Book of Records* as having the world's widest readership in 1990.

Table 12.1 shows how this flurry of publishing, consequent on the freeing of the press, had died down by 1995. There were two main reasons for this, when allowance has been made for an understandable fall-back in enthusiasm as the novelty of the changed circumstances faded. First, the economic reforms from 1992 left most of the population struggling to find the means to support a basic existence, and the cost of a newspaper rose sharply in relative terms. Second, that cost rose also in real terms as the major newspapers and editing houses were fully commercialised. By the same token, they were now unwilling to allow the informal press free or cheap use of their capacity. It is important to note that this fall-back occurred some time before Vladimir Putin became President, and also that even the recovery that came during his first presidency left circulations far short of the position in the latter years of the Soviet Union's existence.

During the presidency of Boris Yeltsin, the journalist profession itself passed through a period of introspection and change. In the Gorbachev years, journalists had developed a keen sense of their social role at this moment of transition, seeing themselves as a 'fourth estate', taking part in the transformation process and not merely reporting and recording it.[1] This elevated view of their mission suffered a blow in the presidential election of 1996, when it seemed possible that the leader of the Communist Party of the Russian Federation (KPRF), Gennadi Zyuganov, might win against Yeltsin in the second round, given the KPRF's strong implantation in the localities. The resulting polarisation drove the recently freed press and television to paroxysms of partisan behaviour, to Zyuganov's great disadvantage. It was commented that there was no point in being impartial about a contest involving someone who would abolish impartiality if elected, even though Zyuganov had by that time accepted that his party's political future depended upon acknowledging the rules of democratic competition. This departure of the media from the standards of responsible journalism did untold and lasting harm.

A further feature of the Yeltsin presidency that was to have an unfortunate sequel was that the vast sums of money accumulating in the hands of financial speculators meant that political influence could now be bought. The mobile political situation offered opportunities for financial gains to be converted into political power. The government needed money, and at the same time Yeltsin and his 'Family' were closely and in many cases personally involved with these financial operators.

A major battle occurred over the auction of Svyazinvest, a holding company into which an extensive spread of telecommunications enterprises had been brought, with a view to privatising them. The struggle pitted the winner, Vladimir Potanin, who had the support of the international financier George Soros, against both Boris Berezovsky and Vladimir Gusinsky, each of them holders of immense funds that they had used partly to build up media empires. Each controlled a leading television channel and each was close to Yeltsin. By the time Yeltsin resigned the presidency, the owners of these holdings were installed in positions of considerable political influence.

In attacking the oligarchs on assuming the presidency, Putin was therefore at the same time asserting the power of the state against powerful private media influences. This chapter records the steps by which he achieved that aim in Russia, while raising a number of issues of a wider relevance concerning the politics of the media and the central question of who is to control these powerful political instruments in an age of mass communications. The position, in brief, after Putin's first presidency is that independent financial holdings still have a substantial stake in the ownership of the media, but that the state is so powerful that – thus far at least – it has been able to cow big business into a role of subservient cooperation with it, and to deprive lesser initiatives and individual journalists of reliable legal protection if they are critical of the holders of power.

Putin's control of the media

It was more important to Putin to control television than the press in view of the former's incomparably wider reach. The printed media continued to enjoy a substantial degree of formal freedom, far more than in Soviet times. But central controls gradually increased during his first presidency, in line with a general return to authoritarianism in other fields. The controls over both these media were exercised:

- through the Ministry of the Affairs of the Press, Television and the Means of Mass Communication (henceforth the 'media ministry'), which Putin put in the hands of Mikhail Lesin;

- through restrictive legislation;
- by taking advantage of financial or other weaknesses of press outlets to bring about their closure;
- through harassment and interference of journalists and press outlets, much of it at local level;
- by an effective withdrawal of judicial protection.

Controlling television

Central control of television was acquired in a number of stages. In the first year of Putin's first presidency, Berezovsky and Gusinsky were forced into exile by the threat of prosecution for financial crimes during the Yeltsin presidency. Berezovsky's television channel fell into the state's hands indirectly, Berezovsky having sold it to another magnate, Roman Abramovich, who then gave it to the state as part of a deal concerning his oil interests, when it became ORT (Russian Public Television). Gusinsky's substantial media holdings, Media-Most, included the popular Independent Television (NTV) channel, which was one of the rare sources of criticism of Putin's policy in Chechnya. Media-Most had run up substantial debts to the giant state-controlled company Gazprom in the years when Gusinsky and Berezovsky were close to Yeltsin. The times had now changed and in the spring of 2001 Gazprom called in the debts, which could not be paid. Gazprom thus acquired Media-Most through the courts. It then created a company, Gazprom-Media, to run all Gusinsky's former media holdings.

The second stage, which again lasted a year, followed with a split among the journalists of NTV. A group of them, led by a major television figure, Evgeni Kiselev, left to form a new channel, TV-6. It was broadcast by the Moscow Independent Broadcasting Company (MNVK), which was owned by Berezovsky. Within a few months, however, it was threatened with a replay of the NTV story. Its failure to run at a profit led to a minority of its shareholders obtaining a court order to close the channel down, which would have the effect of dispossessing its owner, Berezovsky. Its broadcasting frequency was then put out to tender. It was won by a consortium of financial and industrial leaders, Media-Sotsium, on 27 March 2002.

In a third stage, Media-Sotsium put a new station, TVS (Television Sotsium), on air in June 2002. Kiselev became its chief editor and brought with him most of the journalists who had worked at TV-6. However, TVS was unable to generate sufficient income to realise its plans and within a year it, too, was struggling to pay its bills. As funds diminished the staff agreed to work without remuneration but it was only a matter of time before the money ran out. Transmission of TVS programmes was cut off by the Moscow city government in early June 2003 and finally the media ministry closed the station down on 22 June 2003, having offered its broadcasting frequency to a new channel, named Sport TV, which the All-Russia State Television and Radio Company had created at this opportune moment.

With this, independent television broadcasting came to an end in Russia, since the only formally independent channel was NTV, run by Gazprom, which the state is in any case able to control. There remained also some entertainment channels, and much of the print press maintained its independence, but a central part of the Soviet monopoly of power had been re-established. Television news broadcasts from then on regularly started with lengthy accounts of the President's meetings during the day.

As the 2003 Duma elections approached, further revivals of the past occurred. On 15 October 2003, RTR and ORT, both state-controlled television channels, announced that they were planning to broadcast pre-recorded election debates – to allow two different but overlapping programmes to go out at the same time, as they stated, and to allow topical items to be broadcast across the Federation at the same local time. They went back on this idea the following day, but the suspicion that this was yet another step in the return of an authoritarian tradition arose immediately. The head of the Central Election Commission, Alexander Veshnyakov, sagely opposed pre-recording, to avoid possible complaints of censorship at election time from representatives of the political parties.

The central press

Gusinsky's press group Seven Days was taken over by Gazprom-Media with the rest of the Media-Most holdings, including two major publications – *Segodnya* (*Today*) and the news magazine *Itogi* (*Balance-sheet*). *Segodnya* was insolvent and was closed down on 16 April 2001. In *Itogi*'s case the entire staff was simply sacked on the following day, but the magazine reappeared under a new team and its earlier connection with *Newsweek* was severed.

Once assured of his control of television, Putin was prepared to allow the printed press freedom of operation. The circulation of national papers, however, is tiny in comparison with the nationwide television audience. Putin has, moreover, been able to derive a particular benefit from a free press. From his place of self-imposed exile in London, Berezovsky has conducted a spoiling campaign against Putin and his policies, using for the purpose the Russian newspapers that he owns. This has worked in Putin's favour, since Berezovsky is associated in very many people's minds with the profiteering of the privatisation process and with Yeltsin, to whom he was very close.

Even without ownership or outright control, the Kremlin can make its influence felt through the self-censorship of the print media, itself based on the self-preservation of the people who staff the industry from the highest to the lowest levels. For example, immediately after publishing an article entitled 'The Putinisation of the country', Igor Golembiovsky found himself dismissed as editor in chief and general director of *Novye izvestiya* as a result of indirect pressures in February 2003, and publication of the paper was effectively suspended.[2]

Legislation affecting the media

During the first half of 2002 Putin talked more and more about the threat from extremism. This followed in the track of his attacks on terrorist activity after the destruction of the Twin Towers in New York City on 11 September 2001 and his linking of the threat of terrorism to the war in Chechnya. In April 2002 he presented to the Duma a bill on combating extremist activity, which the Duma passed on 27 June. Its definition of extremism included any actions that impede the functioning of the federal authorities by force or other illegal means. Its relevance for the media was not at once apparent but became clear in the aftermath of the Dubrovka hostage-taking crisis of October 2002 (see Chapter 5), when it was used to restrict comment and reporting.

Then, in 2003, as Russia entered a year of elections to the State Duma, the central authorities took steps to tighten the controls on reporting in the electoral field. By that time, a solid majority in favour of the President had been built up in the Duma, and the United Russia party had itself been created and consolidated. In February 2003 the President presented a series of amendments to electoral and media laws to the Duma which would prevent journalists from reporting information that could damage a candidate's reputation, without the media outlet concerned giving the candidate equivalent space or airtime free of charge to present his or her case. The provisions of the bills were in fact not new. What was new, however, was the sanctions that could be applied. If a paper offended twice it could be suspended, right up to the date of the election, and the Central Electoral Commission or local commissions were given charge over which cases should be brought for judgement. Even more alarmingly, the bill restricted the right to campaign in an election to the candidates themselves. It spelled the end of electoral campaigning.

While the legislation was being discussed, representatives of the Industrial Committee of the Media (see below, p. 223) and of the law-enforcement agencies published a 'Convention of the Mass Media Against Terrorism' to cover reporting on terrorist events and on the measures taken in response to them. The Convention placed severe restrictions on future reporting of terrorist incidents and on interviews with participants in them. There was no explicit connection between the media bills and this Convention, but in conveying a suggestion that enemies were at the gates the Convention made it easier for restrictive legislation to be proposed, and the principle that actions of the security services in protecting the population take precedence over a journalist's right to gather information was built into the final amendments.

Mikhail Fedotov, secretary of the Russian Union of Journalists and former State Press Committee chairman under Yeltsin, pointed out that the proposed media law was unexceptionable in itself when applied by a President and Media Minister who respected democracy, but that otherwise it could be used by the less scrupulous as a bludgeon in electoral struggles.[3] Complaints against the legislation were taken to the Constitutional Court by a group comprising a newspaper editor, *Vremya-MN*'s political observer, the deputy editor of Ekho Moskvy (the main central radio station of the Federation), and more than 100 State Duma deputies. The Court began to discuss the bills' constitutionality on 26 September 2003, but before it could pronounce, the future legislation was already being invoked as a basis for administrative decisions. On 30 September the Bryansk oblast election committee issued a warning to three local newspapers: *Bryansk Crossroads* and *Bryansk Facts* were warned for publishing polling results that suggested the possible outcome of the 7 December State Duma elections; and the third, *Right Hand*, was warned for publishing an interview with a candidate on Yabloko's federal party list.[4]

In the end, the Constitutional Court on 30 October overturned that section of the law that restricted media coverage of elections, but it was cold comfort to the opposition parties. Right up to the elections, United Russia's chief rival, the Communist Party, was systematically excluded from the television networks. Such references as were made to it put it in a very poor light, which the few formal slots allowed to it could not dispel, while references to United Russia and its allies were continuous and highly favourable.

Harassment and interference

The harassment of journalists and interference in the daily running of the media are a difficult area to analyse, because it is not always possible to establish clearly the responsibility for particular cases. On the other hand, they are a matter of record and stand as an indictment of the law-enforcement agencies, which clearly offer inadequate protection, itself a mark of the authorities' preferences. The harassment and interference have taken four forms:

- direct interference in programmes and their broadcasting;
- interference with the freedom of the media;
- intervention in newspaper distribution;
- financial constraint.

Direct interference in programmes and their broadcasting

First, there have been cases of direct interference in programmes and their broadcasting, where television or radio programmes are pulled off the airwaves or reshaped to command. This occurred in May 2000 with the satirical *Kukly* programme of Viktor Shenderovich, featuring puppets that crudely but obviously represented prominent public figures, including Putin himself. The Putin puppet was given a very large nose and wore the red neckerchief of the Young Pioneers of Soviet times. In this case NTV informed the press that it had agreed with the Kremlin to withdraw the puppet. Or a radio journalist can find himself peremptorily cut off, as happened to Alexei Venediktov, when he was voicing criticisms of the law-enforcement agencies on Ekho Moskvy during the Yukos affair in July 2003. When he realised that he was no longer speaking live, he began playing jazz, at which point broadcasting recommenced. He made it clear that the interruption was not a fault of the station.[5]

In other cases of this kind, the decision to intervene might have been taken as simply a matter of editorial judgement of the kind that the director of any broadcasting medium anywhere can reasonably take. On the other hand, when obvious political interference is regularly taking place in the world of the media as a whole, such professional judgements can easily appear as a case of it, and indeed there is a good chance that they are exactly that. When Gazprom-Media was exerting pressure on NTV in 2001, the very popular Leonid Parfenov found that his lively programme *Just Recently* had been put under the control of a hostile executive and he had little choice but to resign. Few believed that this was merely a professional decision, given the programme's popularity. Or a regional government may, either unknowingly or disingenuously, misjudge its prerogatives. In June 2003 the Mass Media Committee of the Komi Republic reminded the editors of local newspapers that their publications were getting official financial support. They should accordingly give prominence to important economic and social developments and to issues favoured by the republican government.[6]

Interference with the freedom of the media

Second, regional leaderships frequently interfere with the freedom of the media, by influencing appointments of responsible personnel or by harassing critical outlets. A change in the leadership of a region, for example, can bring changes in the personnel of the regional media, and in important cases the federal centre can itself exercise an influence. As the election for governor of St Petersburg in 2003 approached, Putin made it clear that he favoured a particular candidate, Valentina Matvienko. Coincidentally, the general director of the regional television station, Irina Terkina, resigned, and the *St Petersburg Times* reported on 24 June 2003 that the anchormen of two political programmes had been dismissed. The outgoing governor, Vladimir Yakovlev, was at that time a critic of the federal authorities who had earned himself two rebukes from the media ministry for his outspokenness on press matters. From this case it appears that the federal centre can interfere with the press at regional level to remove impediments to its appointments decisions.

Intervention in newspaper distribution

Third, intervention in newspaper distribution has been a common form of interference with the media in many Russian regions, with regional branches of the federal postal service supporting local power holders against a hostile press by refusing to deliver critical newspapers. In some cases it is not clear that political factors have been involved. According to *Vedomosti*, Oleg Deripaska's Base Element holding company in 2003 had been acquiring control of newspaper and magazine kiosks in large parts of the Federation (often outlets belonging to the press retail network surviving from Soviet days)[7] though there was no suggestion in this case that the purchases were made for political purposes.

Very different was a case of this kind from Bashkortostan that provides an illustration of the many examples of harassment of the press by a regional – in this case republican – leadership. At a press conference in the republican capital Ufa in February 2003, journalists from the opposition newspaper *Fatherland* and representatives of the National Television and Radio Research Centre condemned the Bashkortostan government for restricting the distribution of three major federal newspapers – *Kommersant-Daily*, *Novye izvestiya* and *Trud*. Reporting on this, *Nezavisimaya gazeta* commented that the Russian Union of Journalists had looked into cases of this kind in Bashkortostan and had concluded that no fewer than 17 federal newspapers and magazines had been subjected to direct censorship during the year, and whole editions had never been distributed in the republic.[8]

Financial constraint

Fourth, a very frequent form of interference is exercised through financial constraint. This, as was seen above in the case of NTV and TV-6, is often easy to apply if a media company gets into debt.

The problems of investigative journalism

Physical attacks on journalists, and even their outright assassination, have been frequent in the Russian Federation since the freedom of the media was formally established. At the end of January 2004 the Foundation in Defence of Transparency published its findings for 2003. It found that 20 journalists had been assassinated (up by one from 2002) and that there had been 120 physical attacks on newspapers or their journalists (up by 21).[9] It is rarely possible to ascribe blame in these cases, though journalists are clearly given insufficient protection by the law-enforcement agencies. It is often possible, also, to discern from the circumstances who had an interest in the attacks. Thus, when the editor in chief of the *Tolyatti Review*, Valeri Ivanov, was assassinated in May 2002, he had recently published a series of articles investigating corruption among local officials. In October of the following year his successor as editor in chief, Alexei Sidorov, was also assassinated, but the stories of the police and of Sidorov's colleagues differed.

In other cases where a journalist was killed while exposing corruption, the guilt has been clearly established. In November 1994 Colonel Pavel Popovskikh, a unit commander in the Russian Airborne Troops, and five of his colleagues were charged with the murder of Dmitri Kholodov, a *Moskovsky komsomolets* investigative reporter. They were acquitted by the Moscow District Military Court. The Procurator-General's Office appealed to the Supreme Court against the acquittal, and alleged that the Defence Minister at the time, Pavel Grachev, a major target of Kholodov's enquiries – had encouraged the defendants to kill the reporter. The Supreme Court's Military Collegium upheld the appeal and sent the case back to the Moscow District Military Court for retrial. In June 2004 the court acquitted all six defendants.

The Babitsky case

Journalists covering the war in Chechnya, or defence matters in general, or even those whose reporting has been used by foreign commentators on Russian affairs, have attracted particular attention from the law-enforcement agencies, and especially the Federal Security Service.[10] The case of the journalist Andrei Babitsky accumulated all these characteristics and acquired a particular notoriety. It was as a reporter for Radio Liberty that Babitsky was detained by Russian officials on 18 January 2000. On 3 February he was handed over to the Chechens in exchange for three captured Russian officers and briefly disappeared. He was detained again, this time in Dagestan, but returned to Moscow, to which city his movements were then restricted.[11]

Book publishing

In Soviet days the quality of published books was no more than adequate. Prices were subsidised but particular titles were frequently unavailable, while the shelves of bookshops carried quantities of unwanted stock. Privatisation transformed the position. The quality of production rose and bookshops took on a new life.

Book publishing has not been subject to direct political controls to the same extent as television and the newspapers. None the less, a kind of indirect censorship developed during Putin's first presidency that involved the youth movement Forwards Together, a creation of Putin to fill the vacuum left by the disbanding of the Soviet youth organisation, the Komsomol. For some time Forwards Together had been agitating for the banning of works that it saw as socially harmful and in June 2002 it launched a protest against a work published three years earlier by the novelist Vladimir Sorokin and entitled *Blue Lard*. Objecting in particular to a sexual scene involving Joseph Stalin and Nikita Khrushchev, Stalin's successor as the Soviet Union's leader, the protesters tore up copies of the book and threw them into a giant mock toilet bowl. Sorokin was summoned to appear before the Procuracy on a pornography charge. After the Procuracy had taken advice from three experts, the charge was dropped.

The case is interesting in that both Alexei Volin, a deputy chief of the government staff at the time, and the Culture Ministry itself criticised the Procuracy's original action. It seems likely that Forwards Together was, on its own initiative, voicing widely held conservative views on cultural matters that the government did not share, but which the President would not be averse to soliciting in his own support. Forwards Together's support for overt expressions of Russian nationalism serves the same purpose. Later in the year it distributed leaflets calling for a ban on a work by Igor Plotnik, *A Book of Happiness.*

The structure of the media

As noted, overall responsibility for the running of the media is in the hands of the Ministry of the Affairs of the Press, Television and the Means of Mass Communication. Under Mikhail Lesin, this ministry played a key political role during Putin's first presidency, when the television channels were brought under central control.

The major broadcasting, transmitting and consultative media bodies at central level are as follows:

- The All-Russia State Television and Radio Company is entrusted with the overall running of television and radio broadcasting. It has branches in the regions through which central supervision is maintained.
- In June 2004 a new Federal Tenders Commission of the Culture and Mass Communications Ministry, which was to be responsible for issuing television and radio broadcasting licences, announced its membership.
- Transmission facilities, including broadcast relay stations and cable networks, are run by the Russian Television and Radio Broadcasting System. From 1 January 2002 responsibility for transmission to all cities with a population of fewer than 200,000 was given to this organisation – a decision that had obvious centralising effects but that was designed to minimise financial crises in an industry with very large expenses. It now covers 85 per cent of the Federation. Radio frequencies are allocated by the State Commission for Radio Frequencies and the Ministry for Transportation and Communications.
- On 15 July 2002 an Industrial Committee of the Media was created to represent the interests of the media, under the head of the ORT television channel (later renamed First Channel). The founding members included the directors of the All-Russia State Television and Radio Company, the major television channels, the heads of the press agency Interfax and of the media trade union, and some 20 others. Neither the Media Minister, Mikhail Lesin, nor his deputy was invited to join. The argument of those opposed to their membership was that it would make little sense for them to be lobbying against themselves, which suggests that the Committee intended to maintain a degree of independence from government. There are professional interests to be articulated and the Committee caters to that need. On the other hand, it took the lead in drafting the very controversial and restrictive media legislation of 2003.

223

There is a second layer of media organisation, which comprises commercial broadcasting houses at regional and inter-regional level, but also to a limited extent national level. These are attractive as advertising channels, even though they rarely have a nationwide audience. Of more direct political relevance are the more general regional broadcasting companies. One in particular has entered fully into the political field – TV-Tsentr of Yuri Luzhkov, the mayor of Moscow. So important is Moscow in Russia's political life that in its case the line between the federal and the regional at times becomes blurred. TV-Tsentr broadcasts nationally (just as *Moskovskie novosti* is one of Russia's most read weekly newspapers) and the political use that Luzhkov makes of it parallels that made by the Kremlin of the fully federal television channels. Luzhkov was an early recruit to Unity and then to the United Russia party but, like Mintimer Shaimiev in Tatarstan, he is adept at using a regional power base to defend and promote his political position.

Television

The main television channels are:

- First Channel. This is the successor of Berezovsky's ORT. The state now owns 51 per cent of its shares (through the Property Ministry, the ITAR-TASS press agency and the Television Technical Centre), which gives it a controlling interest.
- NTV. The chequered history of NTV, still part of the Gazprom-Media holding, was recounted above
- REN-TV. The controlling stake in REN-TV passed from LUKoil to the state-owned United Energy Systems in 2000 and was later sold on.
- Rossiya. This is a general-interest channel.
- Kultura. Kultura broadcasts the type of programmes suggested by its name.
- TV Sport. This is the successor to TVS.
- TV-Tsentr. This is a Moscow channel controlled by Moscow's mayor, Luzhkov.

Radio

The main central radio station of the Federation is Ekho Moskvy. Ownership of it was taken over by Gazprom-Media in June–July 2000 and Gazprom-Media now owns 66 per cent of the shares, with the journalists and radio station management owning the remaining 34 per cent. Other radio channels include Radio Mayak and Radio Rossii.

Newspapers and magazines

The central newspapers with the largest circulation are currently:

- *Moskovsky komsomolets*. Founded in 1919, the paper is economically independent and claims a circulation of 1.7 million in Russia and five former republics of the Soviet Union.
- *Izvestiya*. Dating from the Russian revolution and originally the newspaper of the structure of soviets, *Izvestiya* is one of the most informative and editorially balanced titles in the current press. It is attributed a circulation of 235,000. It is owned by Prof-Media, the media-holding arm of Vladimir Potanim's Interros financial group.
- *Argumenty i fakty*. A controlling share of *Argumenty i fakty* was purchased by Promsvyazbank in February 2002. It claims a present circulation of at least 10 million.
- *Komsomolskaya Pravda* (*KP*). Originally the paper of the youth wing of the Communist Party of the Soviet Union, it became one of the liveliest newspapers of the Gorbachev and Yeltsin years. The majority shareholder is Prof-Media. *KP* claims a circulation of 715,000. The Norwegian media company A-pressen acquired a minority stake in 2003.
- *Nezavisimaya gazeta*. Owned by Berezovsky, *Nezavisimaya gazeta* is very informative, partly because of its interest in reporting from behind the scenes. It is attributed a circulation of 125,000.
- *Rossiiskaya gazeta*. This is the official government gazette, but widely read.
- *Sport-ekspres*. This is the major newspaper covering sport.
- *Trud*. *Trud* (*Labour*) was the official organ of the country's trade unions in the Soviet era. It was purchased by Promsvyazbank from Gazprom-Media in August 2003, and this led to a change of editorial policy in favour of the presidential majority.
- *Moskovskie novosti*. This weekly publication, though a Moscow publication ('*Moscow News*'), is read throughout the Federation. In September 2003 it was bought by the Open Russia Foundation, which is financed by Yukos, and the former NTV and TVS editor in chief Evgeni Kiselev was appointed its editor.

There are also newspapers with targeted readerships, including:

- Within the financial/business press, the national *Kommersant-Daily* and the weekly magazine *Ekspert* received the top ratings in a survey of members of the Association of Russian Managers held in July 2003.[12] *Vedomosti* is notable for its pro-Western stance, which led it to support the 2003 invasion of Iraq. It is owned by Interros with Independent Financial, a partner of the *Financial Times* and the *Wall Street Journal*. Other financial papers are *Finansovaya gazeta*, *Profil* and *Ekonomika i zhizn* (*Economy and Life*).
- Papers associated with the Communist Party are *Pravda*, *Moskovskaya pravda* and *Gudok*. *Pravda* (*Truth*) was the newspaper of the Communist Party of the Soviet Union and dates from 1912. When the newspaper was re-registered in the 1990s it kept the newspaper's famous logo and masthead. For several

years, factions on the left wing of Russia's political spectrum have battled for control over it and for a time rival editorial staffs published two different editions of the newspaper. *Konservator* appeals more to the party's concern for the nation and its heritage.

- Catering for a clearly right-wing readership is *Russkaya pravda*. The Procuracy opened a case against it in May 2003, charging it with incitement to ethnic hatred. The nationalist weekly *Zavtra*, purveying a nostalgia for the Soviet Union, is edited by Akexander Prokhanov, who is close to the Communist Party. It has been warned by the media ministry for fomenting xenophobia and ethnic enmity.
- Although targeted at a specialised readership, *Krasnaya zvezda*, the paper of the armed forces, is widely read and has always had particular political topicality.

Other papers that are referred to in this book are *Novoe vremya*, *Vremya novostei*, *Vremya MN* and *Rossiya* (a paper controlled by Luzhkov).

Regional newspapers

Media ministry figures from 2003 show that national newspapers comprised 14.7 per cent of new press outlets launched in the preceding years, with a correspondingly large share for regional, inter-regional and municipal newspapers.[13] This represents a reversal from the position a decade earlier, when the central press dominated the information field. Examples of particularly successful regional newspapers are *The Golden Horn* (Vladivostok),

Figure 12.1 '*The regional press must be accurate and effective*' (*by Yolkin in Izvestiya; courtesy of Courrier International*).

the nostalgically named *Soviet Chuvashiya* (Chavash Republic), *The Marii Pravda* (Mari-El), *Penza News* (Penza), *Saratov News* (Saratov), *Simbirsk Courier* (Ulyanovsk), *Volga Commune* (Samara) and *Time and Money* (Kazan).[14]

Public opinion surveys

While the media were being submitted to increasing controls during Putin's first presidency, the polling of public opinion remained free from substantial interference. A number of organisations such as ROMIR (Russian Public Opinion and Market Research) and FOM (Public Opinion Foundation) produced reliable and mutually supportive findings on a wide range of topics, some of them politically sensitive. Most authoritative of them all was VTsIOM (the All-Russian Public Opinion Research Centre), under the leadership of Yuri Levada, which enjoyed complete freedom in its research and had gained an international reputation for accuracy and responsibility. Government sources referred to the findings of its surveys, while Putin himself has clearly set great store by his ratings in its polls. It may indeed be this very factor that brought a threat to its independence as the elections to the presidential election of 2004 approached. As long as Putin's approval rating hovered around 70 per cent, the polls were his ally, but that would change if his rating slipped, especially during critical moments in the election campaign. There were also factors promising difficulties for the opinion polls in the summer of 2003, and in particular the unfolding of the Yukos affair, which clearly suggested that the forces favourable to a return of the authoritarian tradition were in the ascendant.

On 5 August 2003 Levada told Ekho Moskvy that a new board of directors for the VTsIOM was being formed, to include members of the Administration of the President's Affairs, the Ministry of Labour and Social Affairs, and the Ministry of Property Relations. The fact that VTsIOM was a publicly owned concern made this move possible, though it was noted by commentators that VTsIOM's results regularly showed a lower figure of support for the pro-Kremlin United Russia party than those of FOM.[15] The response of Levada and a substantial number of his colleagues was to leave the VTsIOM and set up a private polling firm entitled Analytical Service VTsIOM, or VTsIOM-A. Levada said VTsIOM-A would finance its research solely through income earned by conducting surveys and analyses. The name of the new organisation was later changed to the Yuri Levada Analytical Centre.

Think-tanks and political commentators

This account of the circulation of information and opinion would not be complete without mention of the numerous influential think-tanks that are an important feature of the political scene in Russia. Often they are the creation of a single commentator who has gathered a team around himself or herself. The recent emergence of the new political order gives a sense of immediacy and urgency to political issues as they arise, which in turn brings journalism and academic work closer together than is the case in more settled political circumstances. These think-tanks and their leaders often work closely with practising politicians – indeed, at one stage Gleb Pavlovsky of the Foundation for Effective Politics was considered to be a part of the Administration of the President's Affairs when Alexander Voloshin was its head.

Some other prominent political analysts and their organisations active in recent years have been:

- Igor Bunin and Boris Makarenko, of the Centre for Political Technologies;
- Mikhail Delyagin, of the Institute for Problems of Globalisation;
- Valeri Khomyakov, general director of the Agency for Applied and Regional Politics (who, in January 2004, took over as head of the National Strategy Council from Stanislav Belkovsky);
- Olga Kryshtanovskaya, of the Institute of Applied Politics;
- Sergei Karaganov, of the Council for Foreign and Defence Policy;
- Sergei Markov, of the Institute for Political Research;
- Galina Mikhaleva, of the Centre for the Study of Contemporary Politics;
- Vyacheslav Nikonov, of the Politika Foundation;
- Dmitri Oreshkin, of the Merkator Research Group;
- Andrei Piontkovsky, of the Centre of Strategic Studies;
- Georgi Satarov, of the INDEM Foundation;
- Mark Urnov, of the Expertise Foundation.

Assessment

The free circulation of information and opinion is central to democracy, and to the efficient functioning of an advanced technology-based society. It was a major plank of the policy of glasnost, launched in 1986 by Gorbachev, and it was at that time that the Communist Party's monopoly control over the media was brought to an end as part of the democratisation process. Putin himself professed an intention to carry forward the move towards democratisation on assuming the presidency as Yeltsin's heir, but his determination to check the slide into disorder of the Yeltsin presidency conflicted with this. The manner in which he pursued his ends included the use of increasingly strict controls. The effects of Putin's notion of 'guided democracy' were felt particularly strongly in the sphere of media freedom.

The dissonance was apparent in his first actions in relation to the media on assuming the presidency, when he forced Gusinsky and Berezovsky to take refuge in exile. This turned out to be the first stage of a sustained period of pressure on the media, which increasingly brought into question Putin's claim to be promoting democracy. In democracy's name he was in fact depriving society of the means to defend itself against the state. Control of the media, and particularly of television, is not unknown in democratic countries, especially when they are passing through a period of exceptional stress. For a time in the 1960s, for example, de Gaulle took television entirely into government hands in France. What is special in the Russian case is that a state monopoly of television broadcasting is backed up by so many other controls that eliminate the accountability of government. On a charitable interpretation, Putin faced the predicament of limiting democracy in order to create the conditions for establishing it. A less charitable view would recall the constant emphasis that the Communist Party of the Soviet Union also placed on future benefits as a fig-leaf to cover the privations of a present state of affairs.

There is another problem concerning the future. Putin may not be a good democrat, but at least his motives can be construed as benign. He has been setting up a structure of government, however, that could be used with tyrannical results by a successor whose motives were less benign.

Putin clearly despises journalists and it must be allowed that the media themselves have not always played a positive role in the promotion of democracy in Russia. It is worth noting that, in the Gorbachev years, many media outlets frequently adopted extravagant and irresponsible stances. Moreover, the media in the 1996 presidential election behaved quite irresponsibly. It is difficult, however, to accuse the media today of abdicating from their responsibility, given the rigour of Putin's restrictions and the lethal risks that investigative journalists run.

Meanwhile, it is also to be noted that the state's virtually complete control of television was the first case of a full return to the monopoly powers enjoyed by the Communist Party of the Soviet Union. One of the reasons for abandoning that Soviet media monopoly was that, in the long run, state controls are counterproductive. Not only do people cease to believe anything that the government says but information channels seize up. It was not for nothing that Gorbachev called for the free circulation of opinion.

Further reading

I. Zasoursky, *Media and Power in Post-Soviet Russia* (London: M. E. Sharpe, 2003).

E. P. Mickiewicz, *Changing Channels: Television and the Struggle for Power in Russia* (Oxford: Oxford University Press, 1997).

T. Rantanen, *The Global and the National: Media and Communications in Post-Communist Russia* (Lanham, MD: Rowman and Littlefield, 2002).

L. Belin, 'The Russian media in the 1990s', *The Journal of Communist Studies and Transition Politics*, 18:1 (2002), 139–60.

M. Wyman, *Public Opinion in Postcommunist Russia* (London: Macmillan, 1997).

Other sources

Post-Soviet Media Law and Policy Newsletter
www.eim.org (European Institute for the Media)
www.medialaw.ru/publications/index.htm (Moscow Media, Law and Policy Institute; site in Russian only)
http://english.fom.ru (Public Opinion Foundation)

Notes

1 I. Zasoursky, *Media and Power in Post-Soviet Russia* (London: M. E. Sharpe, 2003), pp. 11–12.
2 *East European Constitutional Review*, 11:4/12 (1), fall 2002/winter 2003, 47.
3 *Argumenty i fakty*, no. 19, May 2003.
4 *RFE/RL Newsline*, 1 October 2003.
5 www.gazeta.ru, 16 July 2003.
6 *RFER/RL Newsline*, 20 June 2003.
7 *Vedomosti*, 16 July 2003.
8 *Nezavisimaya gazeta*, 21 August 2003.
9 *RFE/RL Newsline*, 6 August 2003.
10 O. Panfilov, 'Putin and the media – no love lost', *East European Constitutional Review*, 9:1/2 (2000), 60–4.
11 For more, see www.rferl.org/specials/russia/babitsky.
12 *VolgaInform*, 9 August 2003.
13 *RFE/RL Newsline*, citing RosBalt, 26 March 2003.
14 *RFE/RL Newsline*, citing VolgaInform, 14 August 2003.
15 *RFE/RL Newsline*, 6 August 2003.

13

Social issues

Background

The record of the Soviet Union in the fields of welfare and social protection was in many ways extremely impressive, but that record has to be set against the political and economic factors that led to the system's downfall. The Communist Party's favouring of expenditure on heavy industry and defence over consumer needs meant that a relatively egalitarian pattern of distribution was pegged at a low level. Since the fall of the Soviet Union, a relative increase in the provision of consumer goods has benefited the few but not the many, as the egalitarianism of the Soviet period has gone, together with much of the social protection in terms of security of employment and subsidised living costs (rents, food and so on). On the other hand, the incidence of crime, narcotics abuse and other social problems has risen sharply. At the same time, the opening of Russia to the world, the break-up of the Soviet Union and the wars in Chechnya have led to a rise of Russian nationalism, which, while it certainly existed in the Soviet Union, was never shown the tolerance that it has enjoyed under Putin's presidency.

Population trends

The figure of 145.2 million for the population of the Russian Federation given by the 2002 census is two million below the figure for 1989, when the previous census was taken. But these figures conceal two contradictory developments.

The first is that a number of factors have been leading to a greater shrinking of the population than the figures suggest. Life expectancy is extremely low, at 65.9 years for both sexes combined, or 58.4 years for men and 71.9 years for women in the provisional results of the 2002 census (though these figures show a rising trend).[1] Women still outnumber men, though the large discrepancy stemming from the deaths in the gulag and the Great Patriotic War (1941–45) has narrowed considerably, especially in rural populations (Figure 13.1). Further, over the last half century the rural population has diminished substantially relative to the urban population (Figure 13.2).

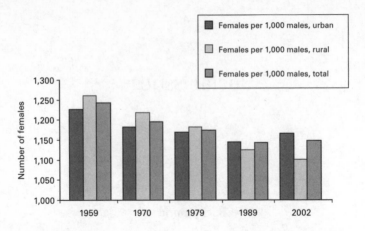

Figure 13.1 *The gender ratio in the Soviet Union and the Russian Federation, 1959–2002. Source: Goskomstat.*

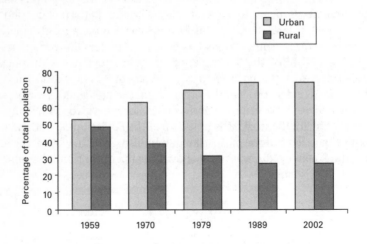

Figure 13.2 *Evolution of urban and rural population in the Soviet Union and the Russian Federation, 1959–2002 (percentages). Source: Goskomstat*

The death rate grew by 10 per cent between 1999 and 2002, and at 13.99 per 1,000 of the population per annum it is far in excess of the birth rate, of 10.09 per 1,000 per annum. Valentin Pokrovsky, head of the Russian Academy of Medical Sciences, suggested that the main reasons for the increasing death rate were alcohol poisoning, accidents, violations of health and safety regulations, the state of the environment and inadequate health provision, to which President Vladimir Putin added, in his address to the Federal Assembly on 16

May 2003, narcotics and new epidemics, such as AIDS.[2] In addition, Russians smoke more than twice the world daily average of cigarettes.

This diminution in the overall population has been only partly compensated for by a second development – an inward migration into Russia chiefly from the former Soviet territories.

Migration and nationalism

Migration into and out of the Russian Federation

The comparatively recent break-up of the Soviet Union into a series of independent states has made the question of migration particularly complex. It left some 20–25 million ethnic Russians outside the new Federation, in the 14 new states that official sources insistently term the 'near abroad'. Should they now be treated as aliens? A second problem has concerned the manner in which immigrants other than ethnic Russians from these newly independent states (Latvians, Ukrainians, Tajiks and so on) should be received. Third, what should be the policy towards immigrants from beyond the 'near abroad', who have been coming to Russia seeking work now that the country is opened to the world economy? These questions all created social tensions and cases of racism.

One result was the passing of the Law on Citizenship in July 2002, which sharply restricted rights to citizenship. In the first nine months from the passing of the law only 90,000 requests for naturalisation were granted, against 470,000 in the previous year. Its restrictive nature was particularly felt by ethnic Russians who were now citizens of countries in the 'near abroad'. In a celebrated case, a grandmother aged 75 years had to travel to a Baltic republic (once a part of the Soviet Union) every three months to get a piece of paper attesting that she had not contracted AIDS.[3]

However, not only Russians were involved. Other cases concerned citizens of the 'near abroad' states who had come to Russia to work. Far from being offered Russian citizenship, they were on occasion unceremoniously repatriated. The potential harm that this could do to the economy was illustrated by cases of Tajiks being repatriated to Tajikistan, despite the publication of a report of a parliamentary commission on Tajik–Russian cooperation that noted the Tajiks' liking for hard work, honesty, conscientiousness and decency, as well as their willingness to do work that Russians shun (and the fact that they do not drink alcohol).[4]

There is also the complex problem of the Meskhetian Turks, who have been the target of repeated pogroms. Though ethnically Turkish, their historical homeland is in Georgia, a former republic of the Soviet Union, but they were resettled by Stalin into areas that are now in the Russian Federation. Krasnodar krai provides the most prominent cases of interethnic conflict involving them. Georgia pledged when it joined the Council of Europe to allow the Meskhetian

Turks to return to Georgia but has not done so, partly for financial reasons and partly because of objections from local residents.

Finally, Russian migration officials have said that by 2010 Russia could have as many as eight million to ten million Chinese residents, which would make them Russia's second-largest ethnic group, ahead of the Tatars. There are significant numbers of immigrants also from Vietnam.

On 24 September 2003 Putin proposed an amendment to the restrictive law of 2002 reversing the exclusion of former Soviet citizens living outside Russia who had become nationals of other states when the Union collapsed. Despite having himself introduced the original 2002 bill into the Duma, Putin was now having second thoughts. In his address to the Federal Assembly in May 2003 he said that 'these people who are coming to us have lived and worked in Russia, participated in its political life, many of them served in the Russian armed forces. Now they are deprived of citizenship in their own country'.

The development of Russian nationalism

The flames of Russian nationalism were already being fanned by a number of political parties when Boris Yeltsin was President,[5] but it took many new forms in Putin's first presidency. There were cases of attacks on foreign embassy staff and foreign students, and the latter led Voronezh State University to establish a special detachment of student volunteers to protect its almost 700 foreign students. A number of extreme right-wing movements arose, which recruited largely among the young and adopted the symbolism of the far right in Western Europe – notably Nazi salutes and insignia, and the closely cropped hair of 'skinheads'. When Russia lost to Japan in the football world championship in June 2002 there was a major riot in the centre of Moscow, where the match had been projected on a giant screen. In the same year a number of regions in the south of the Federation began to close their cities to immigrants. Krasnodar krai, Stavropol krai, Chelyabinsk oblast and the city of Magnitogorsk all took measures against unwanted immigrants from countries in the Caucasus and Central Asia that were once part of the Soviet Union, and early signs of a 'yellow peril' fear appeared in the Russian far east. Yet it was pointed out that this imported labour was needed, and that without attention to immigration policy Russia's population would shrink by a third by 2050.

The problem of racism stemming from immigration has been compounded by the two Chechen wars. The brutality of Russian troops in Chechnya has engaged the attention of human rights campaigners in Russia, but the prevalent attitude of Russians is one of impatience. In particular, the terrorist acts that Chechens carried out in Moscow and other towns outside their republic, including most notably Beslan (Box 2.1), have led to their being demonised. Especially in Moscow there has been a wave of racism, from which many other ethnic groups suffered, as evidenced by attacks on Armenians in the Moscow suburb of Krasnoarmeisk in July 2002 or the numerous assaults on the stalls of non-Russians in Moscow's markets.

It has to be borne in mind that, despite the cases of immigration mentioned in this chapter (some of which in any case concern returning Russians), the population of cities such as Moscow and St Petersburg is predominantly white, to an extent quite unusual in the metropolises of other advanced industrial states.

The ever-increasing expansion of the population of Moscow in the Soviet period was controlled by the requirement of a permit for residence. This was abolished under the new Federation, but Moscow's mayor, Yuri Luzhkov, has reimposed a permit regime. More than that, he took actively to expelling illegal residents: 'Operation Foreigner' was launched in August 1999 under pressure of the first Chechen war and within a month 10,000 people had been deported from the city. Despite two rulings against him by the Constitutional Court, he continued to apply this policy with a major expulsion of non-official residents in the wake of the Beslan crisis of September 2004. Krasnoyarsk, the Altai krai and Sverdlovsk have launched similar operations.[6]

It is possible to suggest a distinction between, on the one hand, a Russian patriotic loyalty that is supportive of the Federation and is a factor of stability in a period of turbulence, and, on the other, pathological expressions of nationalism, which are a negative response to the changes that have been taking place in Russia. The two are connected, and the connection can be located in the demonisation of the Chechens, in which a Russian silent majority has been complicit, and which has provided fodder for a range of extreme nationalist groups.

Political and economic crime

This section is concerned with crime that has a particular relevance to the politics of Russia:

- crimes committed by agents of the state;
- assassinations of public figures;
- economic crime.

Terrorism is treated in Chapter 5 in the Chechen context, since the Chechen struggle for independence is the cause of most significant terrorist acts in Russia; and also in Chapter 14, which deals with the international benefits that Putin has been able to derive from the Chechen conflict.

Crimes committed by agents of the state

In the Soviet period crimes committed against citizens by agents of the state would rarely be reported, and then only if higher authorities wished to make an object lesson of an official or present a scapegoat for their own mis-demeanours. Today there is a good chance that such crimes will be factually reported or given publicity through 'informed sources', but they are still often made to serve as object lessons. In these cases what is important is whether the exposure of a crime is followed by a trial and a court sentence, or simply by an internal enquiry and a token punishment followed by a quiet return to duty for the perpetrator. In the latter case, the effect of publicity having been achieved, the case disappears from view and, as the Russians say, 'the ends are in the water'.

In Chapter 3 it was noted that a number of senior officials of the Moscow Directorate of the Ministry of Internal Affairs were arrested in June 2003, including three colonels and three lieutenant colonels from its Criminal Investigations Department, on charges of blackmail and extortion. The Minister of Internal Affairs, Boris Gryzlov, said that the fight against corrup-tion in the law-enforcement agencies and the organs of state power in general was a priority for him. And, indeed, in this case the offending officials were brought before the courts in February 2004, after the Procuracy had prepared its case.

A case mentioned in Chapter 12 was the murder in November 1994 of Dmitri Kholodov, an investigative reporter of *Moskovsky komsomolets*. His killers were six members of the Russian Airborne Troops, with a colonel leading, though the prosecution charged that they were acting on higher orders. It is hard not to conclude that cases of this kind arise from a double assumption on the part of the holders of power that, first, their crime can escape publicity and, second, that the law-enforcement and judicial agencies will protect the criminal from any adverse consequences.

The assassination of public figures

The history of the young Russian Federation has been studded with a series of political assassinations of public figures, many of which have never been satisfactorily cleared up. The celebrated case of the liberal Duma deputy Galina Starovoitova in 1998 and the more recent case of Sergei Yushenkov, on 17 April 2003, were noted in Chapter 7.

These high-profile cases are but the tip of an iceberg, the major part of which has consisted of very many contract killings of awkward journalists, Duma deputies, mayors and other local officials on the political side, and bankers and business people on the economic side. On the other hand, it is important to note that their number has been diminishing: in the early 1990s the annual figure for contract killings was 600–800, whereas in 2002 it was 70, and the victims were of a lesser prominence.[7]

Statistics on more general violent deaths of political significance in Russia are also presumably of some relevance to these figures for assassina-tions, though the number of political murders that they represent cannot be determined. The death of Duma deputy and journalist Yuri Shchekochikhin, who died on the night of 2–3 July 2003, was generally regarded as a probable case of murder. He had been investigating the possible blame of the Federal Security Service (FSB) for the explosions in apartment blocks in Moscow and Volgodonsk in 1999 (see Chapter 5) – an activity that has been the suspected cause of previous deaths.

In April 2003, *Novaya gazeta* published an investigative survey entitled 'A survey of the Russian killers' market'. It found that the price for a contract killing was roughly $10,000 to $30,000, depending on the skill of the con-tract killer, the status of the victim and how well protected he or she was. The report's author, Roman Shleinov, claimed to discern three categories of hired guns: the 'distinguished professionals', who had been employed in the special units of the former Soviet Committee of State Security (KGB); second, ordinary 'professionals', who were former police officers or veterans of military special forces; and third, ordinary criminals, who were often disposed of after the con-tract had been fulfilled. Shleinov gave among the reasons for the persistence of the phenomenon the fact that 'no one trusts the Russian police, procurators, or the courts', and the fact that the wars in Chechnya had created a large pool of professionals prepared to kill.[8]

Economic crime

Lack of regulation in the newly privatised economy led to a high level of eco-nomic crime during the Yeltsin presidency, which it fell to Putin to deal with. Some of it was crime committed against other citizens, as with fraudulent so-called pyramid schemes, which simply robbed investors of their money. A prominent case was that of Sergei Mavrodi, who, in 1994, started the company MMM. Its capital was provided by incautious investors and holders of priva-tisation vouchers (it had no capital of its own), to whom shares were issued without their having any right to an income from them. Instead, Mavrodi used the income to create other investment schemes (the 'pyramid'). With the eco-nomic crisis of 1998 the company crashed; in three days the value of MMM evaporated – and Mavrodi had disappeared. In 2003 he was eventually brought to trial, but from $312.5 million invested, only $1.6 million was recovered.[9]

In other cases it was the state or its agencies that were cheated, and the challenge for Putin was to claw back as much of the diverted money as pos-sible. There was extensive tax fraud, accompanied by international money laundering as the proceeds were moved out of the country. In other cases, eco-nomic crime has taken the form of a diversion, or simple theft, of resources. The Ministry of Internal Affairs' Investigative Committee stated in August 2002 that over 10 million tons of oil was being stolen each year through criminal dealings on the Russian oil-products market. In 2001, 158 people were arrested in connection with 395 local pipelines that were diverting oil from the state oil network, Transneft.[10]

Corruption

Corruption in the form of bribery is so extensive in Russia that it has become part of the economic system, with conventional rates for particular services or jobs. Georgi Satarov, a former adviser to Yeltsin and later head of the INDEM research foundation, told TV-Tsentr on 13 August 2003 that corruption in government and society continued to grow and was more prevalent than during the Yeltsin years. He said that there was now an unofficial price list for government positions, with $500,000 as the price of an appointment as a deputy minister (his source was people within the administration who wished to compromise each other).[11] The Procurator-General himself, Vladimir Ustinov, has said that Russian officials accept an aggregate of $16 billion in bribes each year and that corruption indirectly caused the economy more than $20 billion in damage per year.[12] Gennadi Raikov, then leader of the People's Party, told the newspaper *Argumenty i fakty* that the average Russian pays R450 a month in bribes (a higher figure than that of Ustinov).[13]

There are two principal reasons for the great extent of corruption in Russia. The first is the low salaries of public servants. The second is the over-regulation of administrative life. Citizens have to pass through so many procedures in arranging their affairs – moving from one flat to another, having a telephone line installed – that the simplest way of getting something done is to offer a bribe. These are not cases of extortion: they stem from the citizen's own wish to settle the affair in a reasonable time or simply just to settle it. Corruption in this case is best seen as an alternative way of allocating the costs of underfunded social services.[14] In other cases, however, extortion is certainly involved, as the examples given in Chapter 3 of police malpractice show.

One of Putin's first acts on assuming his second presidency was to tackle the problem of corruption. First, he increased salaries in the federal bureaucracy by a substantial amount in order to reduce the temptation (or need) to accept bribes.[15] Second, he put in charge of the Duma's Anticorruption Commission Mikhail Grishankov, a United Russia deputy and an FSB lieutenant colonel. The main tasks of the Commission are to ensure that Duma legislation does not leave loopholes that can be used by the unscrupulous and to prevent lobbying in the Duma that is either corrupt or could lead to corruption. The Commission was able to recruit from within the Duma a number of deputies who held, or had held, posts in the FSB and KGB.

Religious issues

One of the Bolsheviks' first acts after the revolution was to separate the church from the state, and a form of militant atheism was instituted. The militancy was slackened in the Great Patriotic War (1941–45), when appeals to patriotism became expedient. But it was not until the fall of the Soviet Union that the Orthodox Church began to recover a real political influence, Yeltsin personally having played an important role in its revival. At the same time, Islam was released from its political fetters and was recognised as more than simply a cultural form related to the development of certain ethnic groups. Under Putin the Orthodox Church was to maintain the momentum of its political gains, while a series of developments presented Russia's Muslims with very particular difficulties.

Policy and legislation

A law of 1997, on Freedom of Conscience and Religious Associations, provided a framework for the practical application of relevant articles of the 1993 constitution. Religious organisations were required to register with the Justice Ministry, and a Department for Public and Religious Affairs within that ministry administered this requirement.

The Orthodox Church's apprehensions of rivalry from other Christian denominations led to its making a distinction between Orthodoxy and Islam as well as between them and other religious formations. When the question of religious instruction in schools arose – as it was sure to do once Orthodoxy was given its freedom – the Education Ministry said that it was prepared to make accommodation in schools available for that purpose, but only to religions that had been legally registered in Russia for at least 15 years (that is, Russian Orthodoxy and Islam). It was for the religious organisations themselves to determine the content of the instruction. It is not clear at the time of writing whether this ruling will be universally accepted by regional authorities, the chairwoman of Moscow City Education Committee for one having challenged it, on the grounds that there were 150 nationalities in the capital and Orthodoxy should not be allowed to diminish the expression of other faiths.[16]

The Orthodox Church

The constitutional separation of church from state has not prevented the Orthodox Church from arrogating to itself some of the characteristics of an established church. It has been able to do this, first, simply through the association of Orthodoxy with Russian culture. There is a historical tradition, and a substantial and revered literature, that attach Orthodoxy to the 'Russian idea'. True, other intellectual traditions in Russian thought contest this version of a Russian idea, and Soviet communism represented an intrusion of secularism that was indeed constitutionally established. However, the communist attack on so many aspects of Russian culture – not only religious beliefs but also social institutions such as the village – has now been succeeded by a backlash, which has reasserted values that communism suppressed, and by a return to Russian roots. This means that people can be culturally Orthodox without attending services. It becomes part of their cultural identity.

Figure 13.3 *'The Orthodox Church defends its territory' (courtesy of* Courrier International*).*

Second, the opening to the world that the fall of communism brought has been welcomed but is also a source of anxiety. This anxiety is fed by the irruption into Russia of so many of the icons of Western culture. Orthodoxy is available as a cultural force to oppose these influences (and Islam is available as an ally in that exercise).

The leadership of the Orthodox Church therefore feels secure in its role as spiritual spokesperson of the Russians but also as a partner of the political authorities. From the moment of Yeltsin's public appearances with the Patriarch of Moscow and All Russia, Alexi II, in the early 1990s, the Church has maintained a prominent political profile. So far, however, this has amounted chiefly to an ability to make its presence, rather than its influence, felt. The Patriarch, for example, was present in the negotiations over a Treaty of Union between Russia and Belarus (dealt with in Chapter 14).[17] 'Of course, by law the church in Russia is separate from the state, but in our souls as well as in our history we are together', TV channels ORT and RTR reported Putin as saying on 7 January 2004. A survey by the Public Opinion Foundation in July 2004 found that some 59 per cent of respondents thought it proper that the Orthodox Church should have a role in state affairs.[18]

The steps that the Orthodox Church has taken to reassert itself in the new favourable climate have included vigorously resisting the development in Russia of its historical enemy, the Roman Catholic Church, which decided in early 2002 to create four dioceses in Russia. From April of that year Catholic priests were being expelled from the country and a visit to Russia by Pope John Paul II planned for the second half of 2003 was cancelled.

Muslim sensibilities

It was noted in Chapter 4 that a substantial population of Muslims has lived peaceably side by side with Russians on the middle Volga since the foundation of the Russian state, while colonial expansion later added to it further Muslim areas in Central Asia and the Caucasus. It is in the latter area that Islam has become a source of real political tension, largely as a result of the Chechen wars, waged against a backdrop of the general rise of Islamic fundamentalism in the wider world, together with 11 September 2001 and the subsequent invasions of Afghanistan and Iraq.

The Chechen struggle was originally a political bid for independence but it acquired an increasingly Islamic character as pressure from Moscow mounted. Then, with the 11 September attacks in the United States, the whole Muslim community of Russia was thrown on the defensive. Islam across the Federation became the victim of a polarisation with an international dimension. This was exacerbated by the invasion of Iraq, and it was seen in Chapter 10 how this led to a call for a jihad against the United States from one of Russia's Muslim leaders. This polarisation is very unfortunate in Russia, where Islam has always had many faces. Historically, the independence-seeking Chechens have always been very different in their relations with the Russians from the Muslim populations of the middle Volga.[19]

Putin and his administration have responded in two ways to this increased Muslim consciousness and its concomitant tensions. On the one hand, by joining George W. Bush's crusade against terrorism, Putin has created nervousness among Russia's Muslims. On the other, he has made overtures to the world of Islam, for example by attending a summit of the Organisation of the Islamic Conference (OIC) in Malaysia in October 2003 – the first at which Russia has been present (Russia was the only major European country invited to participate). He said on that occasion that Russia's Muslims had the right to be part of the global Islamic community, and that participation in the OIC was a way for Russian Muslims to communicate with other Muslims and for Russia to appreciate better what is going on in the Islamic world. While on that diplomatic trip, Putin pointed out that the number of mosques in Russia had grown from 870 to more than 7,000 in what he termed Russia's religious revival of the last decade.[20]

Headscarves

In February 2003, the Ministry of Internal Affairs changed a rule that allowed women to be photographed with headscarves when applying for a passport. The result was that some 3,000 Muslim women in Tatarstan refused to obtain new Russian passports, and ten of them went to court, claiming that the ban violated their constitutional right to freedom of conscience and that the Koran forbids Muslim women from appearing without a covered head in front of un-familiar men. A municipal court in Kazan and the Supreme Court of Tatarstan upheld the Ministry's ban. The women then took their case to the Supreme Court, which pronounced that the Russian Federation 'is a secular state that cannot give preference to any religious norm over other confessions'.[21] Its appelate chamber later reversed this judgement, and the Minister of Internal Affairs signed a decree that allowed women to wear headscarves for their pass-port photographs.

Table 13.1 *Numbers of convictions for illegal narcotics dealing and use (in millions)*

Age of convict	1990	1995	2000	2001
All	7.0	38.6	99.1	126.9
Under 30 years	5.0	26.0	66.5	87.7

Source: Goskomstat.

Narcotics and alcoholism

Putin has taken the problem of narcotics seriously enough to create in March 2003 a new State Committee on Narcotics Trafficking (since renamed the Narcotics Service) and to place in charge of it Viktor Cherkesov, at the time the President's Envoy in the North-western Federal District. The Committee's staff was planned to grow to 40,000, which would double the number in all the country's law-enforcement agencies dealing with narcotics. Cherkesov made it clear that he intended to cover crimes associated with narcotics dealing, such as corruption and money laundering. Table 13.1 shows the rising number of convictions for dealing in narcotics.

The report of a survey by the Education Ministry in May 2003 on the connection between narcotics abuse and other forms of crime, however, painted a brighter picture, with the number of people committing criminal acts under the influence of narcotics since 1999 declining by 41 per cent, and 57 per cent for young people.[22] The extent of the problem of substance abuse among younger people more generally is illustrated in Box 13.1.

Serious as the problem of narcotics trafficking is, it is greatly overshadowed in Russia by alcoholism. This has been historically one of Russia's greatest social ills and is the indirect cause of many others, notably accidents at work, absenteeism and domestic violence. There is a close direct correlation between alcohol consumption per person and the death rate, making alcoholism a demographic problem and adding to the factors that depress Russia's population growth (see above). One of Mikhail Gorbachev's earliest reforms was

---

Box 13.1 Narcotics, drinking and the younger generation

- Four million Russian youths between the ages of 11 and 24 use illegal drugs.
- About one million of them are narcotics addicts.
- The illegal narcotics trade in Russia is worth $5 billion annually.
- About half of all 11–14-year-olds smoke.
- About 80 per cent of young people drink spirits.
- The starting age for smoking has gone down by 3.5 years since 1999 (now 11.5 years of age); for alcoholic drinks by 2.5 (13); for drugs by 3.5 (14).

Source: Education Minister Vladimir Filippov, www.gazeta.ru, 19 May 2003.

an attempt to limit its ravages by restricting access to alcoholic beverages in retail outlets. Apart from being extremely unpopular, this resulted in a run on sugar supplies as Russians took to making their own home brew (*samogon*), which brought its familiar health problems, and the restrictions were lifted. Alcoholism continues to make its ravages.[23]

The environment

Public involvement in the protection of the environment has a history reaching back into Soviet times, when it did not meet the blanket condemnation normally imposed on attempts to organise for political ends. Concern for conservation carried no direct political challenge to the Communist Party's authority, and also the issues around which the movement developed in Soviet days betrayed a none too latent Russian nationalism, as in the case of the movement to preserve the purity of Lake Baikal.[24] However, campaigning on issues more sensitive to the government did not meet with the same indulgence.

There were many causes for concern. The explosion at the nuclear power station at Chernobyl in April 1986 and its wide-ranging effects, and the shrinking of the Aral Sea (both then in the Soviet Union's territory), the latter with its health hazards from polluted drifting dust, were but two of the more prominent. Some 109 million people in Russia live in environmentally threatened zones, while over 30 per cent of samples of water taken in Russia in 2003 failed to meet sanitary standards.[25] The most sensitive issues, however, were those with international implications, such as the mounting risks brought by the disintegrating nuclear submarines in the naval bases at Vladivostok in the east and Murmansk in the north. Cases of journalists being prosecuted for reporting on these risks were noted in Chapter 5. Accused of divulging state secrets, they were in at least two prominent cases imprisoned.

The high sensitivity of such issues, and the extreme sanctions that they have attracted, have set them apart from the mainstream of environmental management, where Russia has been party to many of the major conventions of recent decades and where the critical activities of organisations such as Greenpeace or the World Wildlife Fund are tolerated. Russia for a long time resisted signing the Kyoto protocol on emissions of greenhouse gases and other causes of global warming. The President's economic adviser, Andrei Illarionov, put forward the same arguments as those of the United States: the concept of global warming is controversial, there has been no serious analysis of the Kyoto protocol, and the expenses of implementing it could be higher than the benefits it would bring. 'I am not sure Russia can bear expenses that the richest country in the world cannot afford', he said in June 2003.[26] However, on 30 September 2004 the government took the decision to present legislation to the Duma with a view to endorsing the protocol. It was a change of heart that was likely to improve Russia's chances of joining the World Trade Organization.

Management of the environment has been something of a football in Russian politics. In 2000 the Kremlin liquidated the State Ecology Committee, whose brief was precisely to concentrate governmental policy on the environment, and its functions were transferred to the Natural Resources Ministry. This, some claimed, was tantamount to putting the fox in charge of the hen house, and the transfer was met with a spate of letters and appeals.

At a meeting of the State Council on 4 June 2003, Putin called for a revision of Russia's environmental legislation, and pointed out that Russia had virtually no legal mechanisms for compensation to be paid for damage to the environment caused by industrial enterprises. He called for a single body to manage Russia's environmental policy, noting that it was currently spread across at least five ministries and a myriad of intermediate government bodies. True, elections to the Duma were impending, but the fact that the meeting was held at all was welcomed by environmentalists. The governmental reorganisation of 2004 took these concerns into account.

Gender

In the Soviet Union a Soviet Women's Committee was among the organisations set up by the Communist Party to mobilise strategic sections of society, but whatever political consideration lay behind its creation it did acknowledge the particular interests of women. Women held responsible positions in a number of occupations, including management, though they were extremely rare in politically important posts. A Party of Russian Women, an heir to the Women's Committee, was represented in the State Duma elected in 1993. It failed to secure representation in the following Duma, but by that time women had raised their political profile in another way, with the creation of the Committees of Soldiers' Mothers and the vigorous reaction to the *Kursk* submarine disaster in August 2000.

In the new Russia women are not well represented in political roles. In the Duma elected in December 1999 there were 34 women out of 450 deputies, and in 2003 there were only seven women among the 178 senators in the Federation Council. A woman – Valentina Bronevich – was elected governor of the Koryak autonomous district in 1996, only to be defeated in 2000, while a greater signal of possible advance was Valentina Matvienko's election to the governorship of St Petersburg, after she had already held high office as a deputy Prime Minister.

Not much progress was offered by a bill passed in its first reading by the Duma on 16 April 2003 which sought to ban discrimination by gender, and which grandly declared that men and women should have equal access to property, land and financial resources, and that posts in the State Service should be staffed by both men and women. The bill's provisions were declaratory and did not seem to bind the government, which in fact opposed the bill.

None the less, it was likely to serve, in the event of its being successful, to mark a principle in law. A week later the Minister of Defence, Sergei Ivanov, expressed himself in favour of admitting women as volunteers to combat units under his Ministry's reform plan, since female volunteers should be no different from male volunteers. That his thinking may have reflected expediency more than social enlightenment, however, is suggested by his proposing, at the same time, that citizens of other countries of the Commonwealth of Independent States should be a further source of potential volunteers.[27]

The main issue concerning gender in the Russian Federation, however, has been the growth of prostitution, not only internally but particularly internationally, with young Russian women being attracted to Western destinations by operators who have then effectively enslaved them as prostitutes by holding their passports. This is the less attractive side of a significant emigration of women wooed abroad through the internet.[28]

Dealing with the past

Even before the fall of the communist order, the original names of most of the cities, and streets within cities, that had been renamed in honour of deceased Soviet leaders were being restored. At the same time, the revival of the Orthodox Church and its influence was marked by the restoration of its churches. This process was crowned by the rebuilding of the cathedral of Christ the Saviour in Moscow (known familiarly as the 'big inkpot'). The original had been demolished in 1931 and an open-air swimming pool had been built on its site. The cost of the reconstruction was formidable and diverted a large part of Moscow's construction capacity.

Many statues erected to honour the great figures of the Soviet period were taken down and usually damaged or demolished in the process. Many of the more substantial parts of broken statues in Moscow were placed in an especially dedicated area of the Park of Culture, partly from a sense of nostalgia (and as a political sop to the Communist Party and the nationalists), but as much a matter of not knowing what to do with them.

Nostalgia of a particularly contentious kind was involved in debates that arose over the possible rehabilitation of some of the heroes of the Soviet past. Attention has focused in particular on two emblematic figures – Dzerzhinsky and Stalin. Felix Dzerzhinsky was the founder of the original Soviet political police (the Cheka, distant predecessor of the KGB) and a statue of him had stood since 1958 on Lubyanka Square in Moscow, near the headquarters of the former KGB and now of its successor, the FSB. The taking down of the 15-ton statue in August 1991 was a moment of high symbolism in the process of political change in Russia.

In September 2002 the mayor of Moscow, Yuri Luzhkov, called for its restoration, though he had earlier opposed the idea. Against the proposal it was

Figure 13.4 *'I've been there already!'* *(Vasilev in* Izvestiya, *courtesy of* Courrier International).

argued that playing with symbols begets false fears in some and false hopes in others, and that if the proposal was being made in order to please Putin it was misplaced, since it would simply show the world that the President was a creature of the security services.[29] For many, Dzerzhinsky's name was inseparably linked with the system of concentration camps and the deaths of millions of people. Finally, Vladislav Surkov, a deputy head of the Administration of the President's Affairs, came out against the proposal on the grounds that it would be unnecessarily divisive. Patriarch Alexi II also spoke out against the proposal and it was abandoned.

The fiftieth anniversary of Stalin's death, on 5 May 2003, was an occasion to judge the extent of that former leader's continuing symbolic value. The Communist Party of the Russian Federation was understandably in the forefront of moves to honour Stalin and his historic role. The Saratov regional Communist Party organisation decided in December of that year to erect a statue of him in a Saratov park, while the Communist Party leader in Moscow, Alexander Kuvaev, went so far as to propose that Stalin be cloned (a proposal that so far has had no sequel; Stalin remains unique).

In a less partisan context, a poll by the All-Russian Public Opinion Research Centre of 1,600 adults in 100 towns and cities in 40 regions of the Federation in late February and early March 2003 revealed that 53 per cent of respondents approved of Stalin overall, 33 per cent disapproved and 14 per cent had no position. One-fifth of the sample agreed that Stalin 'was a wise leader who led the USSR to power and prosperity', the same number agreeing that only a 'strong leader' could rule the country in the circumstances of the time. Only

27 per cent agreed that Stalin was 'a cruel, inhuman tyrant responsible for the deaths of millions'.[30]

Gennadi Raikov, until 2004 the populist head of the People's Party, has said of Stalin that he 'died with his boots and overcoat on, never having stolen and having worked for his country' (which underestimates Stalin's role in raising funds for the Bolsheviks before the revolution). For his part, Boris Nemtsov, leader of the Union of Right Forces, has commented that 'When Stalin died, I still hadn't been born ... I didn't know Lenin or Stalin, and during the Khrushchev period I was a child. I was still young during Brezhnev's time. So I can say nothing either good or bad about these people. Let the old Communists evaluate their actions'.[31]

The same year, 2003, marked also the anniversary of the battle of Stalingrad, widely seen as the turning point of the Great Patriotic War. This anniversary revived discussion of the idea of restoring the name Stalingrad to today's Volgograd (few people are still around who can remember its pre-revolutionary name of Tsaritsyn). In this case surveys found that 51 per cent of Volgograd residents were opposed to the idea and 31 per cent were in favour of it. An attempt to introduce a bill into the Duma restoring the name Stalingrad failed.

A gradual change in the attitude to the past was noticeable by the end of Putin's first term in office. By then, the Soviet past had ceased to be evoked in a sharply black-or-white manner. *Izvestiya* reported that of five monuments to Lenin that had been restored in Krasnoyarsk krai over the past 18 months, only one of the restorations had been an initiative of a local Communist Party branch.[32] The report claimed that the restoration work had been carried out by 'simple people' and Russian citizens had learned to treat the symbols of the communist epoch with respect, regardless of partisan attitudes. Similar monuments were being restored in Kaluga, Rostov, Astrakhan and Kaliningrad regions. This nuanced attitude to the past could be noted also in the choice of themes on theatre and opera stages during the year.

Meanwhile, monuments were being constructed to the heroes of the democratic movement who had worked for the abolition of the Soviet Union. A monument to the physicist and human rights campaigner Andrei Sakharov was unveiled in St Petersburg on 5 May 2003 by the city authorities in a square that now bears his name. Sakharov's widow, Yelena Bonner, preferred not to attend the unveiling, calling the event speculation on the part of 'people who want to fill their pockets'.[33]

Assessment

A major theme recurring at many points in this chapter is the rise of a new post-Soviet Russian nationalism. The break-up of the Soviet Union created tensions arising from migration and involving both the majority populations of former Soviet republics and minorities within them. Cultural and religious tensions with ethnic implications have occurred within the Russian Federation itself, stemming from the rise of Muslim fundamentalism and enhanced by responses to the 11 September 2001 terrorist attacks. Most dramatic in its impact on daily life in Russia has been the Chechnya factor. Terrorist acts in Moscow itself, added to the anxieties of the parents of conscripts sent to fight in Chechnya, have led to the demonisation of the Chechens and, by the transmission of prejudice common in such cases, to discrimination against people with a Caucasian name or appearance. Racist attacks by youths on coloured people, particularly in Moscow, have been a further element of the new nationalism.

The connection between this nationalism with a racist content and the populism in the appeals of all the major parties of the 2003 Duma (phrased as 'patriotism' or 'popular patriotism') is that the former is the exclusive version and the latter the inclusive version of the same phenomenon. To appeal to the 'we-feeling' of Russians is to exclude the others. Ironically, the Soviet Union was remarkably inclusive in comparison with today's Russian Federation. Once the ruling party had settled the question of power in its own favour, it was able to allow the many ethnic minorities considerable social advantages, and Russian nationalists, who chafed at this accommodation of minorities, were not given free rein in the way that appears today to be the case.

This is not the only area where the fall of communism and the shift from a planned to a market economy have had regressive effects. In this chapter and Chapter 11, the sharply increased wage differentials, the rise in the cost of housing and communal services, and an upsurge in crime and corruption have been mentioned. The Russian people seem to be getting the worst of both worlds. On the one hand, they have lost the one real advantage of the Soviet system – social protection. On the other, the promise of the political advantages to be had from the turn to the market has not so far been fulfilled. It remains to be seen whether the economic progress seen during Putin's presidency will be used to halt regression in the social and political realms.

Further reading

This list is extended in view of the wide range of topics covered in this chapter. The first three titles are strongly recommended.

O. Shevchenko, '"Between the holes": emerging identities and hybrid patterns of consumption in post-socialist Russia', *Europe–Asia Studies*, 54:6 (2002), 841–66.

A. Ledeneva, *Russia's Economy of Favours* (Cambridge: Cambridge University Press, 1998).

V. Tishkov, *Ethnicity, Nationalism and Conflict in and After the Soviet Union* (London: Sage, 1997).

M. Flynn, *Migrant Settlement in the Russian Federation: Reconstructing 'Homes' and 'Homelands'* (London: Anthem Press, 2004).

H. Pilkington and G. Yemelianova, *Islam in Post-Soviet Russia* (London: RoutledgeCurzon, 2002).

H. Pilkington, *Looking West? Cultural Globalization and Russian Youth Culture* (Pittsburgh, PA: Penn State University Press, 2002).

M. Roman, 'Making Caucasians black: Moscow since the fall of communism and the racialisation of non-Russians', *The Journal of Communist Studies and Transition Politics*, 18:2 (2002), 1–27.

L. I. Shelley, 'The changing position of women: trafficking, crime and corruption', in D. Lane (ed.), *The Legacy of State Socialism and the Future of Transformation* (Lanham, MD: Rowman and Littlefield, 2002).

Z. Knox, *Russian Society and the Orthodox Church* (London: RoutledgeCurzon, 2004).

A. White, *Small-Town Russia: Postcommunist Livelihoods and Identities* (London: RoutledgeCurzon, 2004).

Websites

www.cia.gov/cia/publications/factbook/geos/rs.html
www.unece.org/stats/documents/2003/05/census/wp.1.add.1.e.pdf
(gives the preliminary results of the 2002 census).

Notes

1 *Argumenty i fakty*, no. 15, April 2003; *Nezavisimaya gazeta*, 25 April 2003.
2 www.newsru.com, 23 May 2003.
3 'A migration of sense', *Izvestiya*, 19 May 2003.
4 www.regions.ru, 24 July 2003.
5 In particular the Liberal Democratic Party, the Communist Party of the Russian Federation and, for a period, the Congress of Russian Communities.
6 'Constitution watch', *East European Constitutional Review*, 8:4 (1999), 40.
7 According to Major-General Alexander Gurov, chairman of the Duma's Security Committee, NTV, 20 June 2003.
8 *Novaya gazeta*, no. 30, 2003; *RFE/RL Newsline*, 30 April 2003.
9 *Argumenty i fakty*, no. 8, February 2003.
10 *RIA-Novosti*, 13 August 2002.
11 Interview with TV-Tsentr on 13 August 2003; see also W. H. Webster, *Russian Organised Crime and Corruption* (Washington, DC: Center for Strategic and International Studies, 2000), 37.
12 www.newru.com, 12 March 2003.
13 *Argumenty i fakty*, no. 9, February 2003.
14 A. Ledeneva, *Russia's Economy of Favours* (Cambridge: Cambridge University Press, 1998).
15 *Izvestiya*, 21 April 2004.
16 RenTV, 27 August 2003.
17 E. Bacon, 'Church and state in contemporary Russia', *The Journal of Communist Studies and Transition Politics*, 18:1, 97–116, p. 106.
18 *Yezhenedelnyi zhurnal*, nos 29–30, July 2004.

19 D. Glinski, 'Russia and its Muslims: the politics of identity at the international–domestic frontier', *East European Constitutional Review*, 11:1/2 (2002), 71–83.
20 *RFE/RL Newsline*, 16 October 2003.
21 ITAR-TASS news agency, 6 March 2003.
22 www.gazeta.ru, 19 May 2003.
23 See S. White, *Russia Goes Dry: Alcohol, State and Society* (Cambridge: Cambridge University Press, 1996).
24 Dunlop describes the relatively early emergence of groups concerned with conservation in Russia, in J. B. Dunlop, *The Faces of Contemporary Russian Nationalism* (Princeton, NJ: Princeton University Press, 1983), pp. 3–92.
25 www.newsru.com, 23 May 2003.
26 *RFE/RL Newsline*, 5 June 2003.
27 *RIA-Novosti*, 24 April 2003.
28 See L. I. Shelley, 'The changing position of women: trafficking, crime and corruption', in D. Lane (ed.), *The Legacy of State Socialism and the Future of Transformation* (Lanham, MD: Rowman and Littlefield, 2002).
29 *Izvestiya*, 17 September 2003.
30 *RFE/RL Newsline*, 5 March 2003.
31 *Tribuna*, 5 March 2003.
32 *Izvestiya*, 15 October 2003.
33 *Kommersant-Daily*, 5 May 2003.

Part V

The international dimension

Russia, the Commonwealth of Independent States and the world

Background

Although Russia no longer has the power to sustain the role of superpower of its Soviet predecessor, it remains none the less one of the world's major states by virtue of its size, the wealth of its natural resources and its retained military strength, which includes a substantial nuclear capability. Moreover, since the turn of the century the Russian economy, disrupted by the reforms and the dislocations of the years of Boris Yeltsin's presidency, has been recovering strongly. The Russian Federation has been recognised officially by the international community as the successor state to the Soviet Union, and heir to the latter's hegemonic role in terms of the large scale of its armed forces, its military bases and its nuclear weapons. This is acknowledged by its incorporation into the G8 – the organisation of the world's leading industrial nations.

The collapse of the Soviet Union, however, required a radical rethinking of foreign-policy options – in relations with the United States, the North Atlantic Treaty Organisation (NATO), the European Union (EU), Japan and a rapidly developing China. At the same time, the newly acquired independence of the Central Asian countries on its southern border has meant that Russia has had to contend with an increasingly assertive Muslim radicalism in states that it can no longer directly control.

In its relations with the other major powers, Russia has a source of influence and power that none of them can match – its wealth in fossil fuels. However, the extent to which it can be sure of controlling the routes by which its gas and oil are delivered to consumer countries is uncertain. Here, Russia's relations with the states on its borders that had once formed part of the Soviet Union are determinant. For this, but also for many other reasons, Russia's relations with the Commonwealth of Independent States (CIS) – the organisation that enrols all but three of the former Soviet republics – heavily influence its relations with the rest of the world. Since many in Russia's political class have not fully accepted the loss of these territories, relations with the CIS are part of Russia's internal politics. For these reasons this chapter is divided into two parts. The first deals with the CIS and views Russia's international relations through that prism. The second deals with those aspects of Russia's foreign affairs that do not directly involve the CIS. The distinction between the two, particularly as concerns Central Asia and the Caucasus, is not always easy to sustain. It is often chiefly a matter of two different perspectives, equally important, on the same policy area.

The Commonwealth of Independent States

When the Soviet Union was dissolved at a meeting at Belovezha near Minsk in 1991 (Chapter 1), the three leaders who were gathered there created the CIS (Table 14.1) to serve as a looser successor association which the released former components of the Soviet Union might choose to join. The Baltic republics – Estonia, Latvia and Lithuania – did not so choose, Georgia at first also holding aloof. The leaders of the remaining 11 states met in Almaty in Kazakhstan on 21 December as equal partners at what was the effective foundation of the CIS. In 1993 Georgia finally joined them, at the end of two years of unsuccessful warfare against Abkhazia, a territory within its republic.

The initial attitudes towards the CIS on the part of its members varied from strong support by Kazakhstan, Uzbekistan, Tajikistan and Kyrgyzstan to equally strong reservations from Turkmenistan (where a despot sought his advantage in holding Russia and the CIS at a distance), from Moldova and from Ukraine. In the last of these a determined movement for independence had long existed during the Soviet period. It was strongest in western Ukraine, the territory brought into the republic with the end of the Second World War. Belarus and Armenia were initially equivocal, supporting some initiatives of the new organisation but abstaining from others. Looking ahead, Belarus was to forge the closest political links with the Russian Federation of all the CIS

Table 14.1 *Population of CIS countries*

Country	Population	Year of census/estimate
Armenia	3,326,448	2003 estimate
Azerbaijan	7,830,764	2003 estimate
Belarus	10,350,194	2002 census
Georgia	4,934,413	2003 estimate
Kazakhstan	16,741,519	2002 census
Kyrgyzstan	4,753,003	2000 census
Moldova	4,431,570	2002 census
Russian Federation	145,181,900	2002 census
Tajikistan	6,863,752	2003 census
Turkmenistan	4,603,244	2002 census
Ukraine	48,396,470	2002 census
Uzbekistan	25,563,441	2002 census

states. In time also – in fact in the aftermath of 11 September 2001 – Russia's relations with Uzbekistan, Tajikistan and Kyrgyzstan in Central Asia, and with Georgia in the Caucasus, were to suffer severe political buffetings as a result of interventions from outside the CIS.

Problems stemming from the break-up of the Soviet Union

Three major problems for the CIS followed from the break-up of the Soviet Union, concerning borders, people and material assets, often in close interconnection. One severe case arose while the Soviet Union was still in existence, when in 1988 the Armenian population of Nagorno-Karabakh, an Armenian enclave inside Azerbaijan, attempted to effect a union with their kin state, Armenia. Savage inter-ethnic fighting ensued, including a massacre of Armenians in Sumgait in Azerbaijan.

Less dramatic, but of critical importance to Russia, was the position of the 25 million Russians who, on the break-up of the Union, found themselves subjects of newly independent states. In Soviet days Russians, and to a lesser extent Ukrainians, were spread across the former republics of the Union, partly by choice but more often as a result of political and technical postings. Three concentrations of Russian settlement were to cause especial problems – in the Baltic states, in the Crimea (now part of an independent Ukraine) and in Transdniestria – a strip of land on the left bank of the River Dniestr inside Moldova, separated from the Russian Federation by Ukraine.

The last of these illustrates well the complexities in the fall-out from the collapse of the Soviet Union. Moldova, now independent, contained a population of Russians and Ukrainians in the eastern part of its territory, where privileged establishments of the Soviet defence industry were located. Moreover, pending a resolution on its future, the former Soviet Fourth Army was based there, on the territory of an independent state, Moldova, separated from the Russian Federation by an also independent Ukraine. Resistance on the part of Russians and Ukrainians to being incorporated into Moldova led to open warfare around the Moldovan town of Bendery in 1992, with considerable loss of life. The presence of the Fourth Army helped to defuse the situation, its commander, Alexander Lebed, brokering a peace, and making a name for himself that was to set him on the road to a major role in Russian politics (he was to negotiate also the 1994 peace in Chechnya at Kasavyurt, and to be elected governor of the important krai of Krasnoyarsk), before an untimely death in a helicopter crash in April 2002 removed him from the list of credible contestants for a future presidency.

In the Baltic republics the Russian population found itself subjected to discrimination. The percentage of Russians in Estonia was 30.33 and in Latvia 33.96. Discrimination in these countries took the form of requiring a facility in the state language as a necessary qualification for citizenship, as well as for a range of occupations.

There were also acute problems in Georgia, where three ethnic minorities had been allocated their own territories within the republic in the Soviet period – Abkhazia and Adjaria as autonomous republics and South Ossetia as an autonomous district. In 1991 the Abkhazians took up arms to fight for independence from Georgia, with the connivance of the Russian Federation, which was opposing the Georgian President at that time, Zviad Gamsakhurdia. The struggle ended with the triumphant entry of Abkhaz forces into the territory's capital, Sukhum, on 27 September 1993 with Russian air support, and since then Abkhazia has enjoyed a *de facto* independence. Moves by Adjaria to obtain a similar degree of independence were thwarted through negotiations in mid-2004. Tensions in South Ossetia at that point still escaped a resolution, in good part because of Russia's insistence on maintaining a strong influence in that territory, in large measure through its peace-keeping force there.

Many in Russia refuse to take the break-up of the Soviet territory as final. There are voices in the party-political spectrum – most notably the Liberal Democratic Party – that make plain their support for a restitution of the Soviet territory as a single political space. On 28 November 2003, the Minister of Emergency Situations, Sergei Shoigu, said that he hoped 'to live to see the day when we have one big country within the borders of the Soviet Union'.[1] At the diplomatic level, the Russian Federation has never formally fixed its boundaries with the former Soviet republics. For example, when Kazakhstan ratified its land borders with Turkmenistan, Uzbekistan and Kyrgyzstan in July 2003, the border with Russia was left undefined. While the loss of the Soviet sphere of influence in Eastern Europe has had to be formally acknowledged, together with the eastwards advance of NATO, the very loss of that position has caused the Federation to be especially sensitive about its new western boundary. It is for this reason that, as noted in Chapter 13, the Federation's spokespeople systematically refer to the other former Soviet territories as the 'near abroad'.

The organisation of the CIS

The CIS has a loose organisational structure – necessarily, in view of memories of the Soviet regime. Its central institutions are a Council of Heads of State and a Council of Heads of Government, each of which meets at least twice a year, with the chair rotating. It has an Executive Committee to provide administrative continuity. The summits of heads of state are concerned chiefly with coordination of policy, by some or all of the member states.

The real business of intra-CIS relations is conducted either on a bilateral basis, with Russia usually at the hub, or through groups of states coming together on issues of regional importance, in some cases drafting treaties to formalise a shared interest, with Russia either directly or indirectly playing a role. Despite Russian aspirations at the start there has been no unified military command, nor is there any formal economic planning for the CIS as a whole. The Russian Duma has a Committee for Russians Abroad and CIS Affairs, as has the Federation Council, and the President has an adviser with the same brief.

The CIS in Russia's international relations

Three factors in particular have affected Russia's relations with its CIS partners. First, the United States' war on terrorism brought that power physically into the regions on Russia's southern border, in Central Asia and in the Caucasus. Second, on assuming the presidency, Putin gave relations with the CIS a high priority, and the influence of the *siloviki* (officials with a security background) in Russia's politics added further stiffening to the determination to keep a hold on the CIS countries. Third, Russia needed protection for the routes of its hydrocarbon exports and most of the likely routes lay through CIS states.

The quest for integration

In January 2000, Vladimir Putin approved a document entitled 'The Main Directions of the Development of Russia's Relations with the CIS Member States'. Its chief provisions asserted:

- the priority of the CIS in Russian foreign policy;
- the need for a pragmatic and individual approach to Russia's CIS partners which would take account of their willingness to consider Russian interests;
- the importance of economic cooperation and the promotion of Russia's business interests;
- the need to establish clear priorities in the direction of integration, with a stress on bilateral negotiations.

It has not been an overt aim of the Russian leadership to force integration on the CIS countries. On the other hand, it need not be, given the degree of interdependence that exists, or can be made to exist through leverage stemming from Russia's immense and varied resources.

However, although those who have charge of Russia's diplomacy have no overt aim of absorbing the CIS states, Russia has none the less pursued a policy of integration and bonding wherever possible. A first form of attempted bonding has been through diplomacy, and the signing of a great number of treaties and agreements. Here, very little integration has in fact been achieved. Despite all the signatures placed on imposing documents and all the meetings that have been held to reaffirm loyalty to agreements made, most CIS countries have manifested little motivation for the development of the Commonwealth. From the start it has been looked upon as a means of arranging the multiple divorce that the break-up of the Soviet Union constituted.

A second avenue for seeking increasing integration has been through communication and exchange, promoting where possible the use of the Russian language and a single currency, and through developing trading links. Third, Russia has the natural resources and the military power to win compliance with its interests and has made use of this leverage. Finally, and most recently, Russia has devised complex ways of using Russian citizenship as a means of bonding.

Treaties and agreements

In one case, moves towards integration within the CIS have led to a full constitutional proposal for political union – between the Russian Federation and Belarus. In 1994 negotiations were set in motion to create a Russia–Belarus Union, with a Higher State Council to regulate its affairs. The terms that the President of Belarus, Alexander Lukashenka, sought have been higher than the Kremlin has been prepared to cede. Lukashenka, for example, hoped for parity in running a common currency, but the Russian State Bank insisted on having sole responsibility for it. He also hoped for a rotating presidency (which could have made him President of the Russia–Belarus Union). The cards have always been in Russia's hands, though this is not enough to explain Lukashenka's cantankerous behaviour. By 2003 a crisis had developed over a proposed joint venture which would have involved Russia's taking a stake in Belarus's gas pipeline company, Beltranshaz. As part of the deal Russia was to deliver gas to Belarus at a preferential price. As with the proposed common currency, the deal collapsed when Lukashenka demanded a 50 per cent holding in the joint company, while Russia insisted on holding a controlling stake. A preferential oil contract also fell. The dispute rumbled on into 2004, with Russia stopping and restarting deliveries of gas. When, on 2 April 2004, the Duma unanimously adopted a resolution on the Russia–Belarus Union marking its eighth anniversary, it was a dismal reminder that nothing significant had been done to give the Union any substance.

Beyond this exceptional exercise in constitutional diplomacy, the CIS states have been engaged in extensive treaty making. The treaties have concerned economics and defence as well as simply cooperation and confidence-building measures. At times they have involved a group internal to the CIS states and at other times they have linked a group of CIS countries with the world beyond. Usually Russia has played a key part in their creation, but in some cases has had no direct role at all and in at least one case the aim has been actually to resist Russian domination. Such treaties have included the following:

- An agreement between the Russian Federation, Ukraine, Belarus and Kazakhstan was announced on 23 February 2003 to establish a 'single economic space' covering those four countries and aimed ultimately at creating a regional organisation that other states might see fit to join. It was intended to represent a milestone in the evolution of the CIS, as the creation of the single economic space would accelerate the economic restructuring that the participating countries were engaged in, requiring uniform customs, currency and budgetary policies. An important part of the aim as stated was that the four countries could enter the World Trade Organization as an integrated economic bloc, but this is unlikely to eventuate. Commentators held that combining the four countries – with a total population of 219 million people – was the most ambitious Kremlin initiative since the collapse of the Soviet Union and could lead to the creation of a new regional entity. An agreement establishing the single economic space was ratified by the Russian State Duma on 20 April 2004. It was ratified on the same date by Ukraine and Kazakhstan, and on 23 April by Belarus. The prospects for the single economic space suffered a major setback in the sequel to the 2004 presidential election in Ukraine.

- The Eurasian Economic Community was set up in May 2001 with the Russian Federation, Belarus, Kazakhstan, Tajikistan and Kyrgyzstan as members. In its early days movement towards its aims of creating a customs union and expanding integration in the economic and humanitarian fields was slow, but more solid progress has followed an effort by the Russian Federation and Kazakhstan to move towards greater integration.

- In the mid-1990s a group of CIS states – Georgia, Ukraine, Azerbaijan and Moldova – came together on the basis of their fears of Russian domination. In April 1999 their representatives, together with those of Uzbekistan, whose membership of the group has been intermittent, met in Washington to clarify their shared concerns. The choice of venue indicates a US involvement in the crystallisation of the group, which in its revived form came to be known as GUUAM (the initial letters of the names of its members). With no formal organisation other than a Committee of National Coordinators, set up in 2000, GUUAM's chief aims are to preserve its members' independence, to express and defend shared interests in infrastructure projects, particularly ones involving oil, and cooperation on security matters. A meeting of its Committee in March 2004 was called with the intention of reactivating the group after a period of lacklustre activity.

- The existence of GUUAM and the growing US military presence in Central Asia after 11 September 2001 were instrumental in the creation of the Organisation of the Agreement on Collective Security (ODKB) in Dushanbe in Tajikistan on 28 April 2003. The Agreement revived a treaty dating from 1992 that involved Russia, Belarus, Armenia, Kazakhstan, Kyrgyzstan and Tajikistan (the Collective Security Treaty). The new organisation had the same membership. In its new form it has its own budget, secretariat, military staff and rapid-deployment force. Its main military base is at the Kant airfield in Kyrgyzstan.

Thus the ODKB and GUUAM represent a divergence in defence matters within the CIS, with Uzbekistan playing an equivocal role. It is one manifestation of the sharpening of a rivalry between Russia and the United States in Central Asia and the Caucasus.

A prominent part in this extensive treaty making has been played by Nursultan Nazarbaev, the President of Kazakhstan. He has stalwartly resisted all US blandishments to abandon or qualify his close relationship with the Russian Federation and has emerged as the major figure outside Russia supporting an increased integration of the CIS. As well as being connected with most of the initiatives recorded above, he has been a prime mover in the creation of two further groups, this time looking eastwards, but still concerned with holding US power at bay:

- The Conference on Interactions and Confidence-building Measures in Asia (CICA) brings together the heads of state of China, Mongolia and Russia with their counterparts in 13 other Central, South and South-west Asian states. Its objectives include encouraging cooperation through multilateral initiatives promoting peace, security and stability in Asia, increasing trade and economic links, and the protection of human rights and fundamental freedoms.
- The Shanghai Cooperation Organisation (SCO) was created in 1996 and originally comprised Russia, China, Kazakhstan, Kyrgyzstan and Tajikistan, with Uzbekistan joining later. At first the SCO lacked clarity of both aims and operating structure, but it was given a sense of purpose by the Pentagon's move into Central Asia in the wake of 11 September 2001. This led Russia and China to revive the SCO as a means of responding to the establishment of a US military presence in Central Asia. Uzbekistan's indeterminate allegiances had for a number of years made its role in a number of regional organisations equivocal, but economic and commercial considerations were, by the time of an SCO summit in Tashkent in 2003, dictating an orientation towards Russia.

Making Russian an official language

Russian was not universally spoken throughout the multinational Soviet Union but it was the official language of communication, the elites of all the Union republics spoke it and it was a standard part of the school curriculum. It was the language of command in the armed forces. With the break-up of the Soviet Union, all but two of the CIS states – Belarus and Kyrgyzstan – had disestablished Russian as an official language of state and it was not going to be easy for the Russian leadership to reverse that process. None the less, in June 2003 the State Duma debated the steps that might be taken to have Russian accepted as an official language throughout the CIS, and has called for a programme to be adopted promoting familiarity with it.[2] By then circumstances were developing in Russia's favour. At a time when Russia was opening membership of its armed forces to other members of the CIS, and when Tajiks, for example, were finding employment in the Federation in increasing numbers, an inability to speak Russian was a disadvantage. It was a rational move when the Tajik President, Imomali Rakhmonov, made the study of Russian once again compulsory in Tajik schools with effect from September 2003 (surprisingly, there was already a shortage of Russian-language textbooks in that country).

Defence and peace keeping

Defence links within the CIS have involved far more than diplomacy. As noted, the establishment of an airbase at Kant in Kyrgyzstan contributed a physical response to the presence of the United States in Central Asia – which had itself acquired a Kyrgyz base near Bishkek. The Kant base was a Central Asian addition to Russian military bases already existing in all three of the trans-Caucasian states of Armenia, Azerbaijan and Georgia.

Outside Central Asia, too, military cooperation has been developed in the CIS, as with the Russian early-warning radar installation (intended to become part of an integrated CIS anti-aircraft defence system), the joint naval exercises mounted annually by Russia and Ukraine, and the close cooperation between Russia and Kazakhstan involving the use of the Baikonur space facility; in addition, Russia signed a mutual defence treaty with Kazakhstan in January 2004. Even Azerbaijan, so reticent in its relations with Russia, develops its own defence industry in cooperation with the Russian.

Peace keeping, too, has provided opportunities for Russia to acquire influence and assert its strength, notably in Transdniestria and Georgia. In the latter case its task has been to control events in Abkhazia, in Ajaria and in South Ossetia. CIS leaders have, at a number of their summit meetings, issued statements upholding Georgia's sovereignty over Abkhazia and Russia itself has an interest in maintaining stability in a volatile area that includes Chechnya.

Energy

While some of the economic ties bonding members of the CIS with Russia have been set up through diplomatic means, others simply follow the logic of Russia's commanding position in sources of energy. The withdrawal of a preferential price for gas as a political weapon in Russia's dealings with Belarus was noted above. Many CIS members are dependent on Russia for their energy, which gives Russia leverage over them, particularly when they accumulate debts for energy supplied. In January 2003, Russia's powerful monopoly United Energy Systems (EES) bought 75 per cent of Georgia's energy distribution network from the US company AES, and later in the year acquired 80 per cent of Armenia's power-generating capacity in a debt-for-equity exchange. EES reportedly owns a third of the shares in a Ukrainian–Russian holding company in the power sector. Ukraine, Georgia and Moldova import most of their gas and oil supplies from Russia and have at times accumulated large arrears of payment. Even states that are rich in fuel, such as Azerbaijan, depend on Russian pipelines for exporting it, while the pipelines exporting Turkmenistan's gas are controlled by Gazprom.

Russia has made it clear since the birth of the Federation, in successive versions of its Military Doctrine, that it is prepared to intervene by whatever means necessary to maintain its oil and gas installations in the 'near abroad'. This has raised the spectre of the 'Brezhnev doctrine', proclaimed by the Soviet leadership in justification of the Warsaw Pact's intervention in Czechoslovakia in 1968.

Citizenship

Finally, the Russian leadership has come to see that there is a connection between its policy in the field of citizenship and the chances of increased integration in the CIS. This has been a by-product of immigration into Russia from the CIS countries and the tensions in Central Asia and the Caucasus. It has thus occurred in a roundabout and largely unplanned way, and has involved an important reversal of policy away from exclusion in the sphere of citizenship. In Chapter 13 it was noted that the stringent Law on Citizenship of 2002 caused concerns among demographers, who feared a consequent decline in the population and the workforce, and among those who resented the law's falling on their previous fellow citizens in the Soviet space. The amendments that were passed to relax that law were targeted in particular at former Soviet citizens in the 'near abroad'. This change in policy towards immigration in general had the effect of improving the image of Russia in the 'near abroad' and with it of the CIS as a community. At the same time, the authorities in the Kremlin began to see advantages in recruiting citizens of the CIS countries into the Russian armed forces, which could be expected to have the same effect.

Russia and the wider world

Russia's relations with the wider world from the collapse of the Soviet Union has passed through three phases:

- The first phase was brief – from the collapse of the Soviet Union at the end of 1991 to 1993 – and was a continuation of the opening to the West that had developed in the Gorbachev years. This Western orientation was a natural corollary of the end of the Soviet Union's isolation from the world economy and the end of the cold war.
- The second phase, from about 1993 to 2001, but already prefigured in official statements in 1992, was one of a reaction to this accommodation to the West. The Federation now made clear its interest in maintaining stability in the Soviet Union's former territories and its intention to assert its status as a major power. The Minister for International Affairs of the first

phase, Andrei Kozyrev, remained uncomfortably in that post until 1996, when he was replaced by Evgeni Primakov, a doyen of Soviet diplomacy.
• The third phase, from 11 September 2001 and the terrorist attacks on the United States onwards, contained two strands. On the one hand, there was a further firming up of Russia's oversight of the CIS countries, accompanied by forthright statements of its readiness to use force – including nuclear weapons – in defence of its interests. On the other, US President George W. Bush's war on terrorism, coinciding with Putin's attempts to deal finally with the Chechen question, brought about a relationship between the two leaders that modified Russia's increased self-assertion on the world scene.

In the aftermath of the invasion of Iraq, to which the Federation had been hostile, the broad outlines of the third phase have maintained themselves, but the crisis gave Russia a chance to emphasise its long-standing support for the role of the United Nations. At a conference in May 2003 the Russian Minister for International Affairs, Igor Ivanov, gave his view of how a new system of international relations should be organised. It should, he said, be based on multi-polarity together with multilateral global cooperation. Multi-polarity meant recognising that, in the international arena, power clustered around a number of focal points. He presented Moscow's understanding of multilateral global cooperation as a structure with the United Nations Security Council at its head and its affairs conducted through bilateral discussions among regional organisations. Ivanov had earlier assigned the United Nations a central role in the fight against international terrorism, in first place in a list of what he saw as the principal threats to international security after the close of the cold war, the others being organised crime, narcotics trafficking, the spread of weapons of mass destruction, international financial crises, ecological disasters and epidemics.[3]

In the few words that he devoted to foreign affairs in his address to the Federal Assembly in May 2003, Putin introduced the European dimension, and found room to approve of links with the EU after the ritual assertion of the importance of ties with the CIS countries. This served as a marker of the balance that Russia would have to strike in its relations with the United States, on the one hand, and the EU, on the other, though in the circumstances it was probably a rhetorical rebuke to the United States for setting out to control the Iraqi oil market. The complementarity of their economies, and the fact that Russia and the United States share a responsibility for global security through their nuclear arsenals, mean that Russia must privilege relations with the United States over those with the EU. It must none the less also be a priority of Russian diplomacy to ensure that these preponderant links with US interests do not get in the way of an advance towards closer integration with European structures. Putin has always emphasised the need for ties with Europe. His personal experience in the German Democratic Republic (see Box 2.2, p. 28) and his familiarity with the German language no doubt play a part here.

Relations with the United States

Two factors disproportionately influence Russia's relations with the United States. The first is that the United States is the world's greatest user of energy and the search for secure sources to provide for its needs is a priority in its foreign relations, while Russia has the resources to cater for those needs. It has been estimated that Russia could ultimately supply between one and two million barrels of oil a day to the United States, about 15 per cent of that country's current demand. The second is more recent in its origin; in fact, it came to full prominence only after 11 September 2001. Putin's presidency has been dogged by a failure to solve the problem posed by Chechnya's struggle for independence. Coming to power with a promise to bring the war in Chechnya to a close, Putin had achieved little by the autumn of 2001. The destruction of the World Trade Center enabled him to link his difficulties to the massive emotional response of US citizens to the New York attacks. From that point on, the United States was less outspoken in its criticisms of the way in which the war in Chechnya was being waged, as negotiations about supplies of Russian oil, and mergers between Russian and US producers, moved ahead. A complementarity of interests was bearing fruit.

This has not prevented conflicts of interest arising at a number of points. First, their complementary interests concealed deep sources of competition, which are of more enduring significance. In attacking the bases of Al Qaeda in Afghanistan, the Pentagon was establishing a military presence in Central Asia and was in this way promoting the containment of Russia, which is one of the abiding planks of US foreign policy. The task for Russia has been, in turn, to contain this containment. Georgia, where Russia was negotiating over the retention of two remaining military bases in 2004, here assumes a particular prominence: first, because of the ability of Chechen fighters to operate from bases in Georgia's Pankisi Gorge, which borders Chechnya (this came to be at the forefront of intense diplomacy involving not only Russia and the United States, but also the Organisation for Security and Co-operation in Europe and the EU); and second, because the Caucasus is a crucial area for the routing of oil pipelines from Russia and the Caspian towards the West. There was a time when the British Empire confronted imperial Russia in the Caucasus and Central Asia in what was termed the Great Game. In this new Great Game, the collapse of the Soviet Union has allowed competition between two major industrial giants over energy sources and their supply routes to emerge in the region, and this, in the sequel to 11 September, has fanned the flames of Muslim fundamentalism.

A second area of discord between Russia and the United States concerns nuclear proliferation. Here again, the two countries pursue common goals that conflict in particular cases. Cooperation was evident in the agreement, reached in Vienna in March 2003, that Russia would shut down three nuclear reactors producing weapons-grade plutonium, in Tomsk oblast and Krasnoyarsk krai, in return for assistance from the United States in replacing them with thermoelectric plants elsewhere. But a major difference arose when the United States challenged Russia's policy in helping Iran to complete a nuclear-power installation at Bushehr. This was a long-standing commitment by Moscow to an ally, and Russia had headed off potential hostility to it by insisting that spent nuclear fuel would be returned to Russia. In May 2003, the United States claimed that Iran was instead developing a secret capability for enriching uranium and urged Russia to end its participation in the project. Russia at first refused to comply, but in the end found the political cost of persisting with this project too high, and withdrew its cooperation.

Arms control

The related field of arms control had naturally been transformed with the fall of the Soviet Union. A proposal to cut the number of nuclear warheads at the disposal of each side was discussed during a visit by Putin to Bush's ranch in November 2001. By that time the complementary interests between Russia and the United States over oil and combating international terrorism were beginning to work. It was proposed that each side reduce its long-range weapons by some two-thirds, to 1,700–2,200 warheads by the end of 2012, and in May 2002 an agreement was signed. When the two Presidents met in St Petersburg in June 2003 to exchange the ratification documents, they agreed that their countries would cooperate also in creating an anti-missile defence system and an international space station.

These developments met with resistance from two internal quarters. It came, first, from the Russian military, which strongly resented the United States' presence in Central Asia. Second, when the agreement was debated in the State Duma, the Communist Party took the lead in decrying this sell-out to the old enemy.

The 2003 invasion of Iraq

The clear determination of the United States to invade Iraq with whatever allies would willingly support it or be brought to do so placed Russian diplomacy in a quandary. Putin had to move cautiously, since to fall in with that design would go against Russia's established alignments and would endanger its interests in Iraq itself – in the development of Iraq's oil production and in Iraq's substantial debt to Russia. He had to consider also the implications of being seen by Europe, China and the Islamic countries as having caved in to pressure from the United States. Yet Putin was anxious to preserve the entente that had been built up around the joint commitment to combating terrorism, and he was at pains to justify the joint statement that Russia, France and Germany presented on 11 February 2003 condemning military action against Iraq. Indeed, he turned it to his own account by hailing it as the first brick in the construction of a multi-polar world.

At issue was whether Russia would veto the draft resolution submitted to the UN Security Council in March 2003 by the United States, the United

Kingdom and Spain. It was made clear by US spokesmen that a Russian veto would bring risks to investment, to the anticipated anti-missile defence and to cooperation in security matters, including the battle against international terrorism. Meanwhile, opposition inside Russia to the war was strong. On 5 March the All-Russian Public Opinion Research Centre measured opposition to it at 91 per cent of respondents. There were boycotts of US goods, while restaurants and cafes refused to serve US and British people, and massive demonstrations were held in many cities, large enough to allow occasional charges of manipulation to be discounted. The radio station Ekho Moskvy reported on 13 February that some 2,500 Russian citizens had let the Iraqi embassy know that they were ready to fight in Iraq against any US attack. As noted in Chapter 13, when the attack came, Telget Tadzhetdin, the supreme mufti of Russia and the European countries of the CIS, pronounced a jihad against the United States.

However, in April Russia had to respond to further US pressure when Washington proposed that the sanctions imposed on Iraq under Saddam Hussein be lifted, so that a new administration could use Iraq's oil revenues to finance the reconstruction of the country. Behind Russia's response that this step should not be taken before it had been certified that Iraq was free of weapons of mass destruction no doubt lay Russian apprehensions that it would be badly placed in a reorganisation of Iraq's petro-chemical industry.

In the aftermath of the war, Russia supported the UN Security Council's resolution submitted in May by the United States. While the prerogatives that the draft gave to the United States and Britain in Iraq's reconstruction were extensive, it also included programmes favourable to Russia and made clear the responsibility of any new Iraqi government for the country's debts. It remained for Ivanov to congratulate the coalition that had waged the war for rediscovering the importance and value of the United Nations.

Russia's changing relations with NATO

In mid-February 2000, NATO's Secretary-General, George Robertson, visited Moscow for discussions with the Russian Ministers for International Affairs and Defence. The resulting joint statement was positive in expressed intentions for the future, but it revealed continuing sources of tension, reflecting the turn from Minister for International Affairs Kozyrev's warmth to the West in the Yeltsin presidency. The sources of tension included:

- the bringing of NATO's boundary closer to that of Russia with the proposed accession of new members from the earlier Soviet sphere of influence (in three cases from the Soviet Union itself);
- the continuing damage done to NATO–Russian relations by the war in Kosovo, which removed the accepted barrier against the use of military force in cases of ethnic conflict;

- Western criticisms of the way in which the war in Chechnya was being waged.

The first of these was of the greatest and most lasting importance. In 1997 a NATO–Russia Permanent Joint Council had been created on the initiative of Javier Solana, then NATO's Secretary-General. Set up with an agenda of monitoring weapons of mass destruction, peace keeping and combating international terrorism, it went on to deal with the strains imposed by the negotiations for NATO's admission of a series of proposed new members, and by NATO's bombing of Kosovo in 1999, which led to Russia suspending its contacts with the Council for most of that year.

The next major landmark in the relationship between Russia and NATO has to be seen together with the strategic arms reductions agreed between Russia and the United States on 13 May 2002. On the following day the members of NATO, meeting in Reykjavik, agreed to the establishment of a joint NATO–Russia Council. The Council was established at the Rome summit on 28 May 2002 and opened a new chapter in NATO–Russia relations. Although this Council's brief was broadly similar to that of the Permanent Joint Council which it replaced, the new body was hailed as 'historic' by the NATO Secretary-General (now Lord Robertson) and more generally as marking the final demise of the cold war. Russia would thereby become a partial member of the Alliance and would be for the first time an equal partner in discussions on matters as crucial as military cooperation (including the war against terrorism), nuclear non-proliferation and international crisis management.

The agreement was a major milestone, confirming Russia's shift from being an implacable enemy of the West to being its partner. But, as with so many policy decisions that Russia has had to make since the fall of the Soviet Union, it presented a dilemma. Resentment of Russia's policies in relation to the United States and NATO, on the part of the Russian military but also in a substantial body of public opinion, had already been accumulating as a result of the foreign-policy decisions that Yeltsin and Putin had been taking. Those decisions seemed to subordinate military to economic considerations. But, integrated now into the world economy, and by that token aware of its economic vulnerability, Russia needed as much material help as could be mustered without compromising its security. It was a difficult balance to strike. The new international political atmosphere promised considerable savings in military procurement, but at what political cost and with what certainty that the winds of the new atmosphere would continue to blow so warm?

Russia had been cooperating with NATO for some time on matters such as joint sea-rescue operations, involving the standardisation of procedures and equipment, and training of personnel. At the same time as the 2002 agreement was being signed the Chief of the General Staff, Anatoli Kvashnin, was attending a NATO meeting on European security. Now cooperation could involve combating terrorism, possibly also joint peace-keeping operations, and – with the disaster of the *Kursk* submarine in mind – coordinated rescue operations at sea. Putin hailed as being of historic significance the fact that the Council session was being held in Moscow, and in the exchange of politenesses Robertson said that it would destroy the stereotype of Russia and NATO as adversaries.

The spirit of cooperation, however, could not mask Moscow's concerns about the eastward expansion of NATO, which had already brought Poland, the Czech Republic and Hungary into the Alliance. Now, with Bulgaria, Estonia, Latvia, Lithuania, Romania, Slovakia and Slovenia slated to join, Moscow's diplomacy was directed towards ensuring that NATO forces would not be deployed on Russia's immediate borders. An exchange of letters between the Russian Federation and the NATO Secretary-General in early April 2004, however, provided reassurances about Russia's major concerns and opened the way to future cooperation.[4]

Relations with the European Union

Russia's relations with the EU are based on the Partnership and Cooperation Agreement signed in December 1997, which set out a political, economic and trading framework. This was envisaged as leading to a liberalisation of trade and the establishing of closer relationships, as well as a common security and foreign policy. The EU is Russia's main trading partner, but the EU has a large trading deficit because of its imports of energy.

A common strategy, agreed in June 1999, called for:

- the consolidation of democracy and the rule of law in Russia;
- the integration of Russia into a common European economic and social space;
- cooperation in strengthening security in Europe and beyond;
- a response to common challenges concerning the environment, nuclear safety and the fight against crime.

The expansion of the EU in May 2004 to encompass seven former Soviet republics or satellites – the Czech Republic, Estonia, Hungary, Latvia, Lithuania, Poland and Slovakia – together with Slovenia, Cyprus and Malta, brought a number of problems that required resolution. Moscow was particularly concerned over the loss of preferential trade tariffs after its former Soviet bloc partners joined the EU. The EU, in turn, has been anxious about the control of immigration and international crime. Negotiations over the issues involved in the EU's enlargement led to a two-day summit in March 2004, at which the heads of government confirmed that the Partnership and Cooperation Agreement remained the essential cornerstone of the EU's relationship with Russia. The renewed Agreement was signed on 27 April 2004.

Kaliningrad

A particularly intractable problem has been posed by the fact that the Kaliningrad oblast is an enclave and is separated from the nearest other sub-ject of the Federation by a now independent Lithuania (see map on p. xiv). Kaliningrad shares a border with two states – Lithuania, which was part of the Soviet Union, and Poland, which was not. There has been a historical enmity between both of these and Russia. Lithuania, independent between the two world wars, bitterly resented incorporation in the Soviet Union in 1940 and its struggle for independence during the Gorbachev period was ferocious. In the case of Poland, a historical dislike and suspicion of Russia are today moderated by a certain pragmatism. With the fall of the Soviet Union, a major problem arose because supplies for Kaliningrad, notably for military bases there, had to be transported from Russia across Lithuania, or by sea.

Both Poland and Lithuania are now members of the EU. Russia has pressed very strongly for a special status for Kaliningrad, with a separate visa regime. The matter came to a head in May 2002, when the EU had to make a deci-sion on whether the normal visa arrangements should apply for entry to the territory after the proposed enlargement of the Union. It accepted the case put forward by Poland that Kaliningrad should not enjoy a special status. The oblast adjusted to this negative outcome by offering its residents an annual free visa and one free train ticket – or a discounted airplane or ferry ticket – to the rest of Russia.

One reason for the EU's insistence on strict visa regulations is its fear of substantial and possibly overwhelming illicit immigration across its new eastern border. There are also apprehensions about international crime and the traffic in narcotics. None the less, Russia and the EU have been working towards establishing a visa-free regime for travel between them by 2007. During a preliminary phase, while the regime is being gradually introduced, Russia is cooperating with EU border agencies to deal with questions of crime and illegal immigration.

Kaliningrad could, however, be a major asset for the Russian Federation in its relation with the EU, continuing to generate inward investment from Germany and serving as an entrepot for Russian trade with the EU.

The World Trade Organisation

Russia's relations with the EU have included discussions on Russia's aim of joining the World Trade Organisation, as, for example, at the summit meeting in Rome in November 2003. An issue raised at that summit illustrated one of the factors that have so far stood in the way of Russia's admission – in this case the persistence of subsidies in the reformed economy. One of the EU's key de-mands was that Russia increase its charges to domestic industry for gas, since the gas monopoly Gazprom has been charging domestic customers a price for gas that the EU considers contains a hidden subsidy. Other impediments have been the slow rate of liberalisation and of foreign participation in the economy, inefficiency in the administration of customs, a failure to enforce property rights and a more general weakness in the legislative framework concerning trade. At the time of writing, negotiations for Russia's entry into the World Trade Organisation were continuing.

Russia looks east

China

When the Chinese Communist Party came to power in 1949, there was a brief period of cooperation with the Soviet Union, which was expected to provide a model for rapid industrialisation. The expectation succumbed to a number of factors, in which ideological disputes were overlaid on Chinese resentment at Soviet tutelage. The Soviet advisers and technical experts were withdrawn in 1956, but tension continued to mount until, in 1973, relations between the two countries were broken off. For the best part of a quarter of a century Russia kept China at arm's length, avoiding military conflict and maintaining a minimum of diplomatic contact.

With the break-up of the Soviet Union, a new phase in Russian–Chinese relations opened. The catalyst was the creation, as a result of a series of agreements in 1996, of the SCO, noted above. The chief impulse behind the creation of the SCO was provided by China, which was seeking to increase its regional role. For Russia, the SCO would serve as one of the channels through which integration into the world economy might flow.

A 20-year 'friendship treaty' was signed between Russia and China in July 2001, but it was the visit of the Chinese leader, Jiang Zemin, to St Petersburg on 5 June 2002 for a meeting of the SCO that was the signal that Russian–Chinese relations were entering a new phase – 'A kind of Asian stage is opening in Russian foreign policy', said Alexander Yakovenko, a spokesman for the Russian Ministry of International Affairs.[5] It was preceded by a visit to China by the Russian Defence Minister, and in August 2002 it was the turn of the Russian Prime Minister, Mikhail Kasyanov, to visit Beijing. These various visits had four main concerns:

- Putin was anxious to reassure the Chinese about the rapid development of Russia's ties with the United States after 11 September 2001.
- Russia and China, acting together, offered a chance of successful mediation in the dispute between India and Pakistan, Russia's long-standing ties with India being matched by China's links with Pakistan.
- The intention was partly also to give substance to the SCO itself, with a view to establishing a regional structure for combating terrorism.
- Finally, the growing influence of the United States in the four Central Asian republics was no doubt not far from the minds of both Moscow and Beijing.

Russia's trade with China has been rising, and in May 2003 Putin proposed that the two countries double its volume over the next four to five years. China is the chief purchaser of Russian arms, and armaments account for some 20 per cent of trade between the countries (and some 40 per cent of Russia's yearly exports of arms overall). But more than trade is involved. The result of a visit to China by the Russian Defence Minister, Sergei Ivanov, at the end of May 2003 was a series of agreements covering an expansion of military links and the training of Chinese officers in Russian military establishments, in addition to the supply of new Russian weapons. On that occasion Ivanov was at pains to correct any impression that the recent strengthening of ties to the United States and NATO meant that Russia was neglecting relations with China. In an important development China and Russia signed a bilateral agreement on 14 October 2004 that ended a 40-year dispute over their mutual border.

Japan

Russia's relations with Japan are made difficult by an area of contention that shows no immediate sign of being resolved. Japan contests Russia's sovereignty over the Kurile Islands, which run northwards from Japan to Kamchatka. Since they enclose the Sea of Okhotsk and provide a passage to the ports of Nakhodka and Vladivostok, they are of considerable strategic importance to Russia. Russia has never signed a peace treaty with Japan to close the Great Patriotic War. Whenever the question of a peace treaty arises, the territorial question arises with it.

One of the most prominent factors in Russia's dealings with its neighbours is oil, together with the question of the routes that pipelines conveying it should follow. Japan has an interest in securing a route that would enable it to reduce its dependence on supplies from the Middle East, from which Japan currently imports 88 per cent of its oil.

The politics of oil

The reintegration of Russia into the world economy on the fall of the Soviet Union, at a time when competition for supplies of fossil fuels among energy-poor countries was increasing, was bound to project it into the forefront of the politics of oil. Furthermore, the strategic role of oil in its economy and in its diplomacy alike could only be increased as tensions mounted in the Middle East after 11 September 2001. The account given here concentrates on the vexed question of supply routes, which throws a particularly useful light on Russia's relations with the world beyond its borders.

In Soviet times major pipelines were laid down to carry oil and gas to Central Europe by land – there was no maritime component to this link. These pipelines have been available for extension and present few political problems.

The oil routes in three regions merit attention. The first involves a plan by LUKoil, Yukos, TNK and Sibneft to construct a $4.5 billion oil pipeline from western Siberia to the ice-free port of Murmansk in Russia's north-west, to enable oil and gas from the country's main oilfields in western and northern Siberia to be transported to the United States. The pipeline would pass over Russian territory alone on its way to the Atlantic, and the only major international problem that it raises is the substantial threat of pollution from disasters along Norway's northern coast as tankers take the oil to overseas destinations.

It is oil supply routes in a second region that give rise to the greatest conflicts of interest – those that transport oil from the Caspian to the Black Sea or the Mediterranean, or to the latter via the former. At issue is the question of control. To avoid Russian control of the route, the United States has directed its diplomacy and its pressure towards constructing routes that avoid Russia altogether.

For neither of the two major players is the question simple. For the Russians, the route of their pipeline from Baku in Azerbaijan to Novorossiisk on the Black Sea borders Chechnya (which yields an important perspective on the wars there), and while Azerbaijan is a member of the CIS, its loyalty to Moscow is equivocal. For the United States, while Turkey offers a secure route south-west to the Mediterranean, the existing route through Georgia to the Black Sea is far from secure. The construction of a pipeline through Turkey to Ceyhan in the eastern Mediterranean has therefore been of importance for the United States.

In Russia's east, a pipeline conveys oil to Angarsk near Irkutsk, but the route from there to the eastern seaboard has been subject to debate. The alternatives are, first, to continue on through Russian territory to Nakhodka, from where oil can be shipped by sea to the Pacific coast of the United States, but also to Japan across some 800 km of water. An added advantage of the Nakhodka route is that it would help to supply Russia's own eastern seaboard. The second planned alternative, seemingly the presidency's own preferred option, is to take the line to industrial Dajing in China. As matters stood at the start of Putin's second presidency, the Dajing alternative had been given priority, with the proceeds of that project being used to finance the pipeline to Nakhodka. Japan in any case is standing ready with favourable loans, pressing for the Nakhodka pipeline to have a capacity of one million barrels a day, which would ensure the project's profitability.

Previous chapters have ended with an 'Assessment' of the place that the material of the chapter occupies in a description of Russia's political system today. Russia's international relations are a special case, in that they lie outside the political system itself. At the same time, the political system and Russia's changing place in the world are intimately connected. It is a connection that today presents Russia with a particular challenge, which is treated in the Conclusion to this book, along with the other major challenges that confront Russia today.

Further reading

J. L. Black, *Vladimir Putin and the New World Order* (Lanham, MD: Rowman and Littlefield, 2003).

M. Bowker and C. Ross, *Russia After the Cold War* (London: Pearson, 2000).

P. Duncan, *Russian Foreign Policy from El'tsin to Putin* (London: RoutledgeCurzon, 2005).

R. Fawn (ed.), *Realignments in Russian Foreign Policy* (London: Frank Cass, 2003).

R. Sakwa and M. Webber, 'The Commonwealth of Independent States, 1991–1998', *Europe–Asia Studies*, 51:3 (1999), 379–415.

D. Lynch, *Russian Peace-Keeping Strategies in the CIS: The Cases of Moldova, Georgia and Tajikistan* (Basingstoke: Macmillan, 1999).

S. Cohen, *Failed Crusade: America and the Tragedy of Post-Communist Russia* (New York: Norton, 2000).

H. Grabbe and K. Hughes, *Enlarging the EU Eastwards* (London: Royal Institute of International Affairs, 1998).

M. Webber, *Russia and Europe: Cooperation and Conflict* (Basingstoke: Macmillan, 2000).

Websites

www.ceip.org/files/programs/rea_home.asp (Carnegie endowment)
www.integrumworld.com/eng_test (for CIS and international relations)

Notes

1 *RFE/RL Newsline*, citing RosBalt, ORT and other sources, 1 December 2003.
2 *Izvestiya*, 11 June 2003; see also *RFE/RL Newsline*, 11 June and 26 September 2003.
3 *Rossiiskaya gazeta*, 25 March 2003.
4 On Russia's relations with NATO and the EU see V. Baranovsky, 'Russia: a part of Europe or apart from Europe?', in A. Brown (ed.), *Contemporary Russian Politics: A Reader* (Oxford: Oxford University Press, 2001).
5 *Financial Times*, 7 June 2002.

Conclusion

Three decades after Mikhail Gorbachev gave the initial impulse to the process of change that would sweep away the Soviet Union and the power monopoly of its ruling Communist Party, the Russian Federation faces a series of challenges that, for the most part, could not easily have been foreseen at that earlier point. There is one, though, that certainly could have been foreseen, though not in the form it was to take after the disorder of the years of Boris Yeltsin's presidency and Vladimir Putin's response to that disorder – the difficulty of instituting a democratic polity in a society with a tradition of authoritarian rule and that had just emerged from a period of outright totalitarianism. That was the challenge most in view at the start of the reform process. Any move away from the communist power monopoly spelled progress, and for a decade after Gorbachev's call for glasnost it could be assumed that the foundations of democracy were being laid down.

Yet by the time of the Beslan tragedy in September 2004, a marked return to Soviet political practices was already clear and the regime's reaction to Beslan gave the process a determining impulse. The key feature of this near-complete restoration of the structure of Soviet politics is the acquisition by a single party of the levers necessary to ensure its dominance within the political system – a revival, that is, of the 'leading role of the party'. The two chief levers, as in the Soviet Union, are control of nominations to posts of political importance and control of the channels of communication. This book has recorded in detail the developments that have led to this near restoration, in which United Russia exercises a near monopoly of power, controlling the extent to which other actors can play a role in determining political choices.

- Control of the media, recorded in Chapter 12, is now complete enough to allow United Russia to project its own policy preferences and a view of itself as the sole authentic voice of the social interest, to the effective exclusion of other voices.
- The turning point in an atrophy of the electoral system can be dated to the

aftermath of the Beslan tragedy, when Putin revoked the direct election of regional governors and republican presidents. Interference in elections to the Duma had already deprived them of their free and open nature. If democracy is to develop at all in Russia, it cannot initially be through the operation of free elections. The ending at the same time of the ban on government ministers joining political parties led immediately to a number of ministers joining, or applying to join, United Russia.

- The establishment of control of nominations to key political posts has been less visible and has encountered less criticism. The President's extensive patronage powers are written in the constitution and the quiet development of a *nomenklatura* function in his Administration can reasonably be held to be subsumed under those powers. To that extent, today's *nomenklatura* has acquired a constitutionality that the Soviet *nomenklatura* could not boast. The extension of the President's prerogative in appointments to the posts of regional governor and republican president, however, even if it is held to be constitutionally endorsed, clearly undermines the regime's professed democratic aspirations.

- These developments have each contributed to the formation of a single party capable of perpetuating its own dominance within the political system. It was a significant moment when, on 3 June 2004, United Russia, in a revival of Soviet practice, opened the first of a series of party schools in Moscow, to form the cadres to administer society.[1] Introducing the measure to reporters, Valeri Bogomolov, secretary of the party's general council, also said that the party was considering introducing a test period for new members of the party, reviving the two-year 'candidate status' that recruits to the Communist Party of the Soviet Union were given. An example of how, in United Russia's statements, 'the Party' (with a capital 'P') is distinguished from 'all other political parties' (lower-case 'p') is recorded in Box 9.1 (p. 152). A much more substantial indication, noted above, was the rush of regional governors to join United Russia in the wake of Putin's decision to put their posts on the central *nomenklatura*. The only major distinction remaining between Putin's Russia and the practices associated with the Soviet 'leading role of the party' – the lack in the former of a regional structure of Party committees headed by a first Party secretary – was therewith diminished, and is likely to disappear in all but unimportant details.

These developments concern Russia's political structures. In the partially privatised economy there is no sign so far that the Soviet system of central command planning will be restored, and it is important for Russia to remain open to the world market, with which command planning in its Soviet form is incompatible. It was noted in Chapter 1 that in undertaking political and economic reform simultaneously, Russia has differed from China – a similarly large-scale state facing the same problems of transition from communism. There, the political system has retained its strongly authoritarian nature while economic reform has proceeded with considerable success. Though returning to Soviet political practices in so many ways, Russia has maintained its opening to the world economy and the turn to the market. There have, at the same time, been clear signs of a turn towards the intermingling of the political and the economic systems characteristic of the Soviet power monopoly. Evidence of this can be found in Putin's listing, in August 2004, of over 1,000 'strategic' companies over which the state intended to exercise control, in the increasing use of the President's patronage powers in appointments to key posts in the economy and, perhaps above all, the use of the law-enforcement agencies to intimidate, prosecute and, if thought appropriate, imprison people engaging in economic activity of whom the leadership of the state disapproves.

It must be concluded that, two decades after Gorbachev launched his reforms, the challenge of instituting democratic government remains. At the same time, it must be admitted that a number of circumstances sharply diminished its chances. Two in particular stand out – the pressures stemming from the Chechen wars, and the economic reforms as they were carried out in the Yeltsin presidency.

The Chechen factor has affected almost every corner of Russia's political life. It provided the pretext for the exile of Vladimir Gusinsky (see Chapter 12), whose television channel virtually alone reported adversely on the Kremlin's policy in Chechnya, and for later restrictions on the media as the threat of terrorist actions within Russia grew. The brutality of the Russian forces in Chechnya drew the attention of critical individuals and non-governmental organisations, which were in turn drawn into a stance of dissidence by the over-rigorous reaction of the law-enforcement agencies.

For its part, the shock therapy of the Yeltsin economic reforms, carried out at least partly in the name of promoting democracy, created instead a general penury and a deep perplexity about what was happening. By the end of the 1990s, the Western-sounding word *demokratsiya* had become a symbol of that penury and perplexity, reflecting the fact that there was in Russia only the narrowest basis on which to construct the mechanisms guaranteeing representation and the accountability of government to the people. Comparative studies of transition from authoritarian rule elsewhere in the late twentieth century have recorded the phenomenon of disenchantment as the effervescent optimism greeting the fall of the discredited regime gives way to disappointment, as expectations fall victim to new realities that the new regime is forced to acknowledge. In Russia those realities struck with particular force.

By the end of Putin's first presidency, it was clear to any Russians who thought in such terms that the end of the communist power monopoly did not of itself open the door to democracy. Moreover, the population had other, more pressing priorities, such as stability, which would enable them to engage in economic activity, and an improvement in their standard of living. These Putin had been able to deliver. In sum, the construction of a democratic order could not by then, in the eyes of most Russians, really be considered to be one of the major challenges confronting the country. In any event, had not the democratic mechanisms already put in place demonstrated through free elections that Putin and the party that he favoured had overwhelming support? Frequently overlooked, also, is a historical tendency for the Russia intelligentsia to see democracy in social terms (a pair of shoes is worth more than a Raphael Madonna, as a nineteenth-century writer put it).

While the establishment of democracy in a traditionally authoritarian society presents fundamental challenges with strong cultural implications, other challenges have had a greater immediacy. The transition from communism was revolutionary in the sense that it overturned property relations, though the political conflicts that this upheaval generated were moderated by the fact that the transfer of property went on partly within the existing elite. However, the acquisition by a group of speculators of a significant part of the country's capital in the early 1990s, particularly in spheres of the economy where assets were mobile (banking) or open to purchase by foreign interests beyond the state's control (hydrocarbons), drew a reaction that revealed the extent to which conservative and potentially restorationist people still held positions of power. This was made clear when Putin chose for his governing personnel people drawn from the military and security props of the former elite, who had a strong belief in the primacy of the state in society and a deep suspicion of foreign influences. That statist elite thus confronts a new social force, which owes its considerable economic power to the process of change and which is cosmopolitan in its outlook.

The tension between the governing statist elite and the oligarchs presents particular problems for Russia. First, it inhibits the organic development of a broader business interest, linking manufacturing, trade and distribution with the extractive industries, and it inhibits also the development of a controlled interaction with international economic interests. Second, it serves as a justification for the maintenance in positions of power of military and security personnel who have been brought up to see their role in terms of keeping the foreigner at bay. The internationalisation of the Russian economy remains a point of contention, and the problems that it has been creating will remain a cause of instability until the issue is resolved or an accommodation found. The challenge is partly a short-term one. The oligarchs' booty, or a good part of it, can be recovered. But the challenge cannot be seen merely as a matter of restitution.

A further challenge facing Russia is for the most part more muted. The federal structure put in place by the Soviet Union was based on the idea of creating homelands for each of the ethnic minorities of any size. It had no economic and little administrative rationale, though it had the political aim of dividing the larger and potentially more assertive groups. Needing support in his struggle with Gorbachev, Yeltsin wooed the leaders of some of the larger groups and allowed them privileges that augmented an existing imbalance among the units of the Federation. In confronting the federal question when he became President, Putin adopted a dual policy: first, he set about reducing the asymmetry of the Federation; and second, he reasserted the power of the federal centre against the periphery.

Progress in the first of these policies is being made, with the merging already of two subjects of the Federation and many more projected. This will have the effect of reducing the Federation's ethnic complexity, since the planned mergers will absorb smaller ethnic minorities into oblasts chiefly populated by Russians, so that an existing process of assimilation will progress even faster. The second policy has also been successful, with the aligning of the republican constitutions with that of the Federation. It received a particular boost with the decision in late 2004 to revoke the electoral principle in the appointment of republican presidents and regional governors and to make them subject to effective nomination by the President. Events large and small are constantly confirming Moscow's control over the periphery. The one case where Moscow's writ does not fully run is Chechnya. This exception, however, is unlikely to serve as a growth-point for other claims for independence. Even in the Muslim territories in the Caucasus that neighbour Chechnya, there has been no contagion from that republic. One of the most impressive facts about the whole story of the Russian transition from communism is that, with minor and locally contained exceptions, open warfare has been restricted to that one territory. The Russian Federation's population is truly multinational and yet it is dominated by one of its elements – the Russians. This source of stability is much underestimated, although the stability comes at a social cost borne by other groups.

The evolution to date of the Federation introduces a final, paradoxical, challenge that Russia faces today. Throughout the advanced industrial world, the traditional monopolies of the nation state – over taxation, over the means of waging war, over adjudicating disputes and sanctioning wrong-doers, over representing the state abroad and over political loyalty – have been subject to erosion. The factors involved have included international finance, the development of multinational companies, the shrinking of the world through advanced communications, with the concomitant mutual penetration of cultures, the movement of substantial populations around the globe and the assertion of multiple loyalties. The Soviet Union did not conform to the norms of a nation state, being semi-imperial in nature, but it was sustained by these traditional monopolies. Not only that, but it adhered to them in an extreme form, since the overall monopoly of power not only physically maintained the Communist Party in its directing role but also provided the doctrinal legitimacy for its rule as the historic organ of the workers in their struggle to construct communism.

Even before its collapse, the Soviet Union had been exposed to globalisation and the other forces that have affected the traditional monopolies of nation states. Indeed, they were one of the main reasons for its collapse. The impact they have had on today's Russia is illustrated in many places in this book, from the problems with immigration, to the international academic contacts that so disturb the Federal Security Service, to the most obvious and fateful case of all – the entry of foreign interests into the oil industry of Russia. The rise of Russian nationalism is part of the same evolution and is the counterpart of nationalist movements in many other countries, which similarly represent a pathological response to processes of globalisation. The oligarchs' economic coup must also be assessed in this context.

Russia was bound to be struck with particular force by the challenge of globalisation as the country emerged from a system that had operated as a dam against the intrusion of external influences. Now, two decades after its full exposure to the world economy, Russia appears to be at one and the same time acquiring the characteristics of a nation state (for example, the consolidation around a dominant ethno-cultural element within it, as occurred in the British case) while refusing to accept the threat to its monopolies characteristic of the present predicament of the nation state elsewhere (evident in the spheres of finance, ownership of natural resources and multiple loyalties).

It is in the light of these various challenges that any assessment must be made of the development of democracy and of the inability of society to resist the traditionally strong verticality of the Russian state. The opening to the world means that Western models can be advocated by those interested in doing so inside and outside Russia, in dialogue with each other, though this by no means guarantees a general acceptance of those models, and can equally well cause a reaction against them. Indeed, one of the main features of the 2003 elections to the State Duma was the wide support for 'people's patriotic' formations. The manipulation of those elections and the emasculation of the State Duma, together with the electorate's endorsement of Putin's authoritarian policies, seem to rule out parliament and political parties as the locus of an opening to pluralism. If that is to be sought, it will be found rather in the low-key mobilisation of interest groups in areas where such mobilisation can influence government without causing nervous reactions on the part of a state traditionally inclined to meet attempts at representation with suspicion and severe policing.

For the rest, the medium-term evolution of Russian politics depends to a great extent on the outcome of a duel between a praetorian statist elite drawn somewhat anachronistically from the Communist Party of the Soviet Union's armed supports, on the one hand, and, on the other, new economic elites, whose development has been distorted by the effects of a disastrous mismanagement of the process of privatisation.

Note

1 *RFE/RL Newsline*, 4 June 2004, citing RIA Novosti news agency.

Index

Note: page numbers in **bold** refer to main entries.